THE CONCEPT OF
INTENTIONALITY

A Monograph in

MODERN CONCEPTS OF PHILOSOPHY

Series Editor

MARVIN FARBER

State University of New York at Buffalo
Buffalo, New York

Titles appearing in this series do not necessarily
reflect the thinking of the editor or publisher.
The series has been developed to present *all*
modern concepts of philosophy.
The following titles have either been published in
the series or are in production and will be
published soon.

THE CONCEPT OF INTENTIONALITY

By

JITENDRA NATH MOHANTY

Professor of Philosophy
at the Universities of
Calcutta & Oklahoma

WARREN H. GREEN, INC.

St. Louis, Missouri, U.S.A.

Published by

WARREN H. GREEN, INC.
10 South Brentwood Boulevard
Saint Louis, Missouri, U.S.A.

Library of Congress Catalog Card Number 76-107200

Printed in the United States of America
5B   (189)

PREFACE

My EARLIER BOOK on *Edmund Husserl's Theory of Meaning* (1964) had deliberately restricted itself to a study of Husserl's theory of meaning in its logical aspect and in so far as it bears upon his philosophy of thinking and language. Of course, it had also pointed out the inseparability of such a noematic study from its noetic aspect. But, there was no attempt to examine Husserl's concept of consciousness and his analysis of the intentional act. This lacuna was pointed out by many reviewers. I may only say here that this was not a lacuna but a deliberately imposed limitation of the plan of that study.

The present study, which by no means is concerned with Husserl alone, seeks to make good that inadequacy. It is concerned precisely with the notion of the intentional act, but as it explores the general notion of intentionality it also goes beyond Husserl, as is only inevitable.

The study of European phenomenology is sought here to be supplemented by insights derived from the long tradition of Indian concern with the nature of consciousness. If anywhere, it is in its philosophy of consciousness that Indian thought has made lasting contributions. The present work seeks to combine insights derived from two completely different sources, and shows their beautiful convergence on some key issues.

v

I first discussed the theme of this book in a graduate seminar in the University of Oklahoma during the spring semester, 1967. The students participating in it have in no small measure contributed to the formation of the thesis developed here. Professor William Horosz joined all those discussions, and, although we differed on fundamental issues, his comments provoked me to further thinking. I am grateful to him for this.

Subsequent drafts of the work were read as special lectures at the Centre of Advanced Study in Philosophy, Visva Bharati University, and also at the Indian Academy of Philosophy, Calcutta. The accompanying discussions at both the places have helped me sharpen my formulations and to see some aspects of the problems which I did not see earlier. To all those who took part in those discussions I am grateful. However, I must make special mention of Dr. Pranab Kumar Sen, Dr. Debi Prasad Chattopadhyay and Dr. S. N. Ganguly who raised some most pertinent questions.

I am indebted to Professor Marvin Farber for kindly offering to include this book in a series being edited by him.

J. N. MOHANTY

Calcutta

CONTENTS

PART THREE

THE CONCEPT OF
INTENTIONALITY

PART ONE

CHAPTER 1

BRENTANO'S CONCEPT OF INTENTIONALITY

Whatever might have been the history of the concept of intentionality before Brentano(1), there is no doubt that modern philosophy owes it to him to have both drawn attention to the centrality of this concept for philosophy of mind and given it a formulation which is essentially original. However, since Brentano gave his historic formulation, philosophy has moved ahead; and his concept has been criticised, refined and amended, sometimes beyond recognition, by those who profess allegiance to him. The history of this concept after Brentano is a fascinating story, and forms part of the theme of this book: though the main purpose of this study is not historical survey but systematic understanding. I begin, in this chapter, by taking a close look at the first chapter of the second Book of Brentano's *Psychologie vom empirischen Standpunkt*(2).

I

Brentano wants to find out the character or characters which distinguish mental phenomena (with which alone, he thinks, psychology is concerned) from physical phenomena. He, of course, makes it clear(3) that he is not trying to give a definition in the strict sense, and that what he wants is a clarification *(Erklärung)*, a *Verdeutlichung* of the terms 'mental' and 'physical' (for the present, let us not bother about 'phenomena'), so that any misunderstanding as to their correct application could be avoided. For this purpose, a description may be as useful as a strict logical definition.

One may explain the meaning of the word 'colour' by saying that it is the generic name for red, blue, green and yellow. The word 'mental phenomena' may likewise be explicated with the help of examples. Appropriate examples of mental phenomena would be: an act of representation (as distinguished from the represented object), hearing of a sound (as distinguished from the sound heard), seeing a colour, sensing heat or cold, expecting, believing, doubting, pleasure, pain, fear, love, hatred, desire etc. As contrasted with these, examples of physical phenomena are: a patch of colour, a figure, a landscape, a sound, heat or cold, a smell, and so on. (Curiously enough, Brentano adds to the list he gives: "similar objects which appear to me in phantasy." Is there any character or characters common to all those which we may call 'mental' and absent in all those which we call 'physical'? This is the question with which Brentano starts.

It is worth bearing in mind that according to Brentano intentionality is not the only distinguishing characteristic of mental phenomena. He in fact gives us several others, though he also rejects some other ways of distinguishing between the two sorts of phenomena. The contention, for example, that the distinguishing feature of mental phenomena is their non-spatiality is rejected by him on the ground that certain mental phenomena may be regarded as having extension while there may be physical phenomena which lack it. Even if such cases be set aside as being controversial, and non-spatiality be identified as a distinguishing mark of the mental, it would nevertheless be a negative mark, and it is worthwhile searching for something positive. Brentano himself suggests another distinguishing mark of the mental, though that also is not the sort of thing we are after.

Brentano holds that mental phenomena are either themselves representations *(Vorstellungen)* or are founded on representations. Crucial for understanding what Brentano means by this are the words 'representation' and 'founded': this need not however for the present concern us(4). It suffices for our present purposes to note that this, considered as a mark of the mental, is unsatisfactory. What we do when we put this forward as such a mark is that we divide all mental phenomena into two mutually exclusive and jointly exhaustive groups which again are related in a certain manner, but we would not be thereby singling out any character which these two groups of mental phenomena share in common, unless of course we regard this 'either-or' as designing a disjunctive property.

We are then looking for a property which is common to all mental phenomena and which is neither negative nor disjunctive in character. Brentano gives us *three* such properties:

(1) All mental phenomena, and no non-mental phenomena, are characterised by "the intentional inexistence of an object"(5).

(2) All mental phenomena, and no non-mental phenomena, are such that they can be perceived only in inner awareness(6) and

(3) All mental phenomena exhibit a sort of unity which is not to be found amongst physical phenomena(7).

In other words, all mental phenomena, and no non-mental phenomena, are *intentional* and *reflexive*(8), and always belong to a unity of consciousness. While the concept of intentionality has been much discussed since Brentano drew attention to it, not enough attention has been systematically paid to the concepts of reflexivity and unity of consciousness, and yet for a fuller appreciation of the potentiality and the limits of the concept of intentionality it will be necessary for us to examine these other two concepts as well and to investigate into their relationship to the concept of intentionality.

Brentano, on his own admission, is making use of a scholastic notion. Whereas the scholastics spoke of the 'intentional inexistence of an object' in the mind, Brentano prefers to speak of "the relatedness to a content" (*"die Beziehung auf einen Inhalt"*), "the direction towards an object" *(die Richtung auf ein Objekt"),* or "the immanent objectivity" *("die immanente Gegenständlich- keit").* However, he is also aware that his own expressions are not wholly free from equivocations. We may presume that he was aware of many of the misunderstandings that have actually arisen because of the expressions he used. Perhaps he could not find any better set of expressions, and it is doubtful if his successors have been able to designate the same fact by any completely unambiguous expression. The difficulty becomes all the greater however because Brentano is attached to the Scholastic notion of 'inexistence.' Though he wishes to replace it by the apparently harmless notions of 'relatedness to' and 'being directed towards,' he nevertheless uses 'immanent objectivity' as well, and proceeds even to speak of a mental state as 'containing' *(enthalten)* something as its object, of the psychic *Einwohnung* (which he traces back, rightly, to Aristotle).

An understanding of Brentano's theory requires us to go into his uses of the terms 'object,' 'content' and 'intentional.' In this connection, we have to ask two questions:

Did Brentano distinguish between the 'object' and the 'content' of a mental act?

Further, is the intentionality of consciousness, or of a mental act, according to Brentano, a relation between two terms?

The next two sections will try to answer these two questions.

II

Twardowski and Meinong held the view that the intentional reference of a mental act to an object *is made possible* through the mediation of a peculiar element *in* that act: this element was called by them *'Inhalt'* or 'content.' According to Meinong, the act — as Findlay puts it(9) — makes use of the content to *hit* the object: but precisely how the content makes this possible is left unexplained by Meinong.

Whereas Meinong's position in this regard — quite apart from its tenability — is somewhat unambiguous, Brentano's is not so. From all available evidence, it seems that Brentano did at first draw some kind of distinction between the 'mere object' *(Gegenstand schlechtweg)* and the 'intentional object' or the 'immanent object,' in which case the latter will be the same as the content having a sort of mental existence. The distinction is between the tree as such, as existing out there, and the same tree as an object of my present perception. This-tree-as-an-object-of-my-present-perception has an intentional or immanent existence in my mind, i.e., is a component of my present act of perceiving, though, to be sure, what I am perceiving is not this content but the object, the tree as such, as existing out there. Since Brentano uses the word 'object' frequently in the sense of the intentional or immanent object, i.e., the content,(10) we may attribute to him a threefold distinction, namely that between the mental act, the object or content, and the thing. However, he is clear on the point that the thing does not enter into an analysis of the mental act, and that for two reasons. In the first place, the thing, by definition, is not a constituent of the mental act; secondly, it need not at all exist, as should be evident from the fact that a mental act may very well be directed towards something fictitious or even self-contradictory.

We learn from Brentano's later writings, now available in print, that his view on this point underwent a radical change. He not only comes to reject this view but, strangely enough, even contends that he never held it. The immanent object is now said to be the same as the thing itself, and not the so-called 'object of thought,' not what we have called the content. What we think about is the thing itself, not the object of thought, so that when we think of a horse the immanent object of our thought is a horse and not a contemplated horse. Curiously enough, Brentano still continues (i) to call this thing, the horse, an 'immanent object,' and (ii) to hold the view that the thing need not exist(11). Why does he call the thing an immanent object, when he now believes neither in a content nor in a sort of mental existence of the thing? From his new changed view point, he explains his continued usage of 'immanent' thus:(12) the word 'immanent' is used in order to say that there is an *object*, without implying any further that the object exists whether within or outside the mind. Mental existence of the object has been rejected, extra-mental existence is irrelevant and is not entailed by the fact of being an object. What then is the object?

Does Brentano now assign to the object a curious neutral status? No! Brentano tells us, on the other hand, that its being an object "is merely *the linguistic* correlate of the person experiencing having it as object(13)." Kraus clarifies this(14) with the help of a distinction from Brentano's later writings: a word has 'auto-semantic' meaning when it means something on its own, when it designates or stands for something; when however a word has meaning only as functioning along with other linguistic expressions it cannot be said to designate or stand for anything, it then functions 'synsemantically.' The word 'object' is equivocal, inasmuch as it may function in both ways: when taken as auto-semantic it means what we have above called a thing; when however Brentano speaks of a mental state as having an object the word 'object' is used synsemantically. To say that I have a horse as an object, is to say that I am thinking of a horse: the latter is a less misleading way of saying the same thing(15).

One understands Brentano's serious attempts to get rid of any illusion about there being curious *Zwischenentitäten* like contents, and the more he succeeds in getting rid of such contents, the more does he approximate to an adequate formulation of the concept of intentionality. The language of entities is inescapable, but this by itself need not commit us to admitting entities into our ontology unless we have other good reasons for doing so.

If the concept of intentionality is to serve any purpose, it should be able to dispense with the content *as a medium of reference*: consciousness should be able to refer to its object by virtue of some inalienable power of its own. Whether the notion of content can or cannot be rehabilitated in some other manner and to serve some other purpose within the framework of the intentionality thesis is a question which we shall try to settle in a much later context(16).

III

Brentano no doubt speaks of intentional relatedness. But he is also aware of the insurmountable difficulties that are likely to arise out of treating intentionality as a relation. This is specially clear from the Appendices which the editor has added to the 1911 edition of the second volume of the *Psychologie*. Brentano there tells us(17) that whereas for a genuine relation to hold good between two terms, say A and B, both these terms should exist, this is not the case with mental directedness. If my thought is directed towards an object X, it is not necessary for this directedness to exist that X should also exist. In other words, my thought may very well intentionally refer to something non-existent. Brentano therefore suggests that what we may have here is not something *Relatives* but only *Relativliches*. He, however, does notice that there is nevertheless some similarity between a genuine relation and mental directedness: in both cases, whoever thinks of a genuine relation and whoever thinks of a mental directedness, also thinks of both the relata. If I think of A as being greater than B, I am thinking of both A and B: I am thinking of A *in recto,* directly, and of B in *obliquo,* obliquely. Likewise, when I am thinking of A's thinking of B, I am directly thinking of A's thought though I am also thinking, obliquely though, of B as the object of A's thought. While thus far there is a similarity between a genuine relation and mental directedness, the difference between them is too great to permit an assimilation of the latter under the former.

If mental directedness is not a relation, it is also not a relational property. A relational property is a property which is generated by the subsistence of relations. Of course if A is to the east of B, A has the relational property of being-to-the-east-of-B, and B is not literally a constituent of this property. Likewise, being-directed-to-A may be a relational property of a mental state, and surely A is not a constituent of such a property. There is however this difference between the two cases that whereas in the case of 'being-to-the-east-of-B' the property is generated by a relation between A and B, in the other case there is no such relation: on the contrary, speaking of a relation between the mental state and A presupposes the directedness to A(18).

In view of the above discussions, we may then safely say that many phenomenologoists, while trying to distinguish Brentano's concept of intentionality from Husserl's, have not done justice to Brentano. Landgrebe, for example, in a very influential study(19) makes out, amongst others, two points which I do not think to be tenable. He contends that Brentano knows only of intentional relation between two entities, and — as a corrolary of this — that Brentano's concept of intentionality is based on an assumption of epistemological realism. Now, it is surely true that Brentano was a realist, but it has also to be admitted that in his formulation of the concept of intentionality he did not let this belief in epistemological realism influence him: he does say, for example, that the existence of the object is not necessarily entailed by the fact that it is the object of a certain mental directedness; in other words, he rejects the contention that the thing, be it real or not, enters into the constitution of the mental act. And, as we have shown in the last paragraphs, he did realise the difficulties that arise in case one understands intentionality as relation between two terms: it is at best relation-like, not a relation. Phenomenologists would do well to take Brentano's later theories and self-criticisms more seriously. Again, Spiegelberg in his admirable study on *"Der Begriff der Intentionalität in der Scholastik, bei Brentano und bei Husserl"*(20) recognizes that Brentano had abandoned the use of 'mental inexistence', but notes that he had also dropped the adjective 'intentional' and retained only 'psychic relatedness to the object.' It does not seem to me to be correct to say, as Speigelberg does, that Brentano almost gives up the use of 'intentional' "um nur die mentale Immanenz der psychischen Phänomene noch starker hervortreten zu lassen"(21). It would seem to me that Brentano did most explicitly reject the conception of 'mental inexistence,' and if he also ceased to make use of 'intentional' it must be due to the apprehension that this word was — or had been through his own writings — associated with the idea of mental inexistence. It may also be that even when Brentano did speak of mental inexistence he did not mean a sort of literal being-contained-in. Spiegelberg may be right however in pointing out that for Brentano 'intentional' is an attribute of the object, and not of the conscious act: what then characterises the conscious act in that case is the directedness to its object.

The remarks of the preceding paragraph should not be construed as suggesting that Brentano had before him the full concept of intentionality as subsequently developed by Husserl. Far from it: Husserl did put far more into this concept than could have been anticipated by either the Scholastics or by Brentano. Before we come to Husserl's more explicit criticisms of Brentano, let us direct our attention to the other points of distinction which Brentano sought to draw between mental and physical phenomena.

IV

The second important distinction which Brentano finds between mental and non-mental phenomena is that mental phenomena are directly apprehended only in inner consciousness (*"sie nur in innerem Bewusstsein wahrgenommen werden"*), while non-mental (by which Brentano means 'physical') phenomena are capable of being directly apprehended only in outer perception. Of course, both kinds of phenomena may be known mediately through some kind of inference, as for example when I infer the mental states of another person and when we infer the existence of unperceived material things. But the point of the distinction is that mental phenomena are directly apprehended only through inner consciousness whereas physical phenomena are directly apprehended only through outer perception. Brentano is aware that the distinction, so formulated, is unsatisfactory; it virtually appeals to another distinction, namely that between inner and outer which, it may be said, is part of the explicandum.

However, Brentano also gives us a way of distinguishing between inner perception and outer perception. Inner perception possesses an immediate and unerring evidence which belongs to it alone and which is absent in outer perception. Saying then that mental phenomena are what are directly apprehended only through inner perception is the same as saying that their perception is immediately evident. Brentano even goes further than this, and makes a stronger statement: inner perception alone is perception in the strict sense. The so-called outer perception is, strictly speaking, not perception at all, so that mental phenomena may now be said to be those which alone are capable of being perceived in the strict sense.

Let us for the present leave out of consideration Brentano's *proposal* to use 'perception' in so strong a sense that it would follow analytically from it that only mental phenomena can be said to be perceived. Let us however try to understand what precisely he means by 'inner perception.'

In the chapter on "*Vom inneren Bewusstsein*(22)", Brentano takes up the question: 'Is there any mental phenomenon which is not the object of a consciousness?' This question is the same as: 'Are there unconscious mental acts?' Brentano points out that the word 'unconscious' is used in two senses. 'Unconscious' is sometimes predicated of that which is not conscious of something else. This is the active sense, and in this sense the expression 'unconscious consciousness' is surely a contradiction in terms. But 'unconscious' is also predicated of that of which one is not conscious. In this latter and the passive sense, there is no contradiction in the notion of 'unconscious consciousness.' One who asks, 'Is there unconscious consciousness?' is not asking an absurd question like, 'Is there a red that is not red?' While Brentano rejects as untenable the views of those who contend that the idea of unconscious consciousness in the passive sense of 'unconscious' is self-contradictory, he does not also agree with those who contend that the existence of unconscious consciousness in this sense can be *proved*. The issue is in any case, for Brentano, a factual question and cannot be decided *a priori*. And there is, he holds, no sufficient reason for supposing that there is such consciousness.

I need not consider here the various ways in which Brentano tries to refute the arguments of those who seek to demonstrate the existence of unconscious mental states. I will refer only to one of these arguments in favour of unconscious mental states, and then briefly state Brentano's reply to it. I have selected this argument, because I feel this has a bearing on our subsequent discussions on the nature of consciousness.

It has been argued by those who wish to prove the existence of unconscious mental states that the assumption that every conscious state has to become the object of another conscious state will lead to an infinite regress, which is both impossible and is not testified by experience. If every mental state must *eo ipso* be the object of consciousness, then such a simple mental act like hearing a sound would require an infinite series of mental acts to be completed, which is impossible, and so, as a consequence, we would never come to have the simple experience of hearing a sound! Further, the hearing of the sound will be accompanied by a representation of that hearing. This second mental state, namely the representation of hearing, itself needs to be the object of another mental state, so that we have also simultaneously a representation of the representation of hearing. Thus the person who is hearing a sound has simultaneously three representations: that of the sound, that of the hearing, and that of the representation of the hearing. But even this is not the end of the story. In fact, we will have to accept the existence of an infinite series of such representations as necessarily accompanying the simple experience of hearing a sound.

There is still another dimension in which the situation gets infinitely complicated. As we proceed further in the series from the first act of hearing to the succeeding acts of representation, the number of immanent constituents of the acts increases. In the act of hearing, the immanent object is the sound; in the act of representing the hearing, the immanent objects are the sound heard as well as the hearing of it; and, so on.

One way of resolving this difficulty without assuming the existence of unconscious mental states would be to suppose that the sound heard and the hearing of it are really one and the same thing considered from two different points of view. This would be somewhat like the view held by Russell at one time. Brentano does not consider this view to be correct, and even if it were correct, it does not, according to Brentano, succeed in avoiding the difficulty arising out of the supposed infinite regress(23). It is not correct, because immediate evidence shows that hearing is distinct from what is heard, and also because the sound that is heard does not possess some of the characters by which mental states are distinguished. Further, even if this view were correct it does not help us to avoid the difficulty. For, let hearing be the same as the sound heard; yet, one cannot say the same of other acts like remembering and expectation. Remembering a past event is not the same as the past event that is being remembered, just as expecting a future event is not the same as the future that is being expected. The same difficulty of an infinite regress would therefore arise in connection with mental acts like remembering and expecting even if we grant that it does not arise in connection with acts like hearing.

It is curious, Brentano notes, that though many philosophers including Aristotle have drawn attention to this possibility of infinite regress, very few of them have derived the existence of unconscious states from it. The only philosopher of importance who has based his belief in the existence of unconscious mental states on this supposed infinite regress is Thomas Aquinas, and Brentano does not regard Aquinas's theory in this connection to be very satisfactory indeed(24). Aquinas holds that the senses are not able to apprehend their own acts, for the senses are bodily and so cannot be turned back upon themselves. What then apprehends the acts of the outer senses is, according to Aquinas, an inner sense; but even this inner sense, being no less bodily, is incapable of perceiving its own activities. But Aquinas does not postulate another organ for apprehending the acts of the inner sense, so that in the long run the perceptions of the acts of the outer senses remain unperceived in his system. This leaves room for unperceived perceptions. With regard to the acts of thinking, on the other hand, Aquinas should have a quite different view. For these acts are not bodily, and should have the power to reflect upon themselves. However, according to him, the understanding cannot think of more than one thought at the same time. He resolves this difficulty by holding that the consciousness of a thought is not simultaneous with the thought of which it is conscious, but follows it in time. Since no act of thinking could remain unconscious, there arise, in Aquinas's philosophy, a successive series *ad infinitum* (in place of a simultaneously existing infinite series). Actually however this series cannot come to an end, and so we have to assume some act of thinking, the last member, which remains unconscious.

Brentano finds here several difficulties. In the first place, Brentano is not happy with the way Thomas Aquinas advances one theory for the consciousness of the acts of the outer senses and another for our consciousness of the acts of thinking. Inner experience shows that the two kinds of awareness are alike at least in this respect. Further, it is hard to accept the consequence of the Thomist theory, namely, that we should never be conscious that we are conscious of seeing or of hearing. In the next place, Aquinas treats the inner perception of the acts of the outer senses and the outer perceptions of their respective objects as being precisely of the same kind. He misses the peculiar character of inner perception. His theory of our awareness of our acts of thinking is no more satisfactory. According to his theory, our awareness of our acts of thinking is always retrospective, we always as it were look back to the past and never come to perceive the act as and when it takes place. One cannot in that case speak in the strict sense of an inner perception, and one would not be able to account for the peculiar directness and incorrigibility of the evidence that attaches to inner perception. Lastly, it is to be noted that on the Thomistic theory there should necessarily be acts of thinking, which — as in the case of our knowledge of our acts of the outer senses — remain unconscious or unperceived, for the understanding has not the power to go through an infinite process.

Brentano therefore looks for some other way of resolving the difficulty of infinite regress without however admitting the existence of unconscious psychic states. Our direct experience testifies to the fact that precisely when we are having a mental state we are also aware of having it. Precisely when we are hearing a sound we are also aware of hearing the sound. This seems to be an undeniable fact, and the only question that remains open is how exactly to interpret this fact. One of the questions that arise in this connection is, do we have in such cases many different representations or do we have only one representation? Do we have only one representation, namely that of sound, or do we have at least two, namely that of the sound and that of our hearing of the sound? Brentano seems to hold the view that though there are in this case two representations, these two representations are simultaneous and together constitute *one mental act.* In fact, the two are so intimately connected that we can distinguish between the two representations only conceptually(25). They in fact constitute one and the same mental phenomenon with two distinguishable but not separable, components. In fact, though Brentano does sometimes distinguish between the two representations and speaks of them as two, though inseparable, phenomena, yet at other places he speaks of them as constituting one act whose *primary* object is the sound (in the above example) and whose *secondary* object is the hearing.

However, Brentano does *not* hold the view that we are able to *observe* our own mental states, though surely we do *perceive* them. We can be said to observe a thing only if it is possible for us to be directed towards that object as the primary object(26). We could observe a mental act, say of hearing a sound only if it were possible in a second act to take up that act as the primary object. But the inner perception of hearing a sound is not a second act, but the same act itself simultaneous with it and inseparable from it. The mental act of hearing can only be apprehended as a secondary object, and never as a primary object. It cannot therefore be *'beobachtet,'* though it can be *'wahrgenommen'*.

But may there not be a second mental act, succeeding the act of hearing, in which we apprehend not only the original act of hearing but also the act of apprehending that hearing? In other words, is not there besides the hearing and the representation of hearing (which of course build an intimate unity of their own) also a representation of the representation of the hearing? According to Brentano, there are no other representations, for on his theory, awareness of the representation of the sound and awareness of that awareness are one and the same. What we have in fact is: (1) the representation of a sound = hearing, and (2) awareness of this representation, two inseparable moments of one and the same psychic act. Awareness of (2) is not another distinct act separate from (2), but is (2) itself. The series ends with (2). Thus the mental act of hearing both is an apprehension of the sound (which is its primary object) and also awareness of itself in its totality(27).

In the next chapter bearing the title "*Weitere Betrachtungen über das innere Bewusstsein*", Brentano begins with the following question: 'Is the consciousness which accompanies our mental acts always of one and the same kind, or is it of many different kinds?' In other words, do we have only a representation *(Vorstellung)* of the mental acts, or do we also have judgments about them? Of course, in order that they may be judged they should be represented, for according to one of Brentano's wellknown theories all other kinds of mental acts are based on representations. Therefore, the question which Brentano raises is: 'Are the mental acts simply represented, or are they also apprehended in other ways?'

The fact that we also *know* our mental acts, that for example, we *know that* we perceive or desire or have this or that mental state shows that mental acts may be accompanied not only by a representation of them but also by a judgment about them. But since on Brentano's theory all judgments presuppose representations, the judgments about mental states must somehow be built upon representations of them. A thetic or positional consciousness of them presupposes the non-thetic and non-positional consciousness we always do have of our own mental acts. But while we always, on Brentano's theory, do have a non-thetic and non-positional consciousness of our own mental acts, and we sometimes do have judgments about them, are there cases of mental acts which are not accompanied by such judgments? In other words, are there mental acts of which we are aware in the non-thetic manner but which we do not *know* in the strict sense of 'know'?

The theory that *every* mental act is accompanied not only by a representation of it but also by a judgment about it may be subject to the following criticisms:

It may be pointed out, in the first place, that this would reopen the charge of infinite regress which Brentano has been able to set aside in the case of the accompanying representation. Now Brentano's reply to this charge is that there is no more reason for finding an infinite regress in this case than it was in the previous case. In fact, if Brentano's analysis holds good, then even when a mental act is the object of an accompanying judgment, it has itself in its totality as its secondary object. There is in fact no reduplication or multiplication of conscious acts even when the original mental act is not merely

represented but also known. The knowledge of the first act is
not a second act having the first act as its object, it is the first
act itself having itself as its own object. It is precisely because
of this fact that the relation of our knowledge of a mental act
to this mental act itself is not of the same kind as the relation
of a mental act to its primary object, that our knowledge of
our own mental acts attains to a sort of certainty and indubita-
bility which is absent in any knowledge of a primary object.
The certainty and incorrigibility of our inner perception is not
due to the fact that its object is within us rather than without;
it is rather due to the fact that here the relation of the knowledge to its object, namely to the mental act is not of the same
kind as that of the mental act to its primary object(28).

It may also be argued against the theory that every mental
act is accompanied by a judgment about it, that on this theory
every time we do have a mental act we also need have a judgment accompanying it which connects the mental act concerned
as its subject with the concept of existence as its predicate, and
this seems highly improbable, for the concept of existence is so
vague that we cannot suppose ourselves to be predicating it
every time we are having a mental act. In reply to this objection, Brentano points out(29) that not every judgment connects
a subject with a predicate so that the subject-predicate form is
not an essential form of all judgments but is only an accidental
form of certain sentences. Our knowledge through inner perception provides us with just the example of a kind of knowledge
which being a knowledge is judgmental, but is not of the subject-
predicate form. This judgment of inner perception rather consists according to Brentano in the simple recognition of the
mental act represented within(30).

Brentano in fact holds the view that every mental act is
accompanied not only by a representation of it but also by
a judgment about it, though the proof he tries to give of the
latter part of this contention seems to depend upon a rather
doubtful notion of the degree of intensity of a judgment or of
a representation. However his final view seems to be that every
psychic act is connected with a twofold inner consciousness,
a representation and a judgment. What we call 'inner percep-

tion' is this latter, which is a sort of immediate and evident knowledge of the act(31).

In order to get a final picture of Brentano's views in this regard we have to remember that according to him every mental act is also accompanied by a feeling of pleasure and pain(32), in such a way that this feeling, whatever it may be, is as intimately bound up with the original mental act as are the representation of it and the accompanying judgment about it. Brentano's final position then comes to this: every mental act is conscious (*in fact,* but not on logical or *a priori* grounds). Every mental act has a twofold object, a primary object and a secondary object. The secondary object is nothing other than the act itself. But the act is aware of itself in three different ways: it *represents* itself, it *knows* itself through inner perception, and it *feels* itself as pleasurable or painful. Thus every mental act, however simple, has four aspects: it may be regarded as a representation of its own primary object, it may be regarded as its own representation, it may be regarded as its own knowledge, or finally it may be regarded as its own feeling. And yet these four aspects are so intimately bound up together to constitute one mental act that we are not in need of postulating a series of acts, finite or infinite. In fact, Brentano goes on to add that in the case of every mental act we could even say — without postulating an infinite series of acts — that its self-representation is itself represented, known and felt, its self-knowledge is represented, known and felt, just as its self-feeling is represented, known and also felt(33).

Now this is a very complicated theory in spite of its apparent simplification of the situation. The questions that arise are:

(1) What is the necessity that every mental act should be represented? If there is no logical necessity about it, if the idea of an unconscious mental act does not involve logical contradiction — as Brentano rightly points out — what makes him sure that in fact all mental acts are conscious? What evidence can be brought for this claim?

(2) Do we in fact always *know* — using 'know' in a sense according to which to know is to judge — that we are having a mental act when in fact we are having it?

As regards 2, it is fairly plausible to contend that though we are always aware of having a mental state when in fact we are having it, this awareness does not always amount to judgmental knowledge. If what Brentano means by 'knowledge' in this context is an immediate, direct, evident apprehension, then the non-thetic, non-positional representation would serve this purpose, and we need not suppose that we have always a judgmental knowledge accompanying every mental act. Brentano's analysis in fact *multiplies aspects* indefinitely, and avoids the possibility of infinite regress only by holding that what we have are aspects and not members of a series. But it should be noted that the aspects are not merely four, but go on increasing indefinitely without — this must be added to the credit of the theory — generating a new act at all. This seems to be a deliberate device to accept all that comes — representations, representations of representations, knowledges of representations, feelings of them all, and representations, knowledge and feelings of ever increasing higher orders — without conferring on them the status of new acts and turning them into different aspects of one and the same original act by a kind of inexplicable conjuring trick.

One may therefore want to free Brentano's thesis from this artificiality, and to retain what would seem to be the central core of his thesis, namely that every mental act is always accompanied by a non-thetic and non-positional consciousness of itself, which consciousness is not an act other than itself but is the same act as *self-revealing*. In other words, every act is self-revealing: this seems to be the essence of the situation.

It seems rather strange that Brentano should have included a judgmental knowledge *of* an act within the structure of that very act. I am not objecting to his view that all judgments are not necessarily of the subject-predicate form. What I am objecting to is the view that there is a judgmental knowledge of something, which is not however distinguished from what it is about. I cannot think of a knowledge of . . . ., which does not have the object of which it is a knowledge as its primary object. Yet according to Brentano's theory a mental act never becomes the primary object of an act simultaneous with it(34). Where the object is not a primary object of awareness, I would not use the word 'know,' and even if I did use the word 'know' I would not call such knowledge judgmental knowledge as Brentano surely does.

I would therefore distinguish between a psychic act as self-revealing and an inner perception of it. The psychic act as self-revealing has itself as its secondary object and the original object (e.g., the sound in the case of its hearing) as the primary object. Though this is all that we have in most cases, we may have however an inner perception *of* the original act, but such inner perception then is a different act having the first act as its primary object and the object of the orginal act as its secondary object. This is what, e.g., the Nyāya means by saying that in the *anuvyavasāya* the object of *vyavasāya* is also given but only as *puchchalagna*. Looked at from this point of view, the *Nyāya* theory of *anuvyavasāya* does not contradict but rather supplements the Mimāmsā theory of the *svayamprakāśatva* of consciousness.

It should be noted however that Brentano does not make his contention that every mental act is conscious logically dependent upon his previous thesis that every mental act is intentional. Thus the self-revealing character of a conscious state is not deduced from the intentional character of it. It is rather added as a new feature, logically independent but factually interwoven with the intentionality of consciousness. Nor does he seek to deduce the intentionality of consciousness from this other character. He leaves the two characterisations logically independent of each other.

V

Brentano has still another characteristic of consciousness in his list. This is what may roughly be called 'the unity of consciousness,' to whose elaboration and defence Brentano devotes the fourth chapter of the second Book of his *Psychologie*. In accordance with the purpose of this study, as formulated earlier in this chapter, we can ill afford to ignore this important notion.

Brentano introduces this concept of the unity of consciousness in connection with the distinction between mental and non-mental phenomena. It is often contended that whereas mental phenomena could occur only one after another so that at any one moment one could have only one mental act and not more, many physical phenomena can and in fact do happen simultaneously. Now this formulation is not very happy, for it is not quite clear what is meant by speaking of one mental phenomenon. If it is meant that there can only occur one simple mental phenomenon, we have to find out what is meant by a 'simple' phenomenon. Also it seems undeniable that various mental phenomena do accompany each other. As we have just seen, a representation of an object may and indeed is accompanied by a representation of the representation itself, and possibly by a judgment and a feeling. However, amongst mental phenomena happening simultaneously or successively there is a kind of unity which is absent in the case of the many physical phenomena which surely do take place simultaneously. What therefore characterises mental phenomena is not the supposed impossibility of more than one of them happening at any one moment of one's mental life, but the fact that the mental phenomena always appear within a unity (35). Even simultaneously occurring physical phenomena are not unified precisely in the sense in which every mental phenomenon is. A real unity comprehends the physical phenomena as its parts. But we do not here have a mere totality, a mere collection, but something more, a unity in a more genuine sense.

Whether I have different modes of consciousness in relation to the same primary object (as when I not only barely represent to myself an object, but also judge it and desire it) or whether I have conscious relations to various primary objects (as when I see a colour and hear a sound), these various mental phenomena appear interrelated and as belonging to one and the same comprehensive unity in so far as they all are my states. For how otherwise, argues Brentano, could I, e.g., at all compare or relate these different mental states as being either the same or as different, as being similar or dissimilar, unless they all could somehow be held in one unity. They all belong in common to one real thing, whatever that real thing may be and whatever the sense of 'belonging to' may be. To say that there obtains a real unity amongst the various mental acts is not to say that one mental act, say that of seeing, is identical with another, say the act of hearing. It is also not to deny that some mental acts belonging to the same person may be more intimately connected with each other than some of them are with other mental acts. All that is meant is that the mental acts always appear as belonging to one real thing. They are all partial phenomena of one comprehensive total mental phenomenon.

Brentano is not dogmatically affirming the existence of a soul substance to which all mental states of a person, past, present and future, belong. On the other hand, his elaborations of this notion, as given in chapter IV of the second Book of the *Psychologie* shows that he is strictly on a phenomenological ground. He starts from that minimum unity which each group of simultaneous psychic acts show. He passes on to consider memory which shows that for every moment of the past the group of mental states occupying that moment had a real unity. Memory thus in fact presents us with a whole series of such unified groups, each of which is a real unity, and this series is said to build a continuity though with breaks here and there, breaks which perhaps it is not impossible to overcome. This continuous series is then shown to involve some kind of inner unity in so far as a continuum cannot include a jump. The continuous series of memories brings us to the last member which is always the group which we now perceive in inner perception. The unity of the 'I' remains within the *limits of* this analysis, the unity of this continuous series. More than this Brentano does not claim here. He does not lay claim to an identity other than this(36). Later on, we will draw attention to the relation between this notion of unity of consciousness with the notion of the ego as found in Husserl's later writings.

VI

One great merit of Brentano's *Psychologie* is that he has drawn attention to all the *three* fundamental and distinguishing characters of consciousness. These three are: its intentionality, its self-revealing character, and its peculiar unity. In the history of philosophy, these three properties have been defined, characterised, interpreted, and brought into relationships with each other in many different ways. Philosophers have differed as to which of these is the most fundamental or primitive property. Some have taken the unity as the unity of a substance, and have attempted to understand the other two, i.e., intentionality and selfconsciousness as properties of it. Others, like Samkara, have looked upon the self-revealing character as the basic and innermost nature of consciousness and have denied both substantial unity and intentionality of it. It would seem, at the first sight at least, that in modern phenomenology the concept of intentionality gains the status of being *the* primitive notion, and that the other two have been reduced to derivative functions of it. Some, like Sartre, have retained both intentionality and reflexivity as the two primitive notions, and have denied the unity of consciousness. Also, there is Rāmānuja who makes intentionality and the self-revealing character of consciousness depend upon each other. The Nayiyāyikas have accepted intentionality alone as primitive and have denied the self-revealing character of consciousness and have taken recourse to a substantial unity. In these diverse formulations of their interrelations, the very concepts have got modified, sometimes beyond recognition. It is part of the purpose of this present study to get these notions straight as far as possible both in their historical setting and in their phenomenological self-evidence. In such a project as this, it goes without saying that Brentano's writings constitute the most suitable starting point, for he of all persons saw all aspects of the situation most clearly. No doubt Brentano's thesis as here elaborated has its obvious disadvantages. He, as any reader of the *Psychologie* would know, still operates within the framework of a naturalistic and physiological psychology and in terms of the causal category. Further, he does not attempt the almost bewildering task of relating these three properties, which remain in his system as three primitive notions. However, he poses the problem for us, and we have to go beyond him in search of the solution of our problems.

CHAPTER 2

CHISHOLM AND THE BRENTANO THESIS

Brentano's search for a criterion of the mental has been revived in recent times and given a linguistic turn by R. M. Chisholm in a number of most interesting papers(1). Chisholm's papers not only draw attention to certain new and hitherto unnoticed aspects of the concept of intentionality but have made it imperative to undertake greater conceptual clarifications with regard to it than had been achieved by his predecessors. In this chapter, I shall first make a survey of Chisholm's investigations, and then enquire into the theoretical satisfactoriness both of his approach and of his results.

I

Chisholm distinguishes between two parts of the Brentano thesis(2): an ontological and a psychological part. The ontological thesis is that the object of thought, *quâ* object of thought, has a mode of being "that is short of actuality but more than nothingness": this, according to Chisholm, is the doctrine of 'intentional inexistence' of objects of thought. It has already been shown that though Brentano originally subscribed to some such view, he really did abandon it. It is also doubtful whether such an ontological thesis is entailed by the other part of the Brentano thesis, the thesis namely that all mental phenomena are intentional, and no physical phenomena are so. Given a linguistic turn, the latter thesis becomes: language describing psychological phenomena has certain logical properties not shared by language describing non-psychological phenomena; and whatever else 'intentionality' may mean it surely means precisely these properties. These logical properties would constitute a sure mark of intentionality. Chisholm's papers are concerned with finding out what these properties are.

In his 1956 paper(3), as also in his 1957 book(4), Chisholm offers three criteria of intentional use of sentences. Each of these criteria is individually sufficient for a specified type of sentences. We may call these:

(1) 'The criterion of existence independence.'
(2) 'The criterion of truth-value indifference.'
(3) 'The criterion of referential opacity.'

1. The first criterion gives a sufficient condition of the intentionality of sentences like 'Ram is thinking of Mt. Everest' and 'Diogenes looked for a honest man.' These are simple declarative sentences containing a substantial expression — a name or a description — functioning as the object of the verb. Now if in such a sentence neither the sentence nor its contradictory implies either that there is or that there isn't anything to which the substantial expression truly applies, then the sentence is intentional. All truly psychological sentences which are simple and declarative and which have a substantive expression for the object of the verb exhibit this property; no non-psychological sentence of the same form has this property.

For example, 'Ram is thinking of a horse' does not imply 'There is a horse,' whereas 'Ram is riding a horse' does imply 'There is a horse.' The former sentence is intentional, the latter is not. The criterion may also be called 'Failure of existential generalisation.'

If this criterion is to be accepted then we have to satisfy ourselves (a) that all psychological or intentional sentences of the already specified type are existence independent, and (b) that all sentences (of the specified type) showing existence independence are psychological or intentional.

(a) Psychological sentences describing feelings, e.g., 'I am grateful for the favour,' 'I am excited by the music' are *not* existence independent. 'He is ignorant of . . . . . .' also is not existence independent(5). But with regard to 'I am grateful for the favour' one may argue that what it implies is not that there is a favour but that I believe there is a favour, and the latter is intentional according to criterion 2. With regard to 'I am ignorant of . . . . . .,' one may argue that it really amounts to 'I do not know that . . . . . .,' and if sentences of the form 'I know that . . . . . .,' are intentional by criterion 3, then sentences of the form 'I do not know that . . . . . .' are also so by the same criterion. But one is still left with cases where 'I am ignorant of . . . . . . refuses to take in a *that* clause as also cases where 'I know' is not followed by a *that* clause. 'I know the Principal' is surely of the type which criterion 1 is intended to apply, and yet it is *not* existence independent.

(b) Even if all psychological sentences of the specified type do satisfy the criterion, there are simple, declarative, non-psychological sentences of that type which also exhibit existence independence. For example, 'S resembles a fairy' does not imply that there is a fairy. Similarly, 'India is devoid of dragons' does not imply 'There are dragons.' But these are clearly non-psychological sentences. Therefore, not all sentences of the specified type showing existence independence are intentional.

Criterion 1, therefore, has to be rejected.

2. The criterion of truth-value indifference is meant to be a sufficient condition of the intentionality of non-compound sentences containing a propositional clause. If we have such a sentence, and neither the sentence nor its contradictory implies either that the propositional clause is true or that it is false, then — according to this criterion — the sentence is intentional.

For example, neither the sentence 'Ram believes that there are snow men' nor its contradictory implies either that there are snow men or that there are no snow men. Thus sentences of the form 'Ram believes that p,' 'Ram hopes that p', 'Ram desires that p,' are intentional.

But again, as before, all sentences of the specified type

which are also truth-value indifferent are not intentional(6). The sentence, e.g., 'It is probable that p' is truth-value indifferent, so also is the sentence 'This is consistent with p.' But these are not intentional. Further, not all intentional sentences show truth-value indifference. Thus 'I am grateful that p', though intentional, does not. Nor does 'I know that p,' for 'I know that p' clearly does imply that p. The same seems to be the case with intentional sentences like 'I do not know that p' and 'I do not remember that p.'

Criterion 2 therefore has to be rejected.

3. This criterion is supposed to take care of cognitive verbs like 'know,' 'see,' 'perceive,' but also applies to sentences like 'I believe that p' for which criterion 2 was intended. Suppose there are two names or descriptions which designate or apply to the same thing. Suppose that C is a sentence obtained by separating these two names and descriptions by means of 'is identical with.' Suppose also that A is a sentence using one of those names or descriptions and B is like A except that where A uses one, B uses the other. Now A is intentional if the conjunction A and C does not imply B.

To illustrate: let the two names or descriptions be 'Kalidāsa' and 'the author of *Sakuntalā*. Then,

C = Kalidāsa is identical with the author of *Sakuntalā*. Let A be 'Ram knows that Kalidāsa is the author of *Sakuntalā*,' and B be 'Ram knows that the author of *Meghaduta* is the author of *Sakuntalā*.'

Now A is intentional, for clearly enough: (A.C) does not imply B.

Though this criterion takes care of cognitive verbs which show neither existence independence nor truth-value indifference, yet it is no more satisfactory than the other two. Take a non-intentional sentence, 'It is necessarily true that if Desai were Sashtri's successor, then Desai was Sashtri's successor.' Let this be A. Let C be 'Sashtri's successor is identical with Indira Gandhi', and let B be 'It is necessarily true that if Desai were Shastri's successor, then Desai was Indira Gandhi.' Now surely, the conjunction of A and C does not imply B.

Thus, all the three criteria fail precisely for the same sort of reasons: there are allegedly intentional sentences which do not satisfy the criterion meant for them, and there are admittedly non-intentional sentences which satisfy the criterion not meant to apply to them.

The failure of these criteria has highlighted one important issue. It was found that non-intentional sentences like 'It is possible that p' are both existence independent and truth-value indifferent. A non-intentional sentence like 'It is necessary that . . . . . . ' is characterised by referential opacity. Sentences like 'It is possible that . . . . . . ' and 'It is necessary that . . . . . . ' are intensional but not intentional. This raises the question as to how the two concepts, 'intentionality' and 'intensionality' (or, 'non-extensionality') are related. It would seem that some of Chisholm's criteria for intentionality are criteria for intensionality as well(7).

An extensional sentence is one which, if compound, is a truth-function of its component sentences, and if non-compound has a truth-value which depends only on the extensions of the predicates it contains(8). A sentence which is not extensional is intensional. Thus, in the case of extensional sentences, truth-value is preserved by substituiton of extensionally equivalent expressions, which is not the case with intensional sentences. It would appear then that Chisholm's second and third criteria are *also* criteria of non-extensionality, so that any sentence intentional by either 2 or 3 is also intensional, though all sentences intentional by 1 are not intensional and also all intensional sentences are not intentional. Thus, e.g., 'Ram is thinking of the Mt. Everest' preserves truth-value if we replace 'Mt. Everest' by 'the highest mountain of the world.' Further, some contrary-to-fact conditionals are intensional, but not intentional. Thus, 1 alone would seem to be a criterion of intentionality, 2 and 3 also of intensionality. Neither are all intentional sentences intensional, nor are all intensional sentences intentional. Church's contention therefore that intentional language is nothing but intensional language with a psychological subject matter would seem to be untenable(9).

Under such circumstances, it becomes necessary to find out some criterion which would serve to distinguish intentional sentences like 'I believe that p . . . . . . ' from intensional sentences like 'It is possible that p': both satisfy criterion 2. Chisholm's later papers(10) take up this challenge, and contain interesting results.

Let us call expressions like 'S believes,' 'It is possible,' 'It is true,' as simple sentence prefixes. A simple sentence prefix is not itself a sentence, but the result of prefixing it to a sentence is another sentence. Thus if p be a sentence, 'S believes that p' is a sentence. So are 'It is possible that p' and 'It is true that p.' Chisholm asks, how are sentence prefixes which are intentional to be distinguished from those that are not. He now gives us two criteria, one for sentences which are not quantified, and the other for cases where the prefix is inserted into a quantified sentence. These may be called criteria 4 and 4'.

4. A simple sentence prefix M is intentional if and only if for every sentence p, $M(p)$ is logically contingent.

This rules out prefixes like 'It is possible,' 'It is necessary,' 'It is probable,' from being intentional, for it is possible to find out, in each case, a p such that by prefixing it to p we get a sentence which is either a logical truth or a logical contradiction, and so is not logically contingent. But in case of 'I believe,' 'I know' etc. for every p, $M(p)$ is logically contingent.

4'. Take an intentional prefix 'Ram believes.' Let us also take a propositional function 'x is spiritual,' and write down the two sentences we derive from it with the help of universal and existential quantifiers. Thus we get: 'for every x, x is spiritual' and 'There is an x, such that x is spiritual.' Next, let us insert the intentional prefix 'Ram believes' into these two sentences, in each case in two ways possible — once before the quantificational operator, and once just after it. Thus we get the following four sentences:

Ram believes that for every x, x is spiritual . . . . (1)
For every x, Ram believes that x is spiritual . . . . (2)
Ram believes that there is an x, such that x is spiritual . . (3)
There is an x, such that Ram believes that x is spiritual . . (4)

Now, Chisholm contends that an intentional prefix, as in the present case, shows a peculiar pattern of mutual implication or failure of implication amongst these four forms, and that no non-intentional prefix shows this pattern(11). This pattern is characterised by the distinguishing feature that in it (1) does not imply (2). For 'necessity' and 'possibility,' and for deontic modalities like 'It is obligatory that,' 'It is commanded that,' (1) does imply (2).

We may make the following comments on the last two criteria: Criterion 4 — Chisholm shows that on this criterion 'It is right' is not intentional, for when prefixed to 'There is not anything of which it can be truly said that it is right' it yields a contradictory sentence (which therefore is not logically contingent). But the same could be said of 'I believe,' 'I am sure,' 'I think.' The sentences 'I believe there is no one now of whom it can be truly said that he believes,' and 'I think there is no one now who is thinking' are as much self-contradictory as 'It is right that there is nothing of which it can be truly said that it is right.' To say that the first two are not contradictions in the sense of truth-functional logic would not be any good, because the last one is no more so. There is a sense in which 'X believes at time t that p and not-p' is self-contradictory(12). In other words, if 'p' is replaced by 'p and not-p,' then 'X believes that p' is self-contradictory. It is of course possible to argue that since in this case 'X believes that p' is not contingent, it does not refer to a genuine belief or it is not a genuine belief-sentence. This may be alright, but if criterion 4 is to serve as a genuine criterion for distinguishing, amongst other things, belief-sentences from non-intentional sentences, then this further stipulation that only those belief-sentences are genuinely so which satisfy the criterion would be to move in a circle.

Criterion 4' — It should be noted that on Chisholm's own admission(13), 'stating,' 'asserting,' 'affirming,' and 'commanding' do not conform to the pattern of implication formulated by him, and so are not directly intentional. However, each of them implies believing, and so at least involves what is strictly intentional. The same is also the case with 'love' and 'knowledge,' and also 'acting.' Thus the criterion may at best be sufficient, but not necessary for intentionality. And as Chisholm does admit, intentionality in this sense is at best sufficient but not necessary for the psychological: it is not exemplified in 'He is in pain,' for example.

We may now ask, what precisely is Chisholm doing? It will not of course do to argue against Chisholm that what he is doing is to find out some logical property of intentional *sentences* or of the intentional use of sentences, while intentionality in the true sense, in Brentano's sense also, characterises not sentences, not our uses of them, but mental acts and processes or generally speaking, consciousness. This contention is not of much worth, for Chisholm is also seeking to provide, at the same time, for a criterion of the intentionality of the subject matter of intentional discourse. The linguistic turn is not inconsistent with the original thesis, nor does it render that redundant: it rather presupposes that and illuminates that.

Chisholm is seeking, like Brentano, for a criterion to distinguish between the psychological and the non-psychological. He accepts the Brentano thesis that the psychological is intentional and that nothing non-psychological is so. This makes his search also a search for a criterion of the intentional. Insofar as intentionality itself serves, on the Brentano thesis, as a criterion of the psychological, a further criterion of intentionality would seem to be uncalled for. Since Chisholm is searching for a further criterion of intentionality, what he is doing may be either of the following:

(a) It may be that he simply calls the psychological by the name 'Intentional,' and though he appears to be searching for a criterion of the intentional he is really searching for a criterion of the psychological. Or,

(b) It may be that accepting the Brentano thesis that the psychological is characterised by intentionality he is searching for *some other mark* directly of the psychological discourse, indirectly of the psychological itself.

If (a) be the case, then — quite apart from the question of its tenability his thesis is either redundant or not Brentano's, depending upon whether the property he discovers in the psychological is or is not the same as what Brentano called intentionality. If (b) be the case, then we may ask, how is this mark which Chisholm is searching for related to intentionality in Brentano's sense.

It seems to me that there are again two possibilities here. The mark may be a mere de facto invariable accompaniment of intentionality, or it may be a logical consequence of it. The former possibility is not different from that envisaged under (a). Only the second one therefore need be considered. According to it, Chisholm's thesis is related to Brentano's thesis in this way that if the latter holds good of the psychological domain it would logically follow that the former would hold good of the discourse about this domain. In other words, the features which Chisholm detects in intentional language belong to it because the psychological events, processes and acts are characterised by what Brentano called intentionality. This claim of a logical relationship between the two theses could be substantiated only by taking up each of the criteria and asking whether the claim can be defended in each case. This interpretation if sustainable would provide the best account of the relationship of Chisholm's results to the Brentano thesis.

Fortunately, in the case of the first three criteria, such a connection seems to be detectable. Existence independence, truth-value indifference and referential opacity — all three seem to be closely connected with the phenomenological distinctions between (i) the real object and the intended object, and (ii) the intended object and the object as intended. What the fact that there is an intentional act does entail is that there is an intended object, but not that this intended object is as such real. It may even be that the reality of the intended object is precisely the object of belief etc., but even in such cases one has to distinguish between its reality as such and its reality as intended, i.e., as believed, imagined, thought of etc.. Brentano's original thesis — as distinct from his later thesis in which he sought to do away with this distinction because of the fear that the distinction may lead to a hypostatisation of the intended object as a curious *Zwischenentität* — did not hold that every intentional act has a real object, but only that it has its own intended object. It is this which keeps phenomenology distinct from ontology, and one who would hypostatise the intended objects as curious entities would only succumb to the temptation to ontologise. The phenomenologist here has to tread on a razor's edge, avoiding ontological commitments and describing things precisely as they are given. The doctrine of intentionality implies neither realism nor idealism regarded as ontological theories: it is this *ontological neutrality* whose linguistic correlate is brought out in the first two criteria namely in the alleged facts of existence independence and truth-value indifference of intentional discourse.

The criterion of referential opacity is the consequence of a further phenomenological distinction, namely that between the intended object and the same as intended. One who knows Kalidāsa as the author of *Sakuntalā* and one who knows him as the author of *Meghaduta* know the same person, and in this sense the intended object, the object known, is identically the same. But the object as known is in each case different. Hence the fact that one who knows Kalidasā as the author of *Sakuntalā* does not necessarily know him as the author of Meghaduta. Thus *referential opacity* is present whenever *the respect* in which an object is the intended object is made explicit in the act. Of course, as seen before, 'Ram is thinking of Mt. Everest' preserves truth-value if 'Mt. Everest' is replaced by 'the highest peak in the world'; but this is so only because the sentence 'Ram is thinking of Mt. Everest' does not make explicit the precise mode, the *wie* of Ram's thought about Mt. Everest, or if Ram is thinking of Mt. Everest as being the peak successfully climbed by Tenzing and Hillary, it is not necessarily the case that he is thinking of it as the highest peak in the world. Referential opacity only shows that though the reference may be the same the modes of reference, the meanings (as distinguished from the reference) may yet be different and that substitution of extensionally equivalent expressions fails to preserve truth-value precisely because in intentional sentences not the referent as such but the referent in the precise mode or *wie* of its being so is relevant for truth-value.

While thus the first three criteria seem to be closely connected with, and in some understandable sense following from the Brentano thesis, it is yet not quite clear why non-intentional sentences like 'It is possible that p' should at all satisfy any of them. It may presumably be that these sentences though not wholly intentional involve intentional elements. It may be that 'It is possible that p' has a necessary reference to the 'thought of p' and that the latter is intentional. It may be that in this way all intensional sentences involve intentional elements, or presuppose them.

However, the relationship between the Brentano thesis and the criteria 4 and 4' does not seem at this stage to be at all clear.

The principal defect of Chisholm's thesis derives from that of Brentano: it is a narrow conception of intentionality as characterising only the mental. However, researches after Brentano have shown that not the mental alone but also bodily behavior is characterised by intentionality. Further, Chisholm's procedure seems to be that where anything ostensively non-mental exhibits intentionality, he would show that it involves or presupposes the mental. Unfortunately, this does not always work, and both his and Brentano's thesis fail when faced with bodily intentionality. The search for a criterion thus is destined to fail. The concept of intentionality is not a unitary concept, but somewhat of an analogical concept covering under its scope a whole spectrum of widely differing phenomena.

Chisholm's thesis however has this advantage over Brentano's that it brings out more clearly the ontological neutrality of the concept of intentionality, and is thus nearer to the later phenomenological thought which freed itself from the naturalistic framework of Brentano's psychology.

CHAPTER 3

CAN INTENTIONALITY BE
EXPLAINED AWAY?

I

Generally speaking, the main trend of traditional philosophical thinking runs counter to the thesis of intentionality. Idealists have more often than not maintained that consciousness in its essence is free from reference to objects. They speak of a 'pure consciousness'(1), of subjectivity as 'freedom from attachment to the object'(2). They suspect the intentionality thesis to be a kind of denial of such freedom to consciousness. Idealists of a different brand, viz. the subjective idealists recognise objective consciousness but locate the object *within* consciousness as an idea or a representation, as an *ākāra* of consciousness itself(3). This also is tantamount to a denial of intentionality.

The thesis of intentionality is opposed also by the realists for whom the alleged peculiar reference of consciousness to an object is simply not there. Within the framework of a realistic ontology, there can only be a *real* relatedness of consciousness to its object, both the relata being equally real — their qualitative differences notwithstanding. Intentional directedness is replaced either by a neutral compresence or by a causal relation, or at best by some not to be further analysed relation (a *svarupasambandha*) which is nonetheless real for that.

In this chapter we shall examine the arguments of these philosophers and try to show that the intentionality of consciousness cannot be dispensed with. We shall also examine the contentions of some modern philosophers who would want to deny intentionality altogether.

Why should some idealists regard consciousness as being in its essence non-intentional? They may argue, as Samkara seems to have done(4), that consciousness and object are opposed to each other 'as light and darkness' (*tamahprakāśavad*): the one is self-illuminating or translucent, the other is opaque. Being opposed, the two ought not to be as intimately associated as they in fact are. Therefore, the argument runs, the factual association of consciousness with object, howsoever intimate it may pretend to be, is not logically intelligible and so *should be* regarded as false (*mithyā iti bhavitum yuktam*). Now this argument, ably formulated by Samkara and defended by his commentators and expositors, assumes several things. It assumes, for one thing, that there is an opposition between consciousness and object, analogous to that between light and darkness. For another, it assumes that whatever is logically unintelligible in a certain sense is false although it may nevertheless be a fact. As regards the first, there appears to be no satisfactory argument for showing that consciousness and its object are *opposed* to each other. In fact, the philosophers of Samkara's school have struggled hard to make clear the precise nature of this opposition(5). It cannot be a logical opposition, for first no logical relation could subsist between two real entities, but also because there would seem to be no logical contradiction between two propositions, asserted together, one of which asserts the reality of consciousness and the other asserts the reality of object. Nor can any self-contradiction be detected *within* the structure of the proposition 'I am conscious of an object'. The opposition in question cannot be a factual incompatibility, the impossibility of their coexistence (*sahāvasthāna-sāmarth-yābhāva*), for in fact they do coexist, in the only sense in which it is possible for them to coexist, when there is a consciousness of something. It is not also the case that the one destroys the other; the opposition, in other words, is not one of *vadhyaghātak-abhāva*. On the contrary, the one refers to the other, manifests it, and so on. The only sense in which they may be said to be opposed — as a follower of Samkara concedes — is that, of the two one is incapable of being identified with the other *(tādāt-myasāmarthyābhāva*: it is not possible, for example, to say that consciousness is an object. But this is far from being an index of their opposition, it only shows their radical difference and serves to bring out, rather than refute, the intentionality of consciousness. As to the second assumption, namely the assumption that whatever is logically unintelligible is false, two remarks may be in order for the present. If the word 'false' is being used in its ordinary sense then the assumption is unjustified: there is no reason why what is logically unintelligible should be false for that reason. Moreover, a *fact* cannot involve *logical* contradiction, two propositions alone may contradict each other and a proposition conjoining such contradictories would involve a self-contradiction. If, however, the word 'false' is being used in a special sense — the followers of Samkara, to be sure, use it in the special sense of what is neither real nor unreal nor both *(sadasadbhyāmanirvacaniyam)* — then appeal is made to experiential contradiction (as an illusory content is contradicted in the subsequent experience which corrects it) and no experiential contradiction of intentional consciousness is known to me. In the long run, the philosophers who hold the view that intentionality is fortuitious in respect of consciousness *believe* that it is possible for a man to have a state of consciousness which is non-intentional, when one is aware but not of anything. Now this is an act of faith which at its best may be understood as a *demand* arising out of the belief that the intentional function of consciousness is a product of metaphysical ignorance *(avidyā)*, and is the root cause of all *duhkha* or pain, and so *ought* to be eliminated.

One may also make use of Cartesian doubt to prove the idealistic thesis regarding the essential non-intentionality of consciousness. One will then point out that while it is possible to doubt the reality of any and every object of consciousness, it is not possible to doubt the reality of consciousness itself. But this fact, even if it be the case, — which is doubtful in view of Kant's celebrated counterthesis in his *Refutation of Idealism*(6) — does not prove that the consciousness which is thereby shown to be indubitable is non-intentional. On the contrary, it only confirms our thesis that when I have a thought of an object, my having the thought of the object is logically independent of the real existence of non-existence of it. The Cartesian *cogito* is still intentional. Its peculiar certainty which appears to survive the otherwise universal doubt, derives precisely from its intrinsic intentionality.

The subjective idealist's theory of ideas that are immanent to consciousness, combined with the thesis that consciousness is confined within its own realm and cannot — in fact, need not emerge out of this solitude is both an unnecessary construction and incompatible with facts. It starts with the assumption of a representative consciousness, and also assumes, in addition to it, the so-called *Satz des Bewusstseins*(7). The *Satz* contradicts the fact that consciousness is open towards an other. This openness is not a problem but a phenomenon. It becomes a problem, or rather a pseudo-problem, and then a riddle, once we start with the above-mentioned two assumptions. If we get rid of pre-conceptions, and philosophise in order to capture phenomena, then the assumptions have to be rejected, and the phenomenon of consciousness's essential openness has to be recognised. The supposed representative consciousness is the product of a theory; the intentional consciousness is a phenomenon, not a theory.

II

If the idealistic theory of consciousness, with its denial of intentionality, distorts phenomena for the sake either of faith in a spiritual demand or of theoretical pre-conceptions, the realistic ontology provides no better framework for a satisfactory theory of consciousness. For the realist, mind or consciousness is one object amongst others, qualitative differences notwithstanding(8). Within the framework of such an ontology, intentionality becomes a relation. Or, in the words of Bergmann, only by giving ontological status to the connection between an act and its intention do we provide intentionality with an "ontological guarantee"(9). I am not quite sure of what "ontological guarantee" could mean here, save and except reducing intentional reference to a real relation of some kind between real entities of some sorts. But this ontological founding, it would seem, would destroy the sole point of recognising intentionality.

For almost all Indian philosophers, the intended object is *eo ipso* an existent object. (The only exception to this may be found in the Buddhist *vijñānavādins*, but in their system the intention is a form of the mental act itself, and in any case they do not think there is any extra-mental existence.) This is clear from the accounts they give of error and illusory experience: attempts are made to *locate* the object *somewhere*. Not being able to locate it anywhere in the real world, the Advaita Vedānta calls it *anirvacanīya*, indescribable either as real or as unreal or even as both; but he does not give up ontology. This tendency to ontologise, to hypostatise the intention quâ intention finds its counterpart in theory of meaning: for almost all Indian philosophers — with the lone exception possibly of the *Vaiyākaranikas*, the Grammarians, the meaning of an expression is its reference, every expression in effect is a name. No wonder that the true nature of intentionality escaped their grasp.

As we have said before, a satisfactory concept of intentionality — whatver else it may imply — has to take care of the fact that consciousness's intentional reference does not logically entail the existence of the intended object. Adopting a relational theory of consciousness would not only be tantamount to rendering that motion superfluous, but would also give rise to the well-known difficulties which led Russell to his famed theory of description.

If intentionality is not a real relation, can it be a logical relation?(10) It may be supposed that there can be a logical relation between the existent and the non-existent (e.g., 'It is raining or it is not raining'). But against this, it should be pointed out that though a logical relation may hold good between two propositions, one true and another false, it cannot hold good between two reals which are not propositions, not to speak of an existent and a non-existent. A mental act is not a proposition and so cannot be logically related to anything, existent or not.

It hardly needs to be argued out that the relation between an act and its intended object cannot be a causal relation. Of course, *within* the framework of physiological psychology and the other natural sciences one may, and frequently does, speak of a physical thing, state or event as being the cause of a mental state, e.g., of a perception, a fear, a hatred or a love. One may also speak of a mental cause of another mental state. But that a causal relation holds good between an *object o* and a mental state *m* is neither an explication of the fact that *m* is about *o* or *of o*, or is directed towards it, nor an explanation of it. Being the cause of a fear is not the same as being its object, and though the object of a fear may also be its cause the two concepts are not the same. In other words, the possible identity between the cause of a fear and the object of that fear would be a contingent one and not logically necessary(11). Where the object of a mental state does not exist at all, a causal relation between it and the mental state is inconceivable; in case some other causal processes are produced as explaining the origin of the mental state under consideration, such processes do not in any case explain or explicate the sense in which it is of this object.

The relation between a mental state and its object is not also one of resemblance, nor is the object taken up — in the Aristotelian sense of that expression — into the mind, when the state is one of knowledge, in order to be known. On the Thomist view, when one thinks of a triangle the form *triangular* informs the intellect, or the intellect becomes triangular in the immaterial mode (as contrasted with a wax which can become triangular only in the material mode)(12); on the Advaita Vedānta view, in perceiving an object, the mind *(antahkarana)* goes out and takes up the form of the object, and thereby achieves a sort of (formal) identity with the latter(13). Now both these constructions appear to be uncalled for. Both arise from a felt need for some sort of identity, to be achieved between the act and its object. But why this need? Why is the transcendence and continued otherness of the object felt to be a hindrance to intentional reference or even to a fulfilment of that intention in knowledge? Further, with it we are back with some form of the theory of representative consciousness which we have already discarded.

III

The thesis that the mental phenomena are characterised by intentionality has been taken by many as entailing a distinction between act and content. Russell, in *Analysis of Mind*, criticises the Brentano thesis on the ground that the mental *act* is a fiction and that the content alone is there. Bosanquet in *Three Chapters on the Nature of Mind*, on the other hand, complains that the Brentano-Meinong view does not permit the real world "to enter by virtue of identity into the world of knowledge"(14), and takes the supposed obviousness of the mental content, of the "psychic matter" to be the basis of that view. Both the complaints are unfounded.

Russell in *The Analysis of Mind* recants his earlier sympathy with the Brentano thesis ("Now I no longer believe this, even in the case of knowledge") on the ground that the act seems to him unnecessary and fictitious. "The occurrence of the content of a thought," he writes, "constitutes the occurrence of the thought. Empirically I cannot discover anything corresponding to the supposed act; and theoretically I cannot see that it is indispensable"(15). Now, Russell seems to be thinking that the concept of intentionality is defined in terms of the concept of act, and consequently if there are no acts the intentionality thesis will have to be abandoned. He is wrong, for in fact it is the concept of act that is defined in terms of that of intentionality, and not vice versa. An act is anything which exhibits intentionality, and if empirically it may not be possible to detect anything like a mental activity, it surely is possible to discern the directedness, the *of*-ness, the peculiar about-ness characterising our thoughts and beliefs, desires and wishes, loves and hatred. If Russell is willing to admit mental contents, and if they possess such directedness, then they precisely are to be called 'acts.' The intentionality thesis is not committed

to an analysis of mental states into acts *and* contents. The two
may be one, as with the Buddhists, and this one thing, call it
act or content, may indeed be intentional.

In fact, amongst those philosophers who spoke of mental
acts, one may notice a change of meaning of the word 'act': in
fact, there is whole spectrum of various significations attached
to this word. Whereas Lipps understood mental acts in the
ordinary sense of activities of the *I*, Stumpf understands by
them nothing more than 'psychic functions,' and Stout and Husserl wholly get rid of the sense of activity and mean simply
'modes of consciousness' *(Bewusstseinsweise)*(16). It is in this
last sort of sense that we may admit acts: whether over and
above these there are also mental activities may be regarded
as an additional question to be decided on its own merits.

Just as the act theory does not necessarily imply that there
are mental activities, so it does not imply that there are mental
contents as distinct from the acts. The Nayiyāyikas accepted intentional directedness *(savisayakatva)*, but rejected all contents
of consciousness (which they regarded as being *nirākāra*); the
Buddhists accepted contents of consciousness (which is for them
sākāra) but denied — if they also happen to be idealists — intentionality. Brentano started, as we saw, with a statement of
the doctrine of intentional inexistence which suggests a conception of mental content having a mode of being "that is short
of actuality but more than nothingness"(17). But later on he
seems to have retained the intentionality thesis but outright rejected any suggestion of a duplication of the object in the mind.
Husserl in the *Logical Investigations*(18) attacks the theory of
content interpreted as a *Bildtheorie* and as a thoery of the "immanent object of the act"; though one should allow that there
is an important grain of truth in Oskar Kraus's diagnosis that
"the older doctrine still haunts the *Ideen* (sections 88, 91) and
appears in the correlative fictions of *Noema* and *Noese*"(19).
This at least shows this much that the intentionality thesis is
not committed to a doctrine of contents of the form criticised by
Bosanquet in the paragraph quoted above.

The upholders of the act theory not only differed amongst
themselves regarding the very admissibility of mental content;

even those who admitted both acts and contents, differed amongst themselves regarding the relation between the supposed act and the supposed content(20). Thus while some of them thought act and content to be separable elements (according to Messer, for example, both actless contents and contentless acts are possible), others like Witasek treated the two as inseparable factors of one whole (this act-and-content whole being what is intentional).

We have already emphasized that the intentionality thesis is committed to a denial of the theory of representative consciousness. This much is settled for us. So, if any form of content has nevertheless to be admitted owing to the pressure of facts, then such content cannot be the representative content, it cannot be the image or the picture *(Bild)*. Husserl's analysis of intentionality gives us an alternate version of the content theory which does not entail any form of theory of representative consciousness. On Husserl's theory, the content — if it is a real component of mental life — is the *hyle,* and if it is not to be a real component of mental life, it is the *Noema.* However, we cannot attempt a fair assessment of the question, to what extent Husserl went back to some form of the content theory till we have had a close look at these two concepts — the *hyle* and the *noema,* but we can assure ourselves (i) that he did advocate a form of the content theory and (ii) that he did not revive some form of the theory of representative consciousness.

Husserl's criticism of the imagist version of the content theory (21) is in brief as follows. The theory, Husserl argues, completely overlooks the important point that in the representation of an image *(Bildvorstellung)* we intend the object pictured and not the picture itself. The being-picture of a picture is not an intrinsic character, not a real predicate of the particular thing functioning as a picture. It is not the case that a thing is a picture in the same way as it is red or round. Nor is the being-picture of a picture constituted by mere resemblance of the picture with the object pictured. It is the "representing consciousness" (we may for the present overlook Husserl's references to the representing ego) which makes a picture into a picture, so that, according to Husserl, a picture quâ picture is constituted in a peculiar intentional consciousness. The lesson to be drawn is that an image or a sign becomes an image or a sign only because of a certain intentional consciousness, so that intentionality cannot be said to be itself made possible by the image or the sign.

IV

We may now consider a powerful trend of thought which under the guiding ideologies of physicalism, unity of the sciences and an extensionalist philosophy of language, seeks to do away with all psychological, indeed with all non-extensional, discourse. This thesis is professedly confined to a merely linguistic commitment, but its philosophical consequences reach out beyond a reformation of scientific discourse.

To start with, let us recall certain attempts to reduce intentional sentences to non-intentional ones which have been well taken care of by Chisholm in his "Sentences about believing." Chisholm has been able to show pretty convincingly that such translations into non-intentional language owe their plausibility to the fact that at some stage they covertly use intentional terms. There are two ways of maintaining the intentionalistic position. One may, as Chisholm does, argue that any attempt to translate belief sentences into non-intentional language of specific response or of appropriate behavior, or disposition to expect is either inadequate, or if true will be found on closer examination to be making covert use of the concepts of belief, springs of action, fulfilment etc., all of which are intentional. But I think one can even go further. Even if one does not find any mental concept in the alleged translation, one may still be using intentional concepts for many of our concepts of bodily behavior are intentional. The intentionality thesis as such is not opposed to behaviorism though it surely is opposed to a mechanical concept of behavior. Thus suppose there is a mental word m with an intentional object O, and suppose its behavioristic translation into the language of response is $r(O)$. Let us grant further that the translation is adequate, in other words that the mental word m is dispensable. But $r(O)$ is no less intentional. The truth of the statement 'S makes the response $r(O)'$ logically entails neither the existence nor the non-existence of O. The response r is directed towards O, and the sense of this directedness is closer to the directedness of a mental act towards its object, and is radically different from the relation of 'being caused by.' To bring in the concept of 'being stimulated by O' is of no use, for a stimulus quâ stimulus is not a cause. The concept of 'being a simulus of' is an intentional concept(22).

Feigl concedes that though human behavior may in principle be capable of physical explanation and prediction, yet it may not be possible to give a physical account of how thoughts, beliefs, feelings or desires can be about something(23). He thus separates the problem of physical explanation and prediction of human behavior from the logical problem of reducibility or irreducibility of discourse involving *aboutness* to the langauge of behavioral or neuro-physiological description.

V

There are linguistic critics who would take recourse to a different account which does not necessarily make use of a behavioristic philosophy. We shall now discuss some of these attempts.

Carnap denies any uniqueness to the intentional relation and reduces it to a relation that obtains also amongst terms which are far from being intentional. The latter is the sort of relation which holds good between an element and a relational structure of a certain sort. Other such relations, according to Carnap, are: the relation of a given plant to the botanical system of plants, the relation of a given hue to the system of colours, the relation of a person to his family, his state or his occupational hierarchy. It is not at the first sight quite clear how the relation of an experience to its intentional object is of the same sort as the above-mentioned relations. Carnap's explanation however is as follows. Take the thought of a tree. From the point of view of Carnap's constructionism, the intended tree is "a certain, already very complicated ordering of experiences, namely of those experiences of which we say that the tree is their intended object"(24). The experience which at present intends the tree belongs to the same order of experiences out of which the intended tree is constructed. Thus Carnap requires two conditions to be fulfilled so that the intentional relation may hold good between an experience and an order of experience (which for him is the intended object): for one thing, the former must belong to the latter; for another, "this order must be one of those constructional forms in which real-typical objects are constructed"(25). Unless each object essentially belongs to a certain order of experiences it could not be constructed, it could not be intended(26).

Now it should be obvious on closer examination that Carnap's reduction of the concept of intentionality in fact presupposes it. The intended object is sought to be constructed out of, or analysed into, an order of experiences, "namely of those experiences of which we say that the tree is their intended object." Thus the intended object O is analysed into an order of experiences e_1 e_2, e_3, e_4, ... such that each of these *es* intends the same O. Only if this is so can the proposed construction be meaningful. In fact, as was seen a little before, the order, Carnap stipulates, must be such that real objects could be constructed in it; and this requirement is nothing but this that each member of the order should itself be intentional. Carnap thus fails to eliminate intentionality. The analogy he draws with the relation of a given plant to a botanical system is far-fetched, and does not bring out the essential feature of the very scheme he presents. On his own scheme the relation

$$e \rightarrow O$$

may be restated as:

e is a member of $\{e_1 (o), e_2 (o), e_3 (o), ... \}$

The intentionality reappears within each member of the series, and so the intentionality of e which is a member of it remains unimpaired. Understood in this way, Carnap's constructionism looks surprisingly alike Husserl's later theory of intentionality as constitutive, or of the intended object as being constituted in the noetic acts. This would not be a denial of intentionality, but giving it a new extension or even an explication which we propose to examine in another place in this book.

VI

The view that the objects of intentional attitudes are linguistic entities so that intentional sentences may be replaced
by sentences relating people to linguistic entities has been advocated by Carnap at some places, also by Quine and Sheffler.
We may make two observations on such a view so obviously re-
pugnant to facts(27.) In the first place, it does not as such eliminate intentionality; it shows concern about how to avoid admitting the intended objects with their claim to a curious sort
of being. As emphasized before, the concern is understandable
but avoidable; you do not improve matters by introducing a
linguistic entity − the word 'unicorn,' e.g., in the case of the
thought of a unicorn − as the object of the mental act. The
underlying assumption is that there should be something *real*
towards which a mental act could be directed; if it is not a
real unicorn, if it is not to be a curiously subsistent unicorn, it
can only be the word 'unicorn.' The whole point about intentionality is thereby lost, the fact namely that the real existence
or non-existence of the intended object is not entailed. Further,
as Chisholm has pointed out, the validity of this view depends
upon "the availability of certain semantic sentences corresponding to each intentional sentence, which is indeed hard to sub-
stantiate"(28).

Quine repudiates mental entities, and prefers to construe
consciousness as "a faculty of responding to one's responses"
whereby responses are regarded as physical behavior(29). But
even this is not to eliminate intentionality, for as we have said
before the concepts of response and behavior are incurably
intentional. Sellars formulates a more cautious position(30). He
conceives of a possible situation where men think but do not
know that they think, where their use of language is meaningful because it expresses their thoughts but they do not know
that it is the expression of their thoughts. In such a situation,
they would have no concept of intentionality. The purpose of
this argument is not at all clear to me. Surely every user of
language, though expressing his thoughts and other mental
acts, does not have a fully explicit concept of intentionality, but
this fact does not show that − even if we grant the situation

imagined by Sellars — that the intentionality of linguistic and other forms of human behavior can be theoretically dispensed with, or even that the intentionality of mental acts has to be denied. Sellars, of course, contends that "the categories of intentionality are nothing more nor less than the metalinguistic categories in terms of which we talk epistemically about overt speech as they appear in the framework of thoughts construed on the model of overt speech"(31). Let us try to understand what Sellars could have meant by this. In the ordinary object language where we talk about things, persons, places, events and episodes — inner or outer — we do not use the category of intentionality. Of course, we have beliefs and we express them; we have thoughts and we communicate them. It is only when we talk about our overt speech, and further do so epistemically that the categories of intentionality arise. One may of course talk about overt speech in other ways. One may, for example, talk about its syntax, its grammar and so on, without making use of the concept of intentionality. But one can also talk about overt speech epistemically: thus of an expression 'E' one may say that:

'E' expresses a thought *t*, and *t* is *about p*. The 'about' introduces intentionality. Thus the concept of intentionality is meta-linguistic in origin.

That the categories of intentionality are metalinguistic in origin need not be disputed: this is only the linguistic correlate of the fact that the *concept* of intentionality — not the intentional directedness itself — is a product of reflection on the first order experiences. That it is further a product of an epistemically oriented metalanguage only restates, in the formal mode of speech, the fact that the reflection which reveals intentionality (and so makes its *concept* possible) is a phenomenological reflection, and not an objectively oriented reflection.

VII

The critics of the intentionality thesis are bothered by several quite different things. Some like Quine are concerned about the notion of the mental in general, others like Russell (of 1921) worry not about the mental as such but about the notion of mental acts. Others are bothered by the prospect of having to admit into their ontologies curious entities which are intended in those acts. Now the concept of intentionality does not stand or fall with the concept of the mental in general, it surely is not committed to a philosophy of the ghost in the machine. It is committed neither to a dualism between body and mind (contrary to what Popper maintains)(32). In fact, as Quinton has argued(33), it is compatible with an identity theory according to which the identity between bodily and mental states is not logical but contingent. Which of these theories one is willing to accept would be chosen on its own independent merits, and not merely on the basis of one's acceptance of the intentionality thesis; though having accepted the latter thesis one cannot revert to the mechanistic naturalistic type of thinking about the mind or even about the body. Regarding the mental act, most of the concern felt about it arises from misunderstanding 'act' in the sense of activity, process, episode etc. An act may be any of these, or it may not be. An act is what is characterised by intentionality and it is good to remember that intentional directedness itself, the reference to, the being-about, is not an act.

The concern about the curious entities that one may have to admit into one's ontology should one recognise the irreducibility of intentionality is also unfounded. As has been emphasized, the intentionality thesis is neutral as between realism and idealism, and the true nature of intentionality cannot be grasped unless one stubbornly refuses to ontologise, i.e., unless one takes up the strictly phenomenological attitude which indeed commits one to tread on a razor's edge. We have yet to see whether the phenomenologists themselves succeeded in doing so.

The above discussion also make it clear that the intentionality thesis as a thesis about the alleged criterion of the mental cannot hold its own any more. Whether everything mental is intentional, whether all unconscious states and sensations and bodily feelings are so is disputable. Surely, not the mental alone is intentional, for bodily behaviour and human action are also so.

CHAPTER 4

HUSSERL'S CRITICISMS OF BRENTANO'S CONCEPT OF INTENTIONALITY

Husserl's criticisms of Brentano's concept of intentionality are to be found chiefly in the *Logische Untersuchungen* II.1., V Investigation, Chap. 2; and also in the *Phänomenologische Psychologie* (Husserliana Bd. IX). We shall mainly draw upon these two sources, though we have also to take note of Husserl's many comments scattered in various other places.

1. Brentano, as we have seen, sought to distinguish between the mental and the non-mental phenomena. He had found in intentionality one of the distinguishing features of the mental phenomena. Husserl is not interested in this classificatory project; he is not interested in the project of demarcating the field of psychology, but he is interested in the concept of intentionality as such. To challenge the classification and the principle of doing it would be one thing; to limit the scope of intentionality would be another. Husserl takes up the latter task. It is undoubtedly true from particular instances of intentional reference, e.g., from acts of thinking, desiring, loving etc., we can — through a sort of eidetic abstraction — arrive at the generic notion of experience or *Erlebnis*. But we may then ask, whether all experiences or *Erlebnisse* are intentional or not, i.e.,

whether the generic notion of experience in general and that of intentional experience have the same extension or not. Husserl's own answer to this question is in the negative. For him, all *Erlebnisse* are not intentional. Sensations and complexes of sensations are *Erlebnisse* but they are not intentional(1). When Husserl speaks of 'acts', he is to be understood as specifically referring to the intentional *Erlebnisse* and not to any and every *Erlebnis*(2).

2. Husserl has two major comments to make on Brentano's undoubtedly misleading terminology. In the first place, he objects to Brentano's use of the word 'phenomena' in connection with what Husserl calls intentional *Erlebnisse*. The word 'phenomena' refers to objects that appear or are given, considered as so appearing. When Brentano calls every intentional *Erlebnis* a phenomenon, he evidently means that every such *Erlebnis* has not only an object of its own but is itself the object of another intentional *Erlebnis*, i.e., of what he calls an inner perception. Husserl does not accept this latter proposition(3).

Husserl's next objection is against Brentano's use of 'immanent object.' It is surely misleading to say that the object enters into or appears within consciousness, or that consciousness contains its object within itself. It is also misleading to say — and, as we have found, Brentano was aware of this difficulty — that consciousness enters into a sort of relationship with its object. Brentano indeed was aware of the inadequacy of his terminology, and he in all fairness should not be taken as using them in a strictly literal sense. Husserl warns us against two likely misunderstandings. In the first place, we may be led to think of intentionality as a real process or relation between consciousness or the ego on the one side and the object on the other. What is worse still is to think of intentionality as an intrasubjective relation between two real components of consciousness which surely it is not.

When I have an intentional *Erlebnis*, say a thought or a desire, it is not the case that I have two things given in my experience, the *Erlebnis and* its object. It is only the *Erlebnis* that is present, and the Erlebnis has a certain descriptive character, the character of an intention. The *Erlebnis*, by its very

nature, refers to its object, and the object is intentionally present: the two are only different ways of saying the same(4). The
object may not in fact exist at all. The object is only *meant*.
The *Erlebnis* under consideration consists just in so meaning or
intending its object in the way in which it does so.

I think of or represent to myself the god *Indra*. However
I may analyse my thought or representation, the god *Indra* will
never be discovered as a real component of my mental act. It
is not therefore immanent in my mind. Is it then extra-mental?
It may or it may not be. In the present case, I know from other
sources that there is no such God. But the question of the
real existence or non-existence of the god *Indra* does not in any
way affect the content of what I am thinking about when I
think of *Indra*. Of course, I may think of his existence or of his
non-existence, but that would be a different thought altogether.
My thought of Jupiter and my thought of Bismarck are not, as
thoughts, different, to take Husserl's own example. For the
thinking consciousness it is all the same, there is an object
to it, no matter whether that object further exists or not.

In view of these difficulties arising out of the expression
'immanent object,' Husserl prefers to speak of 'intentional object'
instead(5). But we cannot also any more speak of the *'intentionalen Enthaltensein'* of the object in consciousness.

3. While these are the main points which Husserl makes
in connection with his examination of Brentano's theory — and
it should be clear in the light of our exposition of Brentano
that Brentano himself was aware of many of these difficulties —
Husserl, in the second part of *LU* II, takes up Brentano's thesis
about the inner perception of mental phenomena. Since this also
shall be of interest to our study, we shall attempt here a brief
exposition of Husserl's main criticism of Brentano(6) on this
point.

Husserl looks upon Brentano's findings as important though
they suffer from a lack of phenomenological distinctions and
from a consequent equivocation in terminology. None of Brentano's earlier critics, according to Husserl, have gone into the
real sources of these confusions and equivocations. Brentano's
distinction between inner and outer perceptions is based on the

thesis that inner perception alone is evident, i.e., unerring and indubitable whereas outer perception is fallible. Husserl rejects this thesis. For Husserl, the distinction between evident and non-evident perceptions does not coincide with that between inner and outer perceptions. Every perception of my own inner psychic states is not evident in the sense of being infallible and indubitable. I may well be deceived even with regard to inner perception. The psychic phenomenon as it is perceived to be may not be there at all. And Husserl even allows the possibility of a transcendent perception of psychic states. This in fact is so, according to him(7), when we are in the naturalistic, scientific attitude. It is only when we adopt the phenomenological attitude that the inner is perceived as purely inner, as the pure *Erlebnis,* and this of course may be infallible. Just as inner perception may be subject to error, so outer perception may be in a certain sense infallible. If we mean by 'physical phenomena' not only physical things, events and processes but also — as Brentano certainly seems to have meant — the lived contents of our perceptions of physical things, events and processes, then perception of such contents, even if they are sense-contents, is infallible.

Husserl however grants that if by psychic phenomena we mean the *Erlebnisse* themselves which are "the real constituents of our consciousness" and if one means by 'inner perception' adequate perception i.e. perception wherein the intended object is given exactly as it was intended, in which there is no unfulfilled intention as it were, then of course such inner perception must be regarded as adequate(8). It would seem however that according to Husserl not all inner perception of *Erlebnisse,* whatever precisely '*Erlebnis*' may mean, is adequate, though adequate perception of *Erlebnisse* is possible. All that he here insists on is that Brentano was wrong in simply identifying inner perception with adequate perception. Brentano did not see the possibility of being deceived even with regard to one's own inner perceptions.

It seems that the real significance of much of these will be clear only when we are able to find out what Husserl means by that much used word '*Erlebnis.*' But before we turn to Husserl's own positive conceptions, let us persist for a while with his criticism of Brentano.

4. In his later works, especially in the *Phänomenologische Psychologie*, we find more fundamental criticisms of Brentano. In fact, the criticisms of the *LU* do not go deep enough, and apart from drawing attention to terminological ambiguities and inadequacies, they do not bring out deep and fundamental differences in the understanding of the concept of intentionality. In actual practice, however, the works since the *Ideen* I show a great deal of such fundamental divergence, and before we go into Husserl's positive theory of intentionality it may be fruitful to put together the main points where he would go beyond the Brentano thesis.

(a) Concerned as he was with laying the basis of an empirical psychology, Brentano's interest in the concept of intentionality was that of a psychologist. Here was for him a descriptive character common to all psychic phenomena, and distinguishing them off from physical phenomena. Husserl's interest is not that of a psychologist, though he also made use of the concept of intentionality to characterise a new kind of psychology altogether. Brentano was still working within the framework of a naturalistic psychology for which causal explanation is the explanation *par excellence*. For Husserl, the concept of intentionality demands a complete abandonment of the causal attitude in connection with conscious life. This requires a phenomenological attitude, the attitude of accepting phenomena as they are given. Rejection of a naturalistic psychology — be it of an associationistic, or of the physiological or of the Freudean type — paves the way for the conception of an intentional psychology. The mode of unity which prevails in one's conscious life may be now characterised by the adjective 'intentional.' Conscious states imply each other, lead to one another — not by mechanical association, nor by logical implication but by motivating, anticipating and fulfilling each other. To understand a conscious state in this sense would be to follow all its *intentional implications*.

States of consciousness are not outside each other, and do not influence each other as physical states do. They rather internally refer to each other. It is for the psychologist to decipher such implications. This notion of intentional implication was of course unknown to Brentano.

(b) Brentano of course did classify modes of consciousness in accordance with the modes of intentional reference involved in them. But he did not realise that to each type of object there corresponds a certain type of intentional act. This last mentioned fact has two aspects. On the one hand, there is, for Husserl, a correlation between types of objects and types of intentional reference in the sense that to each type of object there corresponds a certain mode of givenness. In fact, the mode of giveness characteristic of a certain type of object may be used to bring out the phenomenological distinctiveness of that type. In the second place, to each particular object there corresponds a whole series of actual and possible intentional acts which have precisely that object as their intentional object. Two typically Husserlian notions arise out of this latter situation: the notion of *noesis-noema* correlation and that of the constitution of the object in the acts. Both these notions, so central to Husserl's concept of intentionality, are of course not to be expected in Brentano.

From the above it follows that Husserl ascribes to intentionality of the act two important functions: the intentional acts not only may refer to an object, but in a sense make the object possible or constitute it, by (i) synthesising the contents of the various acts, actual and possible, and (ii) by identifying the object as the same object intended in all the various acts. Thus, identification of the object and synthesis of the object are two other functions which Husserl assigns to the intentional act, apart from which the full nature of the intentional function of the act is not grasped. An intentional analysis of an object, or of a type of object therefore requires us to go back to the acts which through their synthetic and identificatory functions make the object or the type of object possible. Husserl makes much use of this method of intentional analysis.

(c) It should be borne in mind that Husserl could introduce these notions because *he did in a way bring back the notion of content* — as distinguished from the intentional object — which, as we have shown, was rejected by Brentano. Once the notion of content is there, one can account for the various ways in which the same object may be given to different acts, and one has to account for how in spite of these different contents one and the same object comes to be intended through all of them for which purpose some action of synthesis is called for. In this respect, the content theory, though inviting complexities, is in an advantageous position, and I would agree with Findlay when he points it out as a defect of Brentano that the latter's concept of reference to objects does not employ any clear cut distinction like Frege's between sense and reference(9).

(d) For Husserl, the decided point of departure is the phenomenological reduction without which the phenomenological attitude cannot come into operation and without which we may not be in a position to appreciate the full significance of the notion of intentionality. Brentano was of course aware that the object referred to may or may not exist, and he too like Husserl saw that the reference *quâ* reference is not affected by the existence or the non-existence of the object being referred to. But this indifference to the existence of the intentional object cannot come to its own so long as we do not give effect to phenomenological reduction by which we put all positing of transcendent things under 'brackets' and view the object *quâ* object, i.e., as it is being intended. This requires in fact putting our entire naturalistic belief in the world under brackets. For though I may be aware that there is no god *Indra* when I am representing one to me, I may still be tempted to take recourse to some kind or other of causal explanation of how this representation could ever arise in me and could at all refer to a non-existent object. Now, such possibilities of and temptations for causal explanation have to be avoided, and the only way to do that is to neutralise our entire naturalistic belief in a transcendent world as causing or stimulating mental states in our psycho-physical organisms. Viewing the object purely as it is intended, and freeing ourselves of the prejudice of a transcendent world (though the world as it is given, as the *noema*, remains), we begin to realise that intentionality is a feature not only of the psychological consciousness characterising this psycho-physical organism but also of transcendental consciousness. This opens up for Husserl the whole gamut of problems with which he was concerned all through his philosophical career. The great difference then between Brentano and Husserl lies precisely here: Husserl's concept of intentionality is not intelligible without following him in his reductions, whereas Brentano — in spite of all his profound insights into the difficulties of conceiving of intentionality on the analogy of a real relation — remained *on the level* of naturalistic belief in a transcendent world.

PART TWO

CHAPTER 1

HUSSERL'S CONCEPT OF
INTENTIONALITY — I

A. CONSCIOUSNESS AND INTENTIONAL ACT

IN THE *Logische Untersuchungen,* Husserl begins the Fifth Investigation entitled *"Ueber intentionale Erlebnisse und Ihre 'Inhalte'"* by trying to clear up the equivocations that so much vitiate our use of the word 'consciousness.' Leaving out of consideration many non-philosophical uses of the word, he concentrates on three philosophical uses or concepts of 'consciousness.' These are: (a) the concept of consciousness as the real (*'reell'*) phenomenological unity of the *Erlebnisse* of the empirical ego; (b) the concept of consciousness as the inner perception of one's own psychic *Erlebnisse,* and (c) the concept of consciousness as the over all name for every kind of psychic act or intentional *Erlebnis.*

I

Each of these three concepts makes use of the term *'Erlebnis,'* and it would be useful if we could go a little into the exact meaning of this term, as used by Husserl. Husserl tells us that according to the psychology of his time the word 'Erlebnis' simply meant the real events (*Vorkommnisse, Ereignisse*) which, changing from moment to moment, constitute — through various kinds of interconnections and interpenetrations — the real unity of consciousness of the psychic life of an individual. In this sense, the perceptions, fantasies, imaginations, thoughts, suppositions, doubts, pleasures and pains, hopes and fears, wishes and desires — all these, as they come and go in our consciousness, are *Erlebnisse*(2). This in fact is Husserl's first and widest sense of 'consciousness'. Anticipating his subsequent findings, we may say that in this sense, the words 'Erlebnis' and 'Consciousness' (which are, of course according to this broadest sense coextensive terms) stand for both intentional and non-intentional experiences, both acts (in the specific sense of that term) and *hyle* (in the sense to be explained afterwards). This wide sense of 'Erlebnis' is somewhat retained in the *Ideas I*. Thus, for example, we are told: "Under *experience* in the *widest sense* we understand whatever is to be found in the stream of experience, not only therefore intentional experiences, *cogitationes* actual and potential taken in their full concreteness, but all the real (*reellen*) phases to be found in this stream and in its concrete sections"(3). In this sense, a concrete act of perception but also the component pure sensation which goes into that concrete act are both *Erlebnisse*.

It should be clear that this is too wide a sense in which the word 'Erlebnis' can be used. Normally we do not say that one has an *Erlebnis* or experience of an object of outer perception, e.g., a tree. I perceive or imagine or may recollect or even think of a tree, but I do not experience one. In Husserl's widest sense of that term, such an usage should be permissible. It is perhaps more in conformity with the ordinary use of that term to say that whereas I perceive or imagine, recollect or think of a tree, I have *Erlebnis* of — or, I *erlebe* or experience — the act of perceiving, or imagining or remembering or thinking. Perception or imagination or memory or thinking, considered as acts, are *Erlebnisse*, but to perceive a tree is not therefore to have an *Erlebnis* of one.

The act itself is an *Erlebnis* in the sense that the act is *erlebt* (while, a tree that is perceived is not thereby a perception). This may be accounted for by the fact that strictly speaking we do not have an *Erlebnis of* an act in the same sense of that word 'of' in which we have perception of a tree. In other words, the act is not an object of *Erlebnis*, but is itself the *Erlebnis* in so far as we, at the time we are having the act (i.e., at the time we are perceiving, imagining etc.), also have an immediate awareness of the act: or, better still, the act is aware of itself. The act and its awareness are the same. It is this essential reflexivity of the act which accounts for its being — over and above being a perception, an imagination, or a memory — also an *Erlebnis*(4).

II

This sense of '*Erlebnis*' however is not the same as Husserl's second concept of consciousness. According to this second concept of consciousness, consciousness is the inner perception that we are supposed to have of our actually present psychic states or *Erlebnisse* in the first and the widest sense of that term. In the first sense, consciousness is the total complex of psychic states or *Erlebnisse;* in the second sense, consciousness is the inner perception of those *Erlebnisse.* In this latter sense, then, consciousness becomes a sort of knowing, a reflective objective awareness of the primary *Erlebnis.* As we have seen, the primary *Erlebnis,* the perception, the imagination, the act of remembering or thinking, is also aware of itself in a more immediate sense and is therefore entitled to be called an *Erlebnis,* but this primary self-awareness of the *Erlebnis* is not yet an inner perception. This primary reflexivity is not yet a reflection. Reflection would turn the primary *Erlebnis* into an object, and the act of reflection would itself then be an *Erlebnis.* This primary reflexive *Erlebnis* has still the form "This is a tree" in case it is a perception, "I had seen it before" in case it is a recognition, and so on. The corresponding reflections would have the form "I perceive a tree" or "I have the perception of a tree," "I recognise the tree," and so on. Reflections on these latter would yield judgments of the

form "I am aware that I am having a perception," "I know that
I am recognising this tree," and so on.

What is important in this is the distinction between the
reflexivity of every *Erlebnis* — the reflexivity by virtue of which
it deserves to be called an *Erlebnis* and also consciousness —
and the fact that every *Erlebnis* may become, but need not
become, the object of an inner perception. Rightly therefore
Husserl rejects this second concept of consciousness both as
being too narrow, and also as being somewhat arbitrary and
finally as involving a *regressus ad infinitum*(5). It is narrow because it is true only of reflective awareness but not of the primary
reflexive *Erlebnis*. I have an immediate consciousness that I
am perceiving before I make this perception an object of reflection or inner perception. It is arbitrary because every primary
Erlebnis need not become the object of an inner perception.
And finally, it leads to an infinite regress, for if every *Erlebnis*
must necessarily be the object of an inner perception then the
inner perceptions themselves must also be objects of other inner
perceptions. Such an infinite series of inner perceptions is of
course not given to us, and so the regress is vicious.

As against the objection that this concept of consciousness
is too narrow in so far as it does not apply to the primary
Erlebnis, it may be answered that the primary *Erlebnis* is con-
scious inasmuch as it is an object of an inner perception while
the inner perception is consciousness itself. But since this concept renders the notion of reflexivity of consciousness redundant,
there remains for it no distinction between the primary *Erlebnis*
and its inner perception: of both we can be conscious only
through an inner perception, of both it holds good that they are
not reflexive. If the inner perception is entitled to be called
consciousness there is no reason why the primary *Erlebnis* also
should not be so called.

Though the second concept of consciousness is narrower,
Husserl reminds us(6) that it may have a certain priority for philosophers in the sense that here in inner perception, as in the
Cartesian *cogito*, the philosopher seems to reach an absolutely
evident point of departure. Can we then say that the Cartesian

cogito is the inner perception of, or reflection on, the primary unreflective but reflexive *Erlebnis?* I would agree with Sartre in giving an affirmative answer to this question. The *cogito,* the 'I think,' certainly does represent the reflective consciousness. It does not represent the unreflective, primary, but reflexive consciousness. The primary perception has the form 'This is a tree' and not the form 'I perceive a tree'(7).

III

In the third sense, 'consciousness' means only the intentional acts themselves. This sense of the term lies midway between the first and the second. It is narrower than the first sense in so far as in this sense not all *Erlebnisse* but only those that are acts, i.e., intentional are conscious. Thus the element of pure sensation, though a component of the act of perception, is not itself intentional and so in this sense is not conscious either. This sense is also wider than the second sense, for whereas in the second sense only inner perceptions of acts are conscious, in the third sense both the acts and their possible inner perceptions are conscious in so far as they both are intentional. This third concept of consciousness establishes its legitimacy by bringing out a certain inadequacy in what was said above about *Erlebnisse* in general. It was said above that an *Erlebnis* is reflexive, i.e., by its very intrinsic nature is aware of itself. This statement has now to be modified in view of the fact that not all *Erlebnisse* are so, perhaps the pure sensation that goes into a perceptual experience as the latter's component is not so. I have an immediate awareness of myself as perceiving and not as having a sensation, though the latter awareness may be achieved through an act of reflection. It is indeed difficult to say if the division of *Erlebnisse* into those that are intentional and those that are not coincides in extension with that into those that are reflexive and those that are not. Acts in Husserl's sense are intentional and reflexive. Pure sensations are non-intentional and non-reflexive. But there may be affective experiences which are non-intentional though reflexive, and there may be psychic states — like the so-called unconscious states which are intentional but not reflexive: they may be intentional in the sense that even an unconscious fear or hatred may be of or about something or some person. One may however prefer to clarify the situation by restricting the use of 'Erlebnis' to those psychic states which are reflexive, whether they are intentional or not: this would be well in conformity with the ordinary use of 'erleben,' and would in effect exclude non-reflexive states like sensations as well as unconscious states, does not matter whether they are intentional or not(8). If we accept this stricter use of 'Erlebnis,' then we could perhaps suggest the following table of classification of psychic states:—

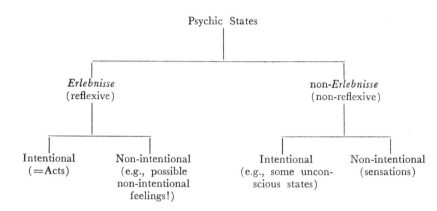

B. ANALYSIS OF AN INTENTIONAL ACT IN THE *LOGISCHE UNTERSUCHUNGEN*

Husserl's own positive analysis of intentionality is developed through various stages. In the *L.U.*II.1 we get what Diemer has called a static analysis of intentionality, whereas in *L.U.*II.2., we get the first glimpses of what the same author calls dynamic analysis. This distinction is on the whole a good working hypothesis, and helps us to find our way through Husserl's writings. We have only to remember that the two kinds of analyses do not exclude each other, and may very well be regarded as being both valid.

Husserl's first step in analysing intentional acts is to distinguish between the real (he uses the word '*reell*' for, as he tells us(9), the word 'real' suggests something like a thing, something that is *dinghaft*) content of an act and its intentional content. This distinction, I should think, is completely basic to his way of thinking, for it shows that the intentional is not a real component of an act. The word 'intentional' (as qualifying not an experience but a thing or an object) may be used as a contrast with 'real': in this sense that is intentional which is not independently real but which owes whatever reality it has to the mercy of the subjective act. In this sense, for example, it may be said that fictitious entities like a golden mountain or logical entities like propositions have a merely intentional existence but do not exist really. Here, however, when Husserl speaks of the intentional content of an act, he is not using 'intentional' in this sense. His preference to avoid the word 'real' as a contrast with the 'intentional' has thus a double advantage: it rules out the possibility of misconceiving the non-intentional components on the analogy of things or thing-like entities, and it also rules out the possibility of misconceiving the intentional content as some thing which depends upon the act for its being, whatever that may mean.

By the real components of an act Husserl understands(10) all those *Erlebnisse* which are parts of the act considered as a totality. To describe these real components of an act would be the task of a descriptive psychology. Descriptive psychology would not stop to consider either their originating interconnections (*genetische Zusammenhänge*) or what they might signify beyond themselves. The attitude of such descriptive psychology would be to give a purely immanent description of the component experiences or psychic states. All that a phenomenologist can do over and above this psychological description is to search for general eidetic structures. But Husserl is well aware(11) that when we talk of the real contents of an intentional act we are talking of 'content' in a sense in which we could also speak of contents of any other non-intentional experience. But when we speak of the *intentional* content we are concerned with intentional experiences as such. The term 'intentional content' however means various things, and we may accordingly distinguish between (i) the intentional *object* of an act, (ii) the intentional *matter* of the act, and (iii) the intentional *essence* of the act. Let us first follow the account given by Husserl of these in the Fifth Investigation and see how that is supplemented in the Sixth one, before we could bring out the changes and developments which were introduced in the *Ideas I.*

In the Fifth Investigation, the concept of intentional matter is explicated by contrasting it with the concept of intentional quality of an act. By the intentional quality of an act, Husserl here means what is common for example to various acts of judging considered as acts of judging irrespective of what they may be about, or what is common to the various acts of desiring irrespective of what they may be about, and so on. Thus, all the various acts of judging have the same intentional quality, all the acts of desiring again have the same intentional quality, all the acts of supposing have the same intentional quality, and so on. But, if we consider two acts of judging about different subject matter, e.g., the act of judging that 2 x 2 = 4 and the act of judging that New Delhi is the capital of India, the qualities of the two acts are the same while that precisely in which they differ, more precisely (for, they might be said to differ also in their complexity or simplicity etc.) the differing content of each, is its intentional matter. It is easy for him to show that acts with different qualities may have the same matter and acts having the same quality may have different matter. For example, the judgment that there are living beings on the Mars, the question 'Are there living beings on the Mars?' and the supposition 'There may be living beings on the Mars' have the same matter, although the acts have quite different qualities. It may be objected at this stage that what the first of the above-mentioned three acts has for its matter is the proposition that there are living beings on the Mars, while the other two acts do not have propositions for their matter. But, this would be to misunderstand Husserl's intention. He is in fact *so defining* 'intentional matter' that from his very concept of it it would follow that these three acts have the same matter in common. In fact, we could even say that what these three acts have in common on the content side is just what is called their matter. From this, it would follow that the proposition does not constitute the matter of an act of judging.

The quality of an act is said to be its peculiar way of referring to the object to which it does refer, its *Weise der gegenständlichen Beziehung;* the matter determines its objective direction, its *bestimmte Richtung auf eine Gegenständliches*(12). But this talk of a determinate objective direction is equivocal. Consider the two concepts 'equilateral triangle' and 'equiangular triangle.' Considered as acts of bare representation (*Vorstellung*), they have the same quality; they also have the same objective direction, inasmuch as they refer precisely to the same object. Yet the two concepts are different concepts. The concept of matter however is sought to be *so defined* by Husserl that when two acts have the same quality and the same matter they may be treated as identical, and not merely equivalent. Therefore, we shall have to say that the concepts 'equilateral triangle' and 'equiangular triangle' do not have the same matter. Accordingly, for Husserl the intentional matter of an act is that element in it which confers on it its objective direction, but also so completely determines this objective direction that through the matter not only the object intended but the mode of intending it is thoroughly specified(13). This shows that the talk of 'mode of objective reference' is somewhat ambiguous. In one sense of it, this mode is conferred by the quality of the act, in another sense of it it is determined by the matter(14).

It of course follows from the above that if two acts have the same matter, the object intended *must* also be the same, whereas if the matter of two acts be different, the object intended may or may not be the same. Further, it would be well to remember that these two factors, quality and matter, are only abstract elements of an act considered as an intentional experience, which means that a quality without matter and a matter without a quality are equally well unthinkable(15).

The concept of the intentional *essence* of an act may now be defined. By the intentional essence of an act is meant the unity of its intentional quality and its intentional matter. Acts which have the same quality as well as the same matter will be said to have the same intentional essence, and even if such acts may, considered as real episodes, occur in different times in the life histories of the same or of different individuals, and so be different, yet for purposes of phenomenological description they would be considered as identical. For, what phenomenology is concerned with is not the real episode but its intentional character as such, and from this point of view two acts having the same intentional essence are the same. In fact, completely identical they are not, for they are sure to have different *real* components. But, if their intentional contents are the same, for our purpose they may be treated as being the same. This concept of identity in intentional essence is not the same as truth-functional equivalence, but truth functional equivalence of two judgments (when the acts are those of judging) is assured by identity of intentional essence.

When the act is one of meaning, i.e., one of meaningfully using an expression or of understanding the meaning of such a use, the intentional essence may be called the meaning-essence (*"Bedeutungsmässiges Wesen"*). It is this which may remain identical even if the other real components of the act, e.g., the intuitive basis, the imagery, the associations and the emotive accompaniments vary.

By the intentional content of an act may also be meant the intentional object. When I am perceiving a house, the intentional object of the act of perception is the house itself. But several phenomenological distinctions have to be made before this notion may be applied to other, and more complicated cases. We have to distinguish in the first place between the object which is intended and the object as it is intended, and in the second place between the object intended by the total act and the objects intended by the component acts. The best illustration for the first distinction may be the pair of descriptions 'The victor in the battle of Jena' and 'The vanquished in the battle of Waterloo': these two refer to the same person, they have the same intentional object, but the object as it is intended in one case is not the same as the object as it is intended in the other. The object as it is intended is of course as much determined by the intended object as by both the quality and the matter of the act. As regards the second distinction, we may consider the judgment "The book is on my table" which no doubt is *about* the book, but the intentional object of the total act of judging is not the book but the fact (*Sachverhalt*) that the book is on my table. The book of course is the intentional object of that component act (of this total act of judging) which corresponds to the subject term alone. Similarly, the total intentional object of an act of wish or desire is again a *Sachverhalt* which is not quite the same as the total intentional object of an act of judging having the same matter in the sense specified above. This shows that the concept of intentional object should not be confused with that of matter, and the concept of *Sachverhalt* is not to be identified with that of fact. The latter identification fails, for whereas the *Sachverhalt* intended by an act of judging or supposal may be called a fact, the *Sachverhalt* intended by an act of wish or desire *may not* be called so.

With these distinctions in mind, let us now proceed to the Sixth Investigation where certain new concepts are introduced. Chief of these is the concept of the *Erkenntnismässiges Wesen* or the *epistemic essence* of an act. First, let us distinguish between objectifying acts and non-objectifying acts. Objectifying acts are either nominal or propositional, they are in other words either representations or judgments, or modifications of them. The nominal act expressing a representation may be either positing or non-positing. It posits when it ascribes to its object some kind of existence or other, it is non-positing when it is a mere representation of a content and does not take any position as regards the existence of the content represented. The propositional act, when it is positing, is called a judgment. When it is non-positing, it is mere entertainment of a proposition, and contains no assertion of existence. Complex acts may be built on these simpler ones by appropriate processes of iteration. Complexities may also arise in another dimension: any of these acts may be either single-rayed or many-rayed(16).

Non-objectifying acts are acts like feeling, wishing, desiring etc. We cannot enter here into a discussion of Husserl's thesis that it is the objectifying acts alone which are the primary bearers of meaning(17). But it should offer no great difficulty to be able to appreciate the fact that there is a sort of basic difference between concepts and propositions on the one hand, and questions, wishes, desires, feelings on the other. When Husserl speaks of the epistemic essence of an act, he speaks only about the former group of acts. Every act, whether objectifying or non-objectifying, has its intentional essence. Only objectifying acts have, in addition, an epistemic essence.

With regard to objectifying acts Husserl maintains that they must always have an intuitive basis. If the act is an act of perception, the intuitive basis of course is clear. If the act is merely one of symbolic thinking, or even of symbolic presentation, the symbol itself must be presented through some kind of intuitive content. If the symbol is verbal, there must be either an auditory or a visual content, sensory or imaginary. Though an objectifying act must have an intuitive basis, the intuitive content may function in many different ways. If the act is one of intuition with no element of symbolic signification in it, the element of intuitive content and the intentional matter of the act (in the sense explained above) remain inseparably juxtaposed. Where the act is symbolic, the intuitive content serves as a mere sign for the intentional matter, there being no internal connection between the content that serves as a sign and the signified matter. There may be acts — like most of our ordinary perceptions — in which both these functions are present in varied degrees.

In view of these, we may now introduce the following terms in accordance with Husserl's discussions in the sixth Investigation:

The intuitive content (of an objectifying act) may be called either the representing content or the *Auffassungsinhalt*. I find the expression 'representing content' less misleading, for the term '*Auffassungsinhalt*' may lead one to suppose that it is this content that is being apprehended in the act which however is not the case: what is being apprehended is the intentional object. The way in which the intuitive content functions in an act — it may act, as we saw, either as a sign or as inseparable from the matter, or in both the ways — may be called the form of representation or the *Auffassungsform*. Thus the *Auffassungsform* of a symbolic representation of an object is different from that of an intuitive presentation of it. The intentional matter of an objectifying act may now be called its apprehended matter *(Auffassungsmaterie)*.

When the representation is merely *signitive* or symbolic, the relation between the matter and the representing content is external. When the act is intuitive, the relation is closer, essential, inner.

We have seen before that the talk of different modes of objective relatedness is equivocal. The mode may be such as is determined by the intentional quality of the act, or it may be such as is determined by the intentional matter. Now we may clarify the equivocation still further. We may say that the mode of objective relatedness may vary *either* with the quality of the act, *or* with the representing content, *or* with the *Auffassungsform*, or with the intentional matter.

Now, when an objectifying act amounts to a *knowledge*, Husserl will say that the intention of the act stands *fulfilled*(18). In other words, when an act is also knowledge-giving, it acquires a fulfilled meaning *("erfüllender Sinn")*. In such a knowledge-giving, act, the fulfilled meaning is bestowed by the intuitive content which now stands inseparable from the intentional matter. We may then define the epistemic essence of an act as consisting in the unity of the act-quality, the act-matter and the intuitive representing content. The first two constitute, as we have already learnt, the intentional essence of an act: the epistemic essence contains this but also, in addition, the intuitive representing content. It should be clear that whereas all intentional acts have their intentional essences, only objectifying ones possess — and that also only if they happen to be knowledge-giving — an epistemic essence. Just as the concept of intentional essence enabled us to have a precise concept of the identity of two acts, so the present concept of epistemic essence enables us to speak of the same knowledge howsoever the knowledges — possibly belonging to two different individuals — may differ otherwise(19).

C. FURTHER ANALYSIS IN THE *IDEAS I*:

In the *Ideas I*, analysis of intentional acts is further enriched. Leaving aside minor changes in terminology, Husserl introduces two new and major notions. In the first place, we meet with the concept of *noema* and its correlative, that of *noesis,* and the correlation between the noetic and the noematic structures becomes the main subject matter for phenomenological description. But also, the idea of act-quality briefly touched upon in the Fifth Investigation is further enlarged, and we have a large mass of interesting discussion on the different possibilities of modifying the act-quality.

Further, Husserl shows awareness of the limits within which all this analysis is being carried out. He in fact tells us that the level in which we are now discussing the nature of intentionality "stops short of descending into the obscure depths of the ultimate consciousness", and "accepts experiences rather as they present themselves in immanent reflexion as unitary temporal processes"(20). We have accordingly to distinguish between intentionality as characterising *constituted* temporal experiences, and intentionality as characterising the *constituting* time-consciousness, and we have to bear in mind that the present discussion, as also that of the Fifth Investigation, concerns the former and is valid only within appropriate limits.

Regarding terminology, Husserl now prefers to use 'consciousness' in a strict sense and clearly rejects the first and the widest sense of it as stated in the *Logische Untersuchungen.* "Consciousness is not a title-name for 'psychical complexes,' for fused 'contents,' for 'bundles' or streams of 'sensations' "(21). The word 'experience' (*Erlebnis*) however is reserved for that wide sense, to stand for "whatever is to be found in the stream of experience, not only therefore intentional experiences, *cogitationes* actual and potential taken in their full concreteness, but all the real (*reellen*) phases to be found in this stream and in its concrete sections"(22). In the strict sense in which he now

uses 'consciousness,' it is not even the same as intentional experiences, and so this sense is even stricter than the third and
the strictest sense of the Investigations. There consciousnesss
was simply identified with intentional experience. Here it is
identified with that part of a concrete intentional experience
which is now regarded as being *meaning-bestowing*, as 'animating' the other and the sensory component of the experience.
Consciousness in this sense becomes the source of all meanings,
the source of intentionality which only *seems* to characterise
the sensory component. In fact, it is now said to be "the source
of all reason and unreason, all right and wrong, all reality and
illusion, all value and disvalue, all deed and misdeed"(23).

With a view to getting at this meaning-bestowing component in each and every intentional experience, we have to
distinguish now between the real (*reell*) components of an intentional experience and its intentional correlate. It should be
borne in mind that when we are going to give a phenomenological analysis we have already exercised the phenomenological *epoche*. We are not any longer concerned with the existence of a real, natural world out there or with the existence
of the experiencer as a real human organism: these beliefs are
simply suspended, set out of action, we do not make any use of
them now. We are concerned with describing the experience
as such, and its intentional correlate as the intentional correlate
of this experience. If it is the perception of the tree over there,
I am concerned with describing both this act of perceiving
with its real components if any and the tree over there as perceived by me. The latter is what Husserl calls the *noema*. The
noema of an act of remembering is the object as remembered,
of an act of perceiving is the object as it is being perceived,
and so on. From this, it is evident that all the things which constitute the naturalistic attitude, the contents of the world out
there reappear as *noema* but with a "change of signature"; and
the *noema* is in a sense *within* consciousness, but not as its real
component but only as its intentional correlate and so in a very
special sense of 'within.'

The real components of an intentional experience are now

shown to be twofold. In fact they are not just two constituents, but rather they build two different strata, one resting on the other. These are the *hyletic* and the *noetic* strata. The concept of *hyle* which Husserl introduces here has been a source of much difficulty for phenomenologists. Many have found in it a trace of uncritical sensualistic empiricism, others have found here a survival of the Aristotelian-Kantian hylomorphic conception of knowledge. Whatever may be its value and historical affiliations, the fact remains that it is there and a proper understanding of its exact role is necessary for understanding Husserl.

We have already seen that in *Logische Untersuchungen*, Husserl held the view that every objectifying act presupposes a representing intuitive content which however may function in many different ways in relation to the intentional matter. It is this concept of representing content that appears in the *Ideas I* as the concept of *hyle* which now applies to all intentional acts and not merely to those that are objectifying. Every intentional experience is a sort of transformation of this purely non-intentional stratum into an intentional experience. Husserl rightly refuses to call it 'sensory data.' For one thing, sensory data that may constitute the real components of an experience are to be distinguished from the sensible qualities belonging to the thing that is being perceived. He is referring not to the objective colour, for example, but to the colour as constituent of the visual experience, to "a colour-like something," to the "sensory colour" in which the noematic, objective colour "manifests itself in varying perspectives"(24). The word 'sensory' is inappropriate inasmuch as we use this word to qualify complete intentional experiences themselves, as when we speak of sensory perceptions. What Husserl is thinking of is some unformed matter which goes into every intentional experience, which is given form and meaning by the meaning-bestowing act, which is consciousness in the pregnant sense, and without which the intentional experience will be of something in general and will not be the concrete and determinate experience that it is. It is this element of matter or stuff that he wishes to be understood by the term 'hyle.' According to Husserl such an element is to be found in all intentional experience, though there is as little unformed *hyle* as there is mere form without matter on which it is imposed.

In all intentional experiences, we have this element of *hyle*. If the experience is one of perception, the *hyle* is roughly what we call sensation. In acts of feeling or evaluation, the *hyle* is constituted by the sensory feelings of pleasure and pain considered only as non-intentional psychic states and as devoid of any intentional reference. In acts of will, the *hyle* may be said to be the desires and impulses and instincts which are of course systematised, organised and given meaning in complete acts of will. In acts of expression, the *hyle* is the sensuous symbol, verbal or otherwise. These elements of stuff have to be separated by an act of abstraction from the concrete intentional experiences in order that we may appreciate the role that consciousness in the specific sense of the meaning-bestowing *noesis* plays in relation to them.

We have spoken of the *hyle* as the matter. This should not lead one to suppose that the concept of *hyle* does the same work here as the concept of 'intentional matter' in the Fifth Investigation. As has been said, the concept of *hyle* is rather an extension of the earlier notion of 'representing content.' The hyle is non-intentional matter, it is pure stuff. Intentional matter on the other hand is intentional, it is formed. The intentional matter is what Husserl will call in the *Ideas I* the noematic *nucleus* as distinguished from the full *noema*.

The *noema* is the object as it is intended, the object as perceived, the object as remembered, and so on. Here then is a sort of unity achieved as contrasted with the large variety of hyletic data constituting the intentional experience having that *noema*. We see a tree unchanged in colour, whilst the variations of perspective may bring about variations in the sensory colour. Perspective variations, Husserl tells us, 'belonging to' the same colour are related to that colour as continuous "variety" is related to "unity"(25). The attainment of this noematic unity out of a plurality of hyletic data — which is *an achievement,* for we cannot refer it back, after the *epoche,* to the thing out there — is due to the meaning-bestowing noetic act.

Within the full *noema,* i.e., the tree as perceived for example, we may further distinguish between what Husserl calls the noematic nucleus and that property of the *noema* which is due to the specific act-quality or thetic character. The nucleus remains the same if the act of perception of the same tree changes over into an act of remembering or into an act of imagining or thinking. The thetic character however changes. From this it follows that different acts having different act-qualities may have the same noematic nucleus though the full *noema* must of course be different. The noematic nucleus is then the same as the intentional matter of the *Logische Unter-suchungen,* the full *noema* being the same as the intentional essence. Like the intentional essence of an act, its full *noema* consists of the nucleus (= intentional matter) and the noematic correlate of the thetic character of the act (= act-quality). Only, as Husserl tells us, he did not bring the noematic-noetic correlation to the forefront in the *Logische Untersuchungen,* where the analysis was still either wholly noetic or wholly noematic and, in any case, immanent-descriptive. The concept of intentionality had not received its full explication.

The noematic nucleus which may remain invariant in many different acts having different act-qualities is now called the *Sinn* or meaning: this identity of meaning is the achievement of the meaning-bestowing component of the act. The full *noema* however corresponds to the full *noesis.*

Both in consciousness as well as in the *noema* there is reference to an object to which it belongs. Consciousness is *of* something. The noematic predicates belong to something. Since we have in the phenomenological attitude bracketed the outer thing, we cannot any more make use of our naive belief in it to account for this objective reference. We have to find a place, within the 'reduced' act and also within its noematic content, for this phenomenon of objective reference. Husserl seeks to locate it in a feature of the *noema* as also in a property of the act as "glancing through" the nucleus towards a "most *inward* phase of the *noema*"(26) which is as it were the "mid-point of the nucleus" and which functions as the bearer of the noematic predicates. What Husserl wants to do thereby is to make room for the conception of a substrate or substance to which the properties of the object belong. Quite apart from the particular metaphysical view about substance which one may or may not like to hold, there is no denying the fact that our consciousness in so far as it is consciousness of something does point to an objective unity underlying the attributes belonging to the intentional object. Phenomenologically, we cannot any more go beyond the *noema*. The *noema* consists of features derived from the various hyletic and thetic components of the act whose *noema* it is. But insofar as the *noema* is a unity and not a mere conglomeration of these features, we have to find a place for this unity within the *noema*. Husserl locates it within the nucleus of the *noema* as its mid-point. Thus, the whole distinction between object and content tends to reopen within the *noema* itself, the supposed mid-point of the nucleus being the object and the noematic predicates constituting the content. It would be wrong to complain that Husserl is thereby going back to a substance metaphysics. What he is doing is only to locate the phenomenon corresponding to the metaphysical conception of substance or substrate.

A large part of the *Ideas I* is devoted to descriptions of the different groups of thetic characters of acts together with possible modifications within each group. The modifications are either attentional modifications or what Husserl calls 'temporalising' (*zeitigung*) — modifications. Let us take a look at these various possibilities without however going into the intricate details of Husserl's descriptions.

Under each head there is a basic primary form round which the possible range of modifications centres. In the case of the thetic acts, the basic form, the *Urform,* is what Husserl calls the *Urdoxa,* the primary belief in the world which underlies and provides the basis for all other attitudes, cognitive, affective or volitional. This of course does not mean that phenomenological bracketing of this belief is impossible. It is rather by bracketing this belief that we come to recognise it as a belief and as the primary belief. Its character as belief is otherwise unknown to us. By exercising the *epoche,* we of course do not make use of the belief, but we certainly come to reflect on it as belief and also as the primary belief. Built upon it are the other thetic characters, even the affective and volitional characters. It should further be remembered that the primary belief as founding all other thetic acts is not yet positing. In other words, this primary belief in the world does not posit the world as an object. Positing is a further modification which takes place within the horizon of the primary *Urdoxa*. The world is not an object whose actuality or reality is posited, but a horizon within which all positing as also all modifications of positing take place.

The thetic characters then fall into two broad groups: the positional and the neutralising acts. It is the positing acts to which the noematic predicate of 'being' or 'reality' owes its existence. The unmodified root form of positing acts is belief, whose preeminent example is the case of perceptual belief. The ontic character of 'real' is the correlate of this act of belief, more accurately of perceptual belief or certainty. Just as all other noetic modalities refer back to this primary certainty as their root form, so all other ontic modalities refer back to the predicate 'real' as their primary root form. Possible modifications of these root forms are, on the noetic side, suggestion or presumption, question or doubt, and on the noematic side, the properties of 'possible,' 'probable,' 'questionable,' and 'doubtful.'

In the neutralised acts, the positing act is set out of action, is made powerless, suspended, so that what we have is a mere awareness of an object without taking up any kind of position with regard to its being or non-being. Modes of neutralisation are two fold: they are either some kind of neutral image-consciousness (*Bild-Bewusstsein*) or fancy. The former is a neutrality-modification of acts of presentation, while the latter is neutrality-modification of acts of representation or recollection. In both, we do not posit but simply have a thought or image or representation.

The temporalising modes are all centred round the primary

mode of presentation ("*Gegenwärtigung*") in which the intentional object is given as *now*. Its chief modification is appresentation ("*Vergegenwärtigung*") whose intentional object is not bodily given here and now but is there in the horizon of what is given. Appresentation always involves some amount of recollection, and may refer to what was given, or may even refer ahead to what is anticipated, or also to what is in the present horizon.

Attentional modifications centre round the contrast between the mode of actuality and the mode of inactuality. In the former mode, the act is in the full sense 'realised.' The actual act is the *cogito* in the explicit sense of 'I perceive,' 'I think,' etc. But, while an act is being lived in the mode of actuality, there are others in the horizon in the mode of inactuality. There is a constant possibility of those in the mode of inactuality coming into the mode of actuality and vice versa. The conceptions of horizon, of the margin and background concern the mode of inactuality.

While these are the principal possibilities of modification of the thetic character, Husserl also draws attention to the numerous ways in which these different groups of modifications may interpenetrate. For example, the thetic modes and the temporalising modes may interpenetrate as a result of which we may have such acts as 'probable memory' or 'a supposition within a remembering.' Further, there may be reiterated modifications like affirmations of affirmations, affiirmations of negations, negations of negations; again, we may have memories within memories, suppositions within suppositions, and so on. These would give rise to corresponding noematic predicates of higher orders. There would be in fact *noematic intentionalities* i.e. noematic predicates referring to other noematic predicates(27).

Further complications arise in the cases of affective and volitional acts which according to Husserl are based on doxic acts and in which there are analogous noetic and noematic modifications.

D. DEEPENING OF THE CONCEPT OF INTENTIONALITY IN THE *VORLESUNGEN ZUR PHANOMENOLOGIE DES INNEREN ZEITBEWUSSTSEINS*

The concept of intentionality receives fresh clarification and even a deepening in the *Vorlesungen zur Phänomenologie des inneren Zeitbewusstseins* partly delivered in Göttingen in 1904/5 but published for the first time in 1928. Martin Heidegger, who edited these lectures, writes in his Foreword that the central theme of the lectures is the temporal constitution of a pure sense-datum (*Empfindungsdatum*) and the self-constitution of "phenomenological time" which underlies such a constitution(28). Heidegger adds that this would not only bring out the intentional character of time-consciousness but would contribute towards a basic clarification of intentionality in general. The concept of intentionality needs such a clarification, for the word 'intentionality' is even now, according to Heidegger, "not a word which solves all problems (*"kein Lösungswort"*) but the title of a central problem."

We have already seen that on Husserl's own admission the analysis of the *Ideas I* is carried out within a self-imposed limit. Husserl had already, in his lectures on time-consciousness, gone beyond these limits, but he seems to have decided not to make use in the *Ideas I* of these explorations. The lectures on time-consciousness antedate the *Ideas,* but in philosophical depth they mark a development beyond it.

Our direct interest here — while attempting an exposition of the lectures on time-consciousness — lies not so much in his views on the nature of time as in finding out the new light they throw on the nature of intentionality. And, they are of course rich in suggestions from this point of view, especially because Husserl's conception of time becomes inseparable from his concept of intentionality.

Let us first try to state his problem. In the *Ideas I,* we have been told that the transcendent *noema* is constituted by the noetic acts bestowing meaning upon the hyletic matter. No further analysis was given of the hyletic matter. The analysis that was given of the noetic acts is somewhat structural in nature: we have the analysis of acts into their intentional matter, act-quality and the resulting intentional essence. The *noema* was also analysed into corresponding structural layers. But the sense in which the *noema* was said to be *constituted* by the acts and the hyletic data is very different from the sense in which an act is made up of its intentional matter, intentional quality and intentional essence. In fact, the question of the constitution of acts as also of the hyletic data was not raised at all. One gets the impression that the question of constitution cannot at all be meaningfully raised with regard to them, for the acts are the original sources of meaning, they bestow meaning and so cannot themselves be said to have derived their unity from some other source while the hyletic data are meaningless stuff and so as such do not possess any sense which could be traced back to some other constitutive source. Either they are in their facticity and in their irrationality absolutely primitive, not further explicable elements of our experience, or they require some sort of causal naturalistic explanation. The latter explanation is of course out of the question within the phenomenological *epoche* which is the standing background for all phenomenological analysis. They would then seem to be absolutely primitive elements, meaningless in themselves and so lacking in any unity or objectivity. It is the acts which confer meaning, unity and objectivity on them. And they themselves are in another sense primitive, inasmuch as they are not constituted but constitute. If we add to this Husserl's doctrine, already referred to, that it is the objectifying acts alone which are the primary carriers of meaning so that non-objectifying acts presuppose objectifying acts in order to produce some kind of objectivity of their own, it would follow that all objectivity is constituted by objectifying acts, i.e., by the acts of apprehension *(Auffassung)* working upon the raw material provided by the so-called hyletic data. It is this neat scheme which collapses in the lectures on time-consciousness. For, now Husserl raises the question about the constitution of both acts and hyletic data regarded as immanent objects, and in the process of answering this question brings out levels of intentionality deeper than what may be called act-intentionality.

Thus we are faced with three different levels of the problem of constitution and so also(29) of the concept of intentionality:

1. The constitution of transcendent *noema*.
2. The constitution of immanent unities (i.e., acts and hyletic data).
3. The self-constitution of the absolute flux of consciousness.

The transcendent *noema*, as has been shown in the *Ideas I*, is constituted by the acts and hyletic data. The problem of immanent unities and their constitution is for the first time raised in the lectures on time-consciousness. The problem of the third and the last level leads us to the concept of the absolute in Husserl's philosophy, and is related to our problem in so far as we not only find here the deepest nature of intentionality but we also begin to realise the inner relation between the intentionality and the reflexivity of consciousness only at this level, i.e., in the notion of self-constitution of consciousness. We have correspondingly three levels of the problem of time: the objective time to which the transcendent objects belong, the immanent time in which the immanent unities are constituted. and the absolute flux of consciousness which is the source of all temporality but cannot itself be said to be in time.

The problem of the constitution of transcendent objects had been dealt with in the *Ideas I* but in a manner which leaves the problem of duration entirely out of picture. In fact, however, the transcendent objects are enduring objects, and the problem of their constitution is only the other side of the question how enduring objects are objects of consciousness, i.e., how they are intended and moreover how such intention comes to be fulfilled. Now Husserl recognises, like Kant, that to be identifiable in recollections is a part of the meaning of temporal objectivity(30). The object in fact is that which can be identified in many different acts. But such possibility of identification is a function of reproduction, and it is therefore no wonder that Husserl would look upon the identity of temporal objects as being constituted through certain possible coincidences of identifications through recollections. This again is connected with the fact — derivable from the nature of immanent time-consciousness — that though each 'now' sinks into the past with its retentions and protentions, i.e., with its total intentional horizon, its mode of givenness changes but its temporal *position* remains unaltered though its temporal interval from the actual 'now' undergoes constant change(31). This fact that each 'now' in spite of its sinking back into the past retains its precise temporal position unaltered and also the fact that we can, in reproductive consciousness, identify it in repeated acts, are but two sides — objective and subjective — of the same phenomenon. This alone however would not account for the possibility of intending or apprehending enduring temporal objects. We have got the possibility of identification of the temporal *position,* but we also need the possibility of identification of the extra-temporal *content* of the object: when both are preserved unaltered, as is evidenced by reproductive consciousness, we have an enduring object. In other words, we could say that enduring, transcendent objects are constituted by reproductive acts of identification on the basis of extra-temporal contents. Several recollections are of the same object when they agree with regard to their intentional content, i.e., with regard to their extra-temporal content plus the temporal horizon. To say that something is an enduring individual, is to say that it is capable of being the common intentional content of an indefinite number of such identifying recollective acts. "The object is a unity of consciousness which in repeated acts (therefore, in temporal succession) can appear as the same"(32).

While the theory of the constitution of the transcendent objects is thus given a temporal twist, what is really new is the problem of the constitution of immanent unities. Acts and hyletic data, like sensations, are also objects in a certain sense. They are surely possible objects of reflection, either of inner perception or of an analytic abstraction or of reflective glance. And insofar as they are objects their constitution needs an intentional analysis. Further, they are temporal unities and in fact belong to what Husserl would call immanent, preobjective time. In searching for the constitution of acts that at first seemed to be not further analysable sources of meaning and for the constitution of hyletic data which seemed to be just meaningless plurality, we are indeed destined to delve into the deeper levels of intentionality.

Neither the acts nor the hyletic data are appearances of anything else strictly speaking. They are however shown to be temporally extended, and herein lies the possibility of exposing their constitution. Immanent objects are made up of temporal phases, and each of these temporal phases is characterised both by a retentive reference to what has been and a protentive reference to what is yet to be and the total immanent object, act or hyletic datum, is what it is only in so far as during its 'actual' duration it has continuously these backward and forward references(33). Husserl seems to be drawing a rather dubious distinction between 'primal apprehensions' (*Urauffassungen*) or 'primal impressions' (*Urimpressionen*) which constitute the full immanent object and the total act or datum that is thereby constituted. The full intentional act in the sense of the *Ideas I* is constituted of partial intentions as it were, and these partial intentions however are not themselves constituted but belong to the basic flux of consciousness(34).

What does Husserl mean by this last distinction? He could have meant that a total act like the perception of a house consists of many partial acts of perceiving different profiles of it, and these again of many primary sensations. The total act is in that case constituted by these partial acts, but in the long run by those primal sensations. But this would be a sort of structural analysis of an intentional act which seems very different from phenomenological analysis, for it would involve analysing a total act into what are supposed to be its constituent elements. It is of course highly dubious to say, from a phenomenological standpoint, that my act of perceiving a house consists of many different partial acts of perceiving the profiles. The profiles are not what I perceive, I perceive through them; the acts directed to the profiles do not constitute the act of perceiving the total object. The total act may be said to be *based on* and built upon these partial acts. One can even go further and say that the total intention is present in each of the partial intentions and makes them what they are, and not *vice versa*.

More in consonance with what Husserl is doing in the lectures on time-consciousness is the following interpretation: each act is a temporal object in the sense that it has a duration in

time. The act of perception, for example, has an extension in
time, however short it may be. Now if it has an extension in
time, it is analysable into a series of 'nows,' each now having its
own retentional and protentional horizon and sinking back into
the past along with this horizon. These 'nows' are the primal
impressions; they are not any more constituted, though they
constitute, in the long run, all other objects, immanent or transcendent.

It has been rightly argued by Sokolowski that this formal
analysis of the constitution of an act leaves it unexplained why
an act should have this quality rather than that. In other words,
it does not provide us with a constitution of the specific quality
of the act, i.e., of its quality as an act of judgment or as an act
of desire or wish, though it at best is an account of the act as a
temporally extended unity(35). I would press the objection still
further, and contend that this does not even provide us with an
adequate constitution of the act *as an intentional* act. In the first
place, it is not at all clear in what sense an intentional act as
an immanent object has a temporal extension. An act of hearing a continuing melody may have a temporal stretch. But an
act of perceiving surely has not a temporal extension. Again,
remembering may in some sense be said to have a temporal
stretch, e.g., insofar as it arouses within itself intentions to be
fulfilled, and in fact may itself consist in the progressive fulfilment of such intentions. Introspection here is not always a safe
guide. Acts may have temporal stretch or they may not have it;
they may be, as acts of perception seem to be, concentrated in a
'now.' This is not to deny that an act of perception usually
awakens further intentions to be fulfilled in time. It is also not
to deny that the 'now' in which an act of perception is concentrated has its retentional and protentional horizon. What I am
denying is that all acts can be resolved into temporal *phases.*
An act of perception cannot be, although it is not in the strict
sense a further unanalysable primal sensation. The total act, as
a total act, is in the 'now.' The point I am driving at is that an
act, *considered as an intentional act,* does not consist in temporal
phases, is not a process, a duration. The intention is compressed
in a point. The component intentions or the resultant intentions

do not break up this character of an intentional act. The partial intentions on which a total intention is built up are not phases of it, they are its supports and media. An intention may give rise to or awaken further intentions, it may press forward to its fulfilment, and in so far temporality enters into its constitution. But we cannot just analyse it into phases and seek to derive its constitution out of the mutual merging of these phases into one another by virtue of their retentional and protentional horizons.

In fact, it would seem to me that when Husserl speaks of the 'constitution' of transcendent *noema* in the acts and also of the 'constitution' of the immanent acts in the temporal phases he is not using the word 'constitution' in the same sense. In the first case, the sense of 'constitution' is genuinely phenomenological for it does not mean analysis of a *noema* into its phases or parts but tracing it back to the constituting acts, i.e., to the intentions. In the second case, we would be decomposing a total act into those phases which go to make it up: the analysis *seems* to be real and not intentional.

It would seem to me therefore that the act is constituted not by temporal phases but by those other simpler intentions, if there be any such, which in any case would remain anonymous behind it. All that Husserl could legitimately say is that it is these simpler, more primitive intentions which constitute time as well, or which are the basic elements out of which time-consciousness is constituted. What are these basic intentions?

These basic intentions are those which figure in what Husserl calls the primal 'now' impression: namely, its reference to what has been and to what is yet to be, to its retentional and protentional horizon. However, the difficulty still remains: how could this retentional and protentional horizon of the primal 'now'-impression serve to constitute the act in the sense of conferring on it its intention which is what makes the act an act? Husserl's account may at best succeed in showing how an act-continuum is possible; it shows how the flow of conscious life to which these acts in one sense belong is made possible. But, it does not explain the act-character of the acts. Now I do not wish to contend that all acts are further irreducible, but I wish to contend that the *sort of intention* which characterises acts is not reducible to the *sort of intention* which characterises the primal 'now'-impression in Husserl's analysis of time-consciousness. Of course, a complex intention of the former sort is analysable into simpler intentions of the same sort, i.e., to other act-intentions on which it is founded, but it is not at once clear in what sense an act-intention is reducible to intentions which are not act-intentions.

Thus, the theory of the constitution of acts in original time-consciousness fails because of the fact that the acts are not temporal in the same sense in which enduring temporal objects are so, and further because the sort of intention which characterises acts or rather makes them what they are is not reducible to the sort of intention which characterises the basic data of time-consciousness.

The acts are of course in time in the sense that they may be temporally located, and also in the sense that certain temporal predicates hold good of them. We may for example say that a certain act occurred after some other act, or before it. But, curiously enough, certain temporal predicates are not meaningfully predicable of them: we cannot for example say that my act of perception of this house before me passes through several temporal phases. This important difference should not be overlooked.

There is another way of approaching the question of a possible constitution of the acts. Seeking to stick to the parallelism between transcendent objects and the acts, one may contend that just as the transcendent object is constituted by the actual and possible acts through which the object comes to be given, so is an act constituted by the modes of its givenness. How then is an act given? An act as an *Erlebnis* is immediately given, in fact it is self-given: it is, by its very existence, given. It should therefore be self-constitutive. One may however contend that the act may be given *as an object* to reflection, and the question of the constitution arises only in so far as it can be given as an object. Well, then the constitution of an act should be sought in the reflection which makes it its object, but then we are only referring it back to another act-intention, for reflection is another act though of a higher type. We do not get down to some other sort of intention *as constituting* the act.

Fink in "*Vergegenwärtigung und Bild*"(1930) sees this distinction between act-intentionalities and intentionalities which are not acts. To the latter type belong, e.g., retentions and horizon-intentionalities. One point of distinction between the two groups is, according to Fink, that the intentionalities which are not acts are *unselbständige,* they cannot be solely by themselves, but always attach to something else, whereas the act-intentionalities are in a sense *selbständig* experieneces. Further, the former kind of intentionalities do not in the strict sense possess an intentional object, though they "constitute the 'condition of the possibility' of every objectivity: the temporal horizon out of which something like an object as an indentity which maintains itself through the flux of temporal phases could at all emerge"(36).

It is significant from our point of view that Fink speaks of the temporal horizon and its intentionalities as constituting the conditions of the possibility of an act-intention as intending an object. The conception of an object is of course that of an identity persisting through time, and it is only in so far as there is a temporal horizon constituted by the basic intentionalities like retention and protention that intending an object like this is possible. Thus the basic intentions of our time-consciousness lay down the conditions of the possibility of objects, and so also of the acts which intend such objects in so far as they intend them, i.e., in so far as they are act-intentions. But to say that we have thereby got the conditions of their possibility is not the same as saying that we have exhibited the constitution of the acts. We are nearer to Kant, and hold that temporality as constituted by the basic intentions which are not acts make it possible for us to intend objects, but they alone do not constitute either the objects or the acts.

The above comments are not meant to uphold the thesis that the only sorts of intentions we can legitimately speak of are the act-intentions. As we shall see presently, there is good ground for saying that there are other sorts of intentions which are in some legitimate sense more basic. We seem to discover these intentions as soon as we enquire about the intentional structure of the socalled hyletic data.

With regard to the socalled hyletic data, the lectures on time-consciousness actually begin with the view of the *Ideas I*: we are for example told that the sensed red is a phenomenological datum which when animated by a certain function of apprehension presents an objective quality(37). But the lectures soon proceed to suggest a certain theory of the constitution of the datum itself. In this connection, the lectures show an inner contradiction, a shifting of views, which is somewhat disturbing, and now we owe it to Boehm to have made it clear(38) that the Heidegger edition of the lectures on time-consciousness (which were largely edited by Edith Stein) includes Husserl's writings on the topic belonging to different periods and so represent many different strands of views which are not all mutually compatible.

In fact, apart from the repetition of the early view as to the nature of the datum as exemplified in the sentence referred to above, we have two other different views:

In the first place, we have the suggestion(39) that the sensed datum, even prior to its being animated by the act of apprehension, *may* already have been constituted. This view is further elaborated in Appendix V belonging to a later date (which suggests that the footnote referred to above may not be of the same date as the text to which it is added!), where we are told that the datum *must* already have been constituted prior to the act which is to animate it, and the reason that is adduced in favour of this view may be said to be the second of the two views which are found in these lectures. The total datum to which the act is applied or which the act is supposed to animate is a totality having a duration and so consisting of several phases. These several phases require to be held together and formed into a total datum, and this is made possible by virtue of the intentional horizon of each primal 'now'-sensation. And obviously this intentionality attaching to every primal 'now'-sensation is not an act-intentionality. What Husserl wants to bring out is the need of some kind of synthesis which makes it possible for the total datum to be present as a totality, as one datum, for the act of apprehension to work upon. This would not have been possible if each momentary datum were completely disconnected with the other, the discrete 'now's would never form a whole, there would always be only one perishing moment. The total datum, as the totality of passing phases, is made possible simply because each moment is not a discrete atom, but an intentional structure, having its own retentional and protentional horizon.

The intentionality of the hyletic datum does not mean that the datum is *of* something, for this reference to the transcendent object is first made possible through the animation by the act. It is the act which is the source of the reference to the transcendent object. The hyletic datum quâ datum is intentional in a quite different sense, namely in the sense that it points beyond itself to the past and the present: its intentionality is simply its temporality. In spite of the improvements effected in these lectures on time-consciousness, the hyletic data remain non-intentional *in the sense* in which they were said to be so in the *Ideas 1*, though a new kind of intentionality is now discovered in their innermost structure. They do not surely possess act-intentionality, they receive it from an act.

Thus it would seem that although some new conceptions of intentionality are introduced, no fundamental change is called for in the scheme of the *Ideas I*. What are required are rather minor alterations and changes in the perspective, in brief a consideration of the whole thing in the light of the all-pervading structure of temporal consciousness.

Sokolowski, as said before, accuses Husserl of giving a formal analysis of time which (i) fails to account for the *quality* of acts as constituted unities, and (ii) fails to account for the material, i.e., content-aspect of the hyletic data(40). And yet Sokolowski rejects Husserl's dualism between the non-temporal content and the temporal form of sense objects, as also his dualism between hyletic data and acts animating them. In fact, he seems to favour the monistic tendency of Husserl's later writings(41). To us it seems however that some sort of dualism is necessary for accounting for the facticity of the constituted unities, whether they are the transcendent objects or the hyletic data themselves: not all their contents can be derived from their temporality. Even if we feel dissatisfied with an absolute dualism between form and matter, there could very well be a sort of relative dualism, in which what functioned as meaning-giving acts on a lower level may just be the matter for further unification at a higher level. An overriding intention may use the more primitive intentions as its matter, so that at every level the distinction between form and matter tends to emerge. The matter-form scheme need not therefore be given up. It may indeed be the most universal scheme illustrated in our experience at all levels. To say that all constitution does not have the apprehension-content form then would mean only that all form is not bestowed by an act-intention, or that there are totally different sorts of meaning-giving, synthesis or unity(42).

The crucial problem for any phenomenologist in fact is: how to retain this dualism without: (a) succumbing to an easy sensualistic empiricism with regard to the *hyle* (which is what we find in Kant, at least in parts of the Transcendental Aesthetic); (b) without surreptitiously escaping from the *epoche* (and thereby appealing to causal explanations), and (c) finally, without identifying all intention with act-intention, all synthesis with active synthesis, all consitution with intellectual moulding. This is no doubt a formidable task, but we cannot shun it, for the alternative to it is the absurd interpretation of constitution as creation.

The lectures on inner time-consciousness affirm — leaving aside the theories of the constitution of the acts and the hyletic data — the theory of the self-constitution of the absolute flux of consciousness. We may now try to understand this very important thesis. The absolute flux of consciousness in which all immanent and transcendent unities are supposed to be constituted is not itself in time, it is not a constituted unity, not an object enduring in time, but is the original source of time-consciousness, and so of all time, objective or inner. In the lectures on time-consciousness, Husserl gives us a number of successive steps — which are not quite the same as successive reductions — by which we may come to exhibit this flux of consciousness in its original purity. Supposing I am hearing a melody, a continuing sound. I am in that case living in the perceiving of the sound. But instead of living in this act, I may attend to the sound as it appears to me, i.e., to the sound as a phenomenological datum. Next, I may attend to the continuities of the shading off of the different phases of this sound phenomenon. Finally, I may attend not to the continuities in the shading of the phases of the sound phenomenon (which is a constituted immanent unity), but to the continuity in the shading of my apprehensions of these phases, whereby I would be attending to the flux of consciousness itself. Now this may suggest that the flux may become an object of reflection or attention, or even of retention. But, first, these reflections, attentions, or retentions themselves belong to the flux itself, and so what we have is the remarkable phenomenon of the flux turning back upon itself. Secondly, the flux is given as a flux even prior to its being reflectively attended to. "Even if reflection is not carried out *ad infinitum* and if, in general, no reflection is necessary, still that which makes this reflection possible and, in principle (or so it seems, at least) possible *ad infinitum* must be given"(43).

It has been previously remarked that every *Erlebnis* as an *Erlebnis* is already reflexively given, that though it may be made the object of reflection or inner perception it nevertheless was already given prior to such objectification. The same we now find true of the flux. We may combine these two findings, and affirm that the *Erlebnis* is no doubt reflexively given prior to objectification, but only in so far as it forms a constituent of this flux. It is the flux that is primarily so given, the isolated *Erlebnis* is so given as isolated but as belonging to the flux. The flux alone then is truely self-given. It alone eludes objectification, for in that very attempt it returns to itself as the underlying flux.

The flux of consciousness is self-constituting. It constitutes its own unity by virtue of intentions belonging to itself. The notion of which Husserl makes special use in this connection is that of "longitudinal intentionality" *(Längs-intentionalität)* by virtue of which the flux is "in continuous unity of coincidence with itself"(44). As every primal sensation changes into a retention, a new primal sensation comes to be conjoined to that retention and likewise in the third moment a new primal sensation comes to be conjoined to the retention of the retention of the first and retention of the second. And the retentions of retentions, of whatever degree of complexity they may be, still contain an intentional reference to the primal sensation which is their originating point as it were. It is by virtue of such properties immanent to the flux that the flux appears to itself as a flux without requiring another flux in which to appear.

The original flux of consciousness is described variously. It is called original *time*-consciousness, it is also called the *absolute* flux of consciousness. We should be clear as to the precise sense of its temporality and its absoluteness. It is of course obvious that it is not in time, neither in transcendent time nor in immanent time. In other words, temporal predicates like beginning and end, before and after cannot meaningfully be applied to the flux as a flux. Further, it does not endure, for all enduring objects are constituted unities. It does not persist in that sense also. It is also not to be conceived in the manner of an objective change consisting of a series of enduring phases each of which can be identified either as transcendent or as an immanent object. Nothing abides in this flux, save and except the formal structure of the flux, i.e., the 'now-retention-protention' nexus, not any particular such nexus but only the bare form of it(45). Rightly therefore Husserl also speaks of it as *timeless* consciousness(46), and refuses to characterise as process(47).

In what sense is it absolute? Taking the remarks in the *Ideas I* together with those of the lectures on time-consciousness, we find the following characterisations of the flux of consciousness which may help us to understand precisely in which sense it may be said to be absolute.

The flux of consciousness is indubitably given, and admits of no illusion, being-otherwise, or doubt(48). It is given without appearances or perspective variations(49). It is a self-contained sphere of being into which nothing can enter from without and from which nothing can go out, which is independent and does not possess mere intentional being as in the case of all transcendent (and immanent) objects(50). The *epoche* does not affect its essential nature even though it disconnects it from the naturalistic attachments; it undergoes some modifications, i.e., the empirical consciousness is transformed into transcendental consciousness, but in its essential nature it remains the same. Further, it is the source of meanings, the realm of "absolute origins," it constitutes all objectivities but is itself self-constituting(51). The appelation 'absolute' may be taken to stand for all these characteristics of the flux of pure consciousness.

However, it should be remembered that even this flux of consciousness is not adequately given, for we still have to "swim after" the *Erlebnisse* in it, and catch hold of them by some kind of retrospective remembrance. This at least seems to be what Husserl says in *Ideas* I(52). In the lectures on time-consciousness one of the points gained in this respect is that the primary retention is not a retrospective remembrance but a direct apprehension of the past as past, it in fact is perception so that in it the just-having-been is directly seen(53). This reduces the difficulty created by the nature of a flux demanding us to "swim after" it. Nevertheless, we never come to have a total apprehension of the flux *sub species aeternitatis,* but are within it even as we are aware of it, for our awareness is also a part of this flux. This precludes a completely adequate mode of givenness of the flux as a flux, though as it is given it is given immediately and directly and not through perspectives or appearances.

We have distinguished above, following Husserl, between (i) the objective time to which transcendent objects belong, (ii) the immanent time — also objective, being constituted — to which the immanent constituted unities like acts and hyletic data belong, and (iii) the absolute flux of consciousness which is the source of all temporality and cannot itself be said to be in time. In view of the exposition of the details of Husserl's thought that we have given in the foregoing pages, this list of three levels is somewhat inadequate. We need to recognize a level of temporality which is to be placed between (ii) and (iii), and which is to explain how (iii) constitutes itself into (ii). This is the level of what Husserl often calls "pre-phenomenal" or "pre-immanent" time in which the phases of the flux are arranged in a rather "quasi-temporal" manner *(quasizeitlich)*(54). Thus, while the absolute flux of consciousness is not at all temporal, is in fact 'timeless', by virtue of its own intentional structure it is given to itself as quasi-temporal ordering of its phases, and it is in this quasi-temporal ordering, in this pre-immanent time that the immanent objectivities and immanent time are constituted. The two, however, namely the absolute non-temporal flux and the quasi-temporal ordering, are not identical, nor are they different. The latter is how the former appears to itself(55).

CHAPTER 2

HUSSERL'S CONCEPT OF INTENTIONALITY — II

A. INTENTIONALITY AS NOETIC-NOEMATIC CORRELATION

W E HAVE ALREADY noticed how within the period of the *Ideas* I Husserl has already effected a transition from the concept of intentionality as the simple reference to an object to the conception of it as noetic-noematic correlation, and from the latter to the conception of it as constitution. Of these three conceptions the first is not abandoned in favour of the second, nor is the second abandoned in favour of the third. On the contrary, the second and the third are introduced as successive phenomenological explications of the first, as answers to the question, "what the 'claim' of consciousness to be really 'related to' an objective, to have an objective 'reference' properly comes to?"(1). For Husserl the conception of intentionality as noetic-noematic correlation (henceforth to be called simply 'correlation'), presents only a halfway house in the final explication of the concept of intentionality, a necessary and important phase but not the final and adequate explication. Its validity is not sublated, just as the validity of the initial naive conception of reference to an object is also not sublated. Only like the latter it is taken up into a wider body of doctrines wherein it receives fuller phenomenological clarification.

Gurwitsch, more than any one else, has emphasized the centrality of the notion of correlation in Husserl's concept of intentionality. "The noetic-noematic correlation is what the term intentionality must signify"(2). Further, "All structures of intentionality rest upon the noetic-noematic correlation which, for this reason, is the most universal structure"(3). It characterises all forms of mental activity, and so is also the most fundamental and the most universal structure. Gurwitsch's further interpretation of this correlation is both novel and interesting. He finds here a two-level theory of consciousness, a theory according to which consciousness is not a uni-dimensional flow but a correlation between two levels, "on the one hand, the level of multiple acts, psychological events, which take place in time; on the other, the level of meanings, of significations, of noemata"(4), between a level of real temporality and a level of ideal unity.

This thesis is surely valid to a certain extent. Granted that the correlation and the consequent bi-dimensionality characterise, according to Husserl, consciousness at all levels, one may yet contend that intentionality in the sense of directedness towards an object is also equally universal a structure. At the same time, it has also to be recognised that so far as Husserl is concerned the correlation as little provides us with a final explication of the intentionality thesis as does the notion of being directed towards an object. At the same time, it is even doubtful whether the correlation does characterise — or can be meaningfully said to characterise — the intentionalities other than the acts. It does not seem to hold good of the deeper intentionalities revealed by the lectures on time consciousness. Further, Husserl speaks of noematic intentionalities, and surely the idea of correlation cannot be extended to these. If then we are to gain a comprehensive understanding of Husserl's concept of intentionality we have to go beyond the notion of correlation.

Let us now consider a few important points in connection with the idea of correlation:

1. The relation of *noesis* to *noema* is *not* the same as the relation of consciousness to its object(5). Consequently, intentionality understood as correlation is not a substitute for intentionality understood as reference. The reference of consciousness to its object is *made possible* through (a) the correlation, (b) the noematic nucleus with its "necessary midpoint" "by means of" which the *noema* also refers to the object, and (c) the consequent noematic intentionality. If this be so, it will not be correct to identify the *noema* with the intentional object. When I perceive a tree, the tree is the object of my perceptual act. The *noema* of that act is the tree as perceived. Of course, the intentional object is not *eo ipso* the apprehended object(7). But apprehending the intentional object and apprehending the *noema* are two entirely different activities. The intentional correlate of an act of loving may become an apprehended object through a distinctively "objectifying" turn of thought(8). But the apprehension of the corresponding *noema* requires that all affirmations bearing on actuality must be suspended(9). It would not also be correct to hold that the concept of *noema* does the job of the more familiar concept of content. In fact, for Husserl "the distinction between 'content' and 'object' must be drawn not only in the case of 'consciousness,' of the intentional experience, but also in that of the *noema* taken in itself"(10). The *noema* refers to its object through its nucleus which may be regarded as its content.

2. What is the mode of being of the *noema?* Husserl uses various expressions in this connection: the *noema* lies "immanent" in the experience(11), but is not "reell" contained in experience(12). The *noema* is a "dependent object," its *esse* is *percipi* — not in Berkeley's sense, Husserl adds, "since here the *percipi* does not contain the *esse* as a real *(reelles)* constituent"(13). The perceptual *noema* "belongs to" the perception inseparably(14), and so in all other cases. Now Husserl's use of the words 'immanent' and 'transcendent' is varied, and we need not here bring out all the different senses in which he uses them(15). This much is clear that the immanence of the *noema* is not what Husserl often calls real immanence(16), not immanence in the sense of absolute givenness (for things other than

the *noema* may be absolutely given, and there is a sense in which the *noema* is not), not immanence in the sense in which the *noesis* and the hyletic data are immanent in an *Erlebnis,* and obviously not immanence in the sense in which Husserl speaks in the *Ideas* I (§ 38) of immanent perceptions. It can only be immanence in the sense of *"intentionalen Beschlossenseins,"* a sense which is not opposed to any mundane transcendence. But even here, in order that the specific peculiarity of the concept of *noema* is not overlooked, we should recall that also transcendent things of the natural world are, according to a well known conception of the *Ideas* I (§ 47), correlates of consciousness. There should, therefore, be an important difference between the sense in which natural things are correlates of consciousness, and the sense in which the *noema* "lies immanent" in experience: both kinds of immanence are characterisable as intentional *Beschlossensein,* and both are compatible with mundane transcendence. One way of bringing out this difference is this: according to the doctrine of the *Ideas* I (§§47-51), the natural world is necessarily related to consciousness, but consciousness is "essentially independent of all Being of the type of a world or Nature, and it has no need of these for its *existence"*(17): the relation is not a necessary correlation. Between *noesis* and *noema* however there is a necessary correlation: the immanence here is greater, the transcendence lesser. In fact, of the three: the real tree out there, the intentional object of my act of imagining the tree, and the same tree as imagined (or, the *noema* of the act of imagining it) there is a subtle difference which is likely to be overlooked. They differ not merely with regard to the sort of immanence and transcendence they enjoy with regard to consciousness, but also in the modes of their apprehension and also in their ontological status.

The *noema* is not also the same as essence(18). In the first place, the *noema* of an act of perception is different from the essence of the perceived object — as may easily be seen. Secondly, apprehension of the *noema* and apprehension of the essence are very different sorts of apprehensions: the former requires a phenomenological attitude, the latter an ontological(19).

The concept of *noema* therefore cuts across ontological

regions of individual thing and essences, the existent and the non-existent, simply because it itself is not an ontological concept but a genuinely phenomenological one, and presupposes the phenomenological bracketing of all ontic positing(20).

3. Can we say that the *noema* is meaning, signification? Husserl of course does say many things to that effect. The intentional object of an intentional experience is said to be its "objective meaning"(21); the perceived tree as such — as distinguished from the tree plain and simple — is said to be the perceptual meaning belonging to the act of perceiving inseparably(22). Here, both the intentional object and the *noema* are said to be meaning, and of course we have argued that they are different. The word 'meaning' is ambiguous enough to permit this equivocation. We might suggest that the intentional object is 'meaning' in the sense of 'reference,' whereas the *noema* is 'meaning' in the sense of 'sense.' It is this latter alone, the sense as distinguished from reference, which is meaning in the strict sense, and we may therefore say that it is the *noema* and not the intentional object which should be called the meaning. In the *LU*, Husserl uses the word '*Gegenstand*' to mean reference, and the words '*Bedeutung*' and '*Sinn*' indifferently to mean 'sense.' In the *Ideas* I (especially in § 124), Husserl proposes to use the words '*Bedeutung*' and '*Sinn*' differently: '*Bedeutung*' is used for 'meaning at the conceptual level,' i.e., for logical meaning, whereas '*Sinn*' is used for meaning in the broadest sense. The former applies especially to acts of expressing, the latter to all acts(23). The noematic nucleus is the *Sinn* of the noetic act, but not for that reason to be taken for a conceptual or logical meaning. However, every noematic nucleus may be raised to "the realm of the "Logos," of the "Conceptual," and so can be "expressed" "(24).

The full *noema* is not the meaning, it rather contains an inner core, the nucleus, which is "its" meaning(25), but which is also the meaning of the act (whose *noema* is under consideration). In any case, it is not meaning in the sense of logical or conceptual meaning of expressions. It is thus that we have to understand the following statement of Husserl: "*das Noema überhaupt ist aber nichts weiter als die Verallgemeinerung der*

Idee der Bedeutung auf das Gesamtgebiet der Akte" (26). What
we have elsewhere said of 'meaning' holds good of the noema;
it is both subjective and objective — in the words of Adorno,
"ein Zwitter subjektiver Immanenz und transzendenter Objek-
tivität" (27).

4. After having considered the nature of the *noema*, let us
take a brief look at the concept of *noesis*. Although Husserl is
using *'noesis'* for 'consciousness,' he is using 'consciousness' in a
rather strict sense. According to this strict sense, consciousness
is the same as intentional experience in general. But again an
intentional experience has two *real* components: the *hyle* and
the meaning-bestowing component which 'forms' or 'animates'
the *hyle*, and thereby "brings in the specific element of intentionality" (28). Thus in the strict sense *'noesis'* designates not
the completed intentional experience but that component of it
which bestows sense on the unformed *hyle*. This is alright, but
we are still to take note of certain peculiarities of this conception.

First of all, we should bear in mind that Husserl often
refers to the noetic phase as a stratum of "the stream of phenomenological being" (29), or as a real component of the *pure*
experience, i.e., "of what remains over as phenomenological resi-
duum, when we effect the reduction to 'pure immanence' "(30).
What these suggest is that the *noesis* is not to be regarded as a
real component of a concrete mental act regarded as a real concrete event in the life history of a real individual man, e.g., of
this act of perceiving by me here and now. You do not reach
the *noesis* by analysing this act of perceiving into its real components. The experience has first to be "reduced" into a pure
experience, to "pure immanence." But once we do this, does it
any more make sense to speak of a *real* component of pure experience, when for real analysis we treat an experience as an
object like any other? (31). The entire noetic-noematic analysis
would require an attitude that seems to be radically different
from the attitude of real analysis of a whole into its component
elements. Further, though Husserl does use the word 'component,' he also uses the words 'strata' and 'phases,' and the
last two would seem to be more appropriate, for the *hyle* and
the noetic act cannot by their very nature be regarded as co-

ordinate elements, constituting a whole. They are not merely different elements, but *as elements different*.

Though thus Husserl's use of 'real component' is unfortunate, his intention is clear and justifiable: he rightly sees, and wishes to express, the undeniable difference that subsists between an immanent element of a subjective experience and a transcendent correlate of that experience.

The difficulty that we have been pointing to is but an aspect of a much deeper problem concerning Husserl's philosophy, the problem namely of the relation between the psychological and the phenomenological experiences (or even between the empirical and the *a priori*). The problem is, to what extent is the noetic correlate of a *noema* a pure act?(32). In the *Ideas* I, it must be admitted, the noetic correlate is still regarded and understood *on the analogy* of a psychological act, or at least as a real component of such an act. The purely noetic is still a real component of a concrete noetic experience, their difference notwithstanding(33). Transcendental subjectivity as meaning-conferring and so as constituting is still a component of psychological subjectivity: only it is to be discovered through a phenomenological reduction and an intentional analysis.

5. How are we to understand the celebrated doctrine of noetic-noematic correlation? It is summed up in one sentence: "no noetic phase without a noematic phase that belongs specifically to it"(34). But this is not as simple a statement as it looks like. In fact, Husserl is aware that there are several parallelisms and that they all are beset with great difficulties(35). Let us try to make the situation as much clear as possible, making use of Husserl's various analyses and taking the more convenient case of perceptual acts and perceptual *noemata*.

Let us consider my perception of the tree over there. In every perception, as I move around or orient myself differently or take a different perspective, I have both a different perceptual act and a different perceptual *noema*: however, in all these cases, I am perceiving the same tree, the intended object is the same. Let these acts be $A_1, A_2, A_3, A_4, \ldots\ldots$, and let their respective *noemata* be $N_1, N_2, N_3, N_4, \ldots\ldots$ Thus, there is *both* a noetic multiplicity and a noematic multiplicity. But as Gurwitsch has well argued, the two multiplicities are on different levels(36). For to each *noema* there corresponds a multiplicity of actual and possible and possible acts. In other words, many different acts may have identically the same *noema*. Thus, let A_1 be the act of perceiving the tree from the perspective (to simplify matters)p_1. Now, from the same perspective, many different perceptions of the same object are possible, all these acts will have the same *noema* N_1. If these acts are A^1_1, A^2_1, A^3_1, A^4_1, ... , then all these acts (having the same subscript) have the same *noema* N_1. These acts may differ from each other in their temporal positions. I may have a whole series of successive perceptions of one and the same object, the *noema* remaining the same.

Thus, although each act has it own *noema*, and different acts may have different *noemata*, it is also possible that different acts have identically the same *noema*. Further, different *noemata* may contain reference to identically the same object. The situation may be represented in the following manner:

$$[A^1_1, A^2_1, A^3_1 \ldots \ldots] \rightarrow N_1$$
$$[A^1_2, A^2_2, A^3_2 \ldots \ldots] \rightarrow N_2$$
$$[A^1_3, A^2_3, A^3_3 \ldots \ldots] \rightarrow N_3 \rightarrow \qquad O$$
$$\ldots \ldots \ldots \ldots$$
$$[A^1_i, A^2_i, A^3_1 \ldots \ldots] \rightarrow N_i$$

As should be obvious, there are various relationships involved in this situation. These are:

(a) Each act has its own intended object.

(b) Each act has its own *noema*.

(c) Different acts may have the same *noema*.

(d) Different *noemata* may refer to the same object.

To these we add a fifth one:

(e) Each act *phase* has its own noematic *phase*(37).

Let us consider briefly these five relationships. These relationships show that it would be an error to identify the noetic-noematic parallelism with the parallelism between the unity of the intended object and the constituting formations of consciousness(38). Further, the relationship between *noesis* and *noema* is not a simple one-to-one relationship. It is at one level one-one, at another many-one. Though each act has its *noema,* to each *noema* there corresponds a multiplicity of acts — so that in the noematic level there is achieved a unification which raises the *noema* above the temporality and particularity of acts: one sense in which the *noema* may be said to be irreal. ('Irreal' is here to be distinguished from ideal being. The ideal being, as for example, of the essences is still being. The *noema* is neither being nor non-being, as Gaston Berger has emphasised). We begin to see the affinity of this category with that of logical meaning(39), and a partial justification of calling the *noema* the meaning *(Sinn)* of the act.

While the unitary *noema* in its irreality stands over against a multiplicity of real acts, a multiplicity of *noemata* — curiously enough — refers, through passive synthesis of identification, to an identical real or ideal object. Thus the irreal *noema* mediates between real intentional acts and the real or ideal referent of those acts. In relation to the correlative multiplicity of acts, the *noema* is an identity; in relation to the correlative noematic multiplicity, the intentional object is an identity. The consitution of the intentional object by its correlative noetic acts may then be said to be mediated by two constitutions: constitution of the identical *noema* by the correlative noetic acts, and constitution of the identical intentional object through synthesis of the correlative *noemata.*

Let us now turn to the last of the five relationships listed above. The source of the diffculty here is the conception of 'noetic phase' and also the correlative conception of 'noematic phase.' If Husserl's statement to the effect that there is no noetic phase without a noematic phase that belongs specifically to it means simply that to the structure of the *noema* with its content, quality and the central core there corresponds a noetic structure, and that to every noetic modification — attentional temporalising etc. and their interpenetrations — there corresponds a noematic, we understand it. But it would seem that Husserl means something more. This is what he has further to say:

> ". . . to every component which "objectively" directed
> description picks out in the object, there corresponds

a real *(reelle)* component of the perception. . . . Also
we can indicate all these noetic components only by
falling back on the noematic object and its phases, and
referring shall we say, to the consciousness . . . . " (40)
The tree that I am now perceiving has its colour, the colour of
its trunk let us say. The noema of the act of perceiving has,
amongst its component predicates, the noematic colour. Corresponding to the noematic colour there is a whole multiplicity
of sensory colours. These sensory colours or *hyle* are 'animated'
by noetic meaning-bestowing acts which transform them and
unify them into objective, noematic predicates. So in the case
of each of the noematic predicates.

Let A be the act of perceiving, N its noema, O the object
perceived. Let S_1, S_2, S_3 . . . . . . be objective properties of O. (S_1
may designate the colour of O, S_2 its texture, S_3 its shape, and
so on). Further, let s'_1, s''_1, s'''_1 . . . be the hyletic data
correlative to the noematic predicate N_{s1}. Likewise let s'_2, s''_2,
s'''_2 . . . . . . be the hyletic data correlative to the neomatic predicate N_{s2}. Similarly with the other noematic predicates. Now
s'_1, s''_1, s'''_1 . . . . . . need a noetic meaning-bestowing act or
act-phase in order to constitute the noematic predicate N_{s1}.
Let us call this noetic phase a_1. The act-phase which constitutes the hyletic plurality s'_2, s''_2, s'''_2, ... into the noematic
predicate N_{s2} is a_2. We have thus noetic phases a_1, a_2, a_3,
a_4, ... In general, the noetic phase a_i animates the hyletic data s'_i, s''_i, s'''_i . . . . . . and constitutes the noematic
predicate N_{s_i} which corresponds to the objective property S_i
apprehended in the original act of perceiving O. In fine, every
generically homogenous group of hyletic data (sensory colour,
sensory shapes, etc.) requires a specific noetic phase to animate
it and to constitute the correlative noematic phase.

Now if this be Husserl's theory rather succintly stated in §97
of the *Ideas* I, several points need to be taken care of. In the
first place, assuming that every noematic phase N_{s_k} has a correlative noetic phase a_k, one may wonder if an over-aching
noetic act A is needed which would unify the phases a_1, a_2 . . . . . .
and which would be required to account for the unity of the
noematic predicates in one noema N. Even leaving this apart,

one is bothered by the thought, to what extent such an analysis may claim to be strictly phenomenological. May it not be reasonably suspected that this analysis is an unwitting victim of the much maligned constancy hypothesis and objective prejudice which phenomenologists like Gurwitsch and Merleau-Ponty have so effectively criticised. For, is not Husserl assuming that there is a noetic component corresponding to every component of the object? Of course, he adds: "but only in so far, be it observed, as the description holds faithfully to the object *just as* it "stands before us" in this perception itself." This suggests that what he has in mind is not a component of the real tree I am perceiving, but a component of the noema: but I think his doctrine makes use of both. Even if we take the noematic colour, the noematic shape etc., to suppose that corresponding to each of these there is an appropriate noetic act-phase is, in a way, to bring in the constancy hypothesis and the objective prejudice. It is to miss the unity of the perceptual act and the unity of the *noema,* and to dissolve them into the supposed multiplicity of noetic and noematic phases. There is no doubt that the notion of the *hyle,* as stated by Husserl in §97, requires this. The notion of the *hyle,* I believe, has a certain relevance and need, but it cannot be retained in the form in which Husserl formulates it here.

To what extent Husserl in the paragraph quoted above is under the influence of a sensationalistic psychology is borne out by the fact that the act-phases a_1, a_2, a_3, ... are not all as such given. I am aware of perceiving the tree, and not of having all these acts of apprehending the sense data. The noetic phases can be identified, talked about, even defined by no other way save in relation to the noematic phases. I suspect here a remnant of the theory of *unbemerkte Empfindungen* in the form of act-phases lived through but not noticed!

There is difference between saying that an act is founded on some other act or acts, and saying that it has some other acts as its component act-phases. Is an act-phase itself an act? Is it intentional? How many act-phases are there in a given act? How to identify and enumerate them? I think there is neither phenomenological evidence nor theoretical reasons for assuming them, unless of course one is initially committed to an atomistic theory of *hyle* like the one found in §97 of the *Ideas* I.

B. INTENTIONALITY AS CONSTITUTING FUNCTION:

The transition from the conception of intentionality as noetic-noematic correlation to the conception of it as constituting function never meant, as said before, abandonment of the correlation thesis. It meant taking it up into a much wider theory. The basis of this is already laid in the hylo-morphic scheme according to which the noetic act 'animates' or 'confers meaning' on the meaningless hyletic data, and therefore constitutes the objective *noema*. This is the first stage of the theory of constitution which — by its own inner logic inevitably leads beyond itself, so that we have not one but two conceptions of constitution. These are:

(a) The conception of constitution as meaning-bestowing or *Sinngebung*; and

(b) The conception of constitution as transcendental production.

Let us call these constitution$_1$ and constitution$_2$ respectively.

(a) The Conception of Constitution$_1$.

We have already had occasion, in connection with the correlation thesis, to look closely at the conception of constitution$_1$. However, a few more critical remarks may nevertheless be in order. In the first place, this conception of constitution applies to act intentionalities and to act-phases, but not to intentionalities other than acts. It is valid therefore within a limited perspective(41). It looks upon *hyle* and acts as further unanalysable ultimates, whereas in fact — as the lectures on time consciousness showed — they too are constituted. Their constitution is not constitution$_1$. Thus the major presupposition of the doctrine of constitution$_1$ is the doctrine of *hyle*. With the transition to the doctrine of constitution$_2$ this doctrine of the *hyle* is sought to be abandoned. As we have already seen, the lectures on time consciousness seem to unravel the intentional constitution of the hyletic data: the notion of *hyle* was rejected by Husserl as being a remnant of the influence of sensualistic empiricism.

In order to assess the nature of the conception of constitution₁ let us consider the two components of it: the conception of *hyle* and that of the meaning-bestowing act, a little more closely.

(α) Complaints against the doctrine of *hyle* have been various.

(i) According to Sartre, though Husserl came to recognise the hyletic component of consciousness in order to account for the element of passivity in knowledge yet the doctrine itself creates more difficulties than it solves.

"The *hyle* in fact could not be consciousness, for it
would disappear in translucency and could not offer
that resisting basis of impressions which must be sur-
passed towards the object"(42).

Sartre's difficulty is genuine, provided one accepts his basic thesis that consciousness is wholly transparent to itself. We have not as yet taken up this issue which is reserved for a future chapter.

(ii) One may also complain that Husserl should not have found place for non-intentional *hyle* within the real structure of consciousness which is, on his own theory, intentional. One may even suspect that the non-intentional *hyle* would frustrate the intentionality of consciousness.

"Even if we grant to Husserl that there is a hyletic
stratum for the noesis, we cannot conceive how consciousness can transcend this subjective toward objectivity"(43).

Now, so far as this objection is concerned one may want to defend Husserl by saying that the *hyle* is not needed to facilitate the self-transcending reference of consciousness but to account for the facticity, the determinateness and the element of passivity in it. The *hyle* is not supposed to be the medium of reference, it is not to do the job of the concept of content of the theory of representative consciousness. The content, in Husserl's philosophy, is not the *hyle* but the *noema*. How consciousness can transcend the *hyle* towards objectivity could not be an issue, for this precisely is the job of the noetic component of an experience: it transforms the non-intentional datum into an intentional *noema*, thereby making the reference possible. The truly difficult point then is not that the *hyle* threatens to block the intentional reference but that it should at all be there within consciousness when consciousness is supposed to be out and out intentional. Either one retains the latter thesis and expels the non-intentional *hyle* out of consciousness; or one modifies the thesis of the intentionality of consciousness to make room for impressional matter within consciousness; or one may retain both the theses but so modify the latter, by exhibiting the intentional structure of the *hyle*, that it is not any longer incompatible with the former. Husserl takes to the last alternative in the lectures on time consciousness. Sartre chooses the first. We shall attempt to suggest a solution along the second. Our solution will take care of the objection under (i), and will try to connect the two notions of intentionality and reflexivity of consciousness.

(iii) What Gurwitsch finds fault with is the "alleged independence of a hyletic stratum"(44). We do not have, according to him, any sensuous material that is not articulated and structured, that is not already meaningful. On the contrary, what is immediately given is already meaningful, it is already structured and formed. Thus writes also Merleau-Ponty:

"Every sensation is already pregnant with a meaning inserted into a configuration, and there is no sense — datum which remains unchanged from illusion to truth"(45).

Gurwitsch also argues that it is not true that the material remains the same through change in interpretations. The data themselves change with change in the acts. To take his very appropriate illustration: if Chinese letters are presented to one who knows Chinese and one who does not, the letters *look* different to the two persons, the sensuous appearance and not merely its interpretation is different in each case.

Now both the contentions of Gurwitsch are incontestable. It cannot be denied that we never get down to the formless given, that the given at any level we choose is always structured. It is also true that the sensuous aspect of the given changes with the change of the act — which shows that there is no independent, identical, sensuous stratum. Granted all this, it is nevertheless doubtful if this wholly dispenses with the need of some conception of *hyle*, though it surely does show the unsatisfactoriness of some of Husserl's statements in the *Ideas* I. It need not be a part of the doctrine of *hyle* that the *hyle* is given as unformed. On the other hand, the *hyle* may simply be regarded as a presupposition of the fact that anything is given at all. To this it may be objected that the supposition that the *hyle* is not given is inconsistent with the supposed transparency of consciousness, but in order to take care of this one may need to modify the naive and unconditional assertion that consciousness is wholly transparent to itself.

(iv) Asemissen draws attention to two major flaws in Husserl's conception of sensation(46). In the first place, according to Asemissen Husserl defines sensation not by what it is but by what it does, i.e., through its function which again it does not in itself possess but first comes to have through the noetic act. This, Husserl does when he defines sensation as those sensuous components of an experience because of which an objectivating apprehension — through the corresponding noetic intention — comes to correspond to the objective appearances. Now this function of making objective reference possible does not belong to sensations as such but is conferred upon them by the noetic act: in fact it belongs to both together, and not to any one of them separately.

"Die Husserlsche Empfindungsdefinition spiegelt den Umstand wieder, dass er die Empfindungen als Empfindungen gar nicht untersucht hat. Er benutzt einen unüberprüften Empfindungsbegriff, um mit seiner Hilfe die Eigenart intentionaler Erlebnisse, so fern es sich um Wahrnehmungen handelt, verständlich zu machen"(47).

What this criticism, if valid, amounts to is not that Husserl's conception of *hyle* has to be totally rejected but that his conception of sensation is unsatisfactory. In fact, at least in the *Ideas* I he never carefully thought through the latter conception.

Asemissen's second point has considerable weight: sensations have properties which make them unfit for being real components of consciousness. They have — and Husserl recognises this — spatial properties, and further they are intimately connected with the body. In the *Ideas* I Husserl had not yet developed the conception of body which he does in his later works. He is still operating with a naive conception of body and brackets it in order to reach pure consciousness, so that he feels obliged to accomodate the sensations within consciousness. Body is still external to consciousness, though empirically conjoined with it into "a natural unity"(48).

The much beaboured doctrine of the *hyle* has had very few defenders amongst Husserl's followers. It is also true that Husserl himself has disowned the version of the *Ideas* I. But it cannot also be straightaway denied that some form of the doctrine has to be recognised by any phenomenology of consciousness. Sartre's fear that to locate the *hyle* within consciousness would amount to inserting into the all-transparent consciousness a "centre of opacity" would be justified only if we assume that consciousness is in fact all-transparent. But this is an assumption which one may very well question. In fact, from the foregoing discussion it would seem that if the doctrine of the *hyle* has to be retained in some form or other one has to do a rethinking of the thesis of consciousness as being out and out intentional and also as being out and out transparent to itself. The points raised by Gurwitsch and Merleau-Ponty are more serious, but they are directed against an atomistic sensualistic conception of *hyle*. The supposed discrete sensation is quite possibly a myth — a product of theory and not a datum of consciousness. The most elementary data may exhibit intentional structures of various sorts. Nevertheless the basal thesis that there is some kind of impressional matter does not stand or fall with the conception of sensation, and it is in this form that the doctrine of the *hyle* may still survive. An attempt such as Landgrebe's(49) to get rid of the atomistic and sensationalistic conception of *Empfindung* which persisted both in Kant and Husserl(50) by construing *Empfinden* as "a structure of the Being-in-the-world" may be right in appealing to facts (the fact, e.g., that sensation is closely connected with movement) which are undeniable, but is surely wrong in thinking that the general notion of 'Being-in-the-world' is adequate to account for the particularity and the variety of the sensuous matter. Furthermore, as Ricoeur has shown(51), this doctrine may be indispensable for those phenomenologists who would like to take the psycho-analytical concept of the unconscious more seriously.

Regarding the relation of the sensations to the body, it has been pointed out that in the *Ideas* I the body is still regarded as external to consciousness, and serves as a connecting link between pure consciousness and the real world(52). He does recognise there however that states like a state of pleasurable feeling have an intentional reference to the '*Mensch-Ich*' and the human body, but adds that when abstraction is made from this reference the state concerned undergoes an alteration such that it finds place in pure consciousness and looses all natural significance(53). It is this abstraction from what would otherwise seem to be an essential bodily reference which leads him to locate all *hyle* directly within pure consciousness as its real component. The second volume of the *Ideen* contains Husserl's first systematic phenomenology of body(54). We need not consider here all the different levels of understanding body which Husserl elaborates: body as the "zero-point of orientation"(55), body as the field of localisation(56), body as the organ of will(57) etc. But we can detect a clear realisation that a large part of the hyletic stratum (e.g., touch) is directly founded in the body and that through it the intentional components (e.g. touching) also receive an indirect localisation(58). This localisation entails for Husserl(59) that the body is already more than a material thing and possesses a psychic layer, so that when we speak of the physical body we are abstracting from the total body. He even calls the body "*das subjektive Objekt*"(60).

We may therefore conclude: (i) that the concept of *hyle* is indispensable to account for the concrete fullness of the content of our human conscious life; (ii) that it may and should be freed from the atomistic-sensualistic form which the *Ideas* I gave it; (iii) that the conception is also needed to take into account the psycho-analytical concept of the unconscious within the framework of phenomenology; and (iv) that the concept needs to be founded on an adequate phenomenology of body and its psychic stratum. These considerations will have a profound influence on the notions of intentionality and reflexivity or transparence of consciousness, as we hope to be able to show later on.

(β) The other component of the concept of constitution$_1$ is the concept of the meaning-bestowing act. This latter concept itself involves the concept of meaning which needs some comments. Husserl has, in fact, two concepts of meaning-bestowing act: one in the *Logische Untersuchungen* and the other in the *Ideas* I. The former is the narrower one and applies to expressions carrying logical meaning; the latter is the wider one and applies to any intentional act whatsoever. What is common to both is, in the first instance, that a sensuous complex that is presented is transformed into a significant whole referring beyond itself, and further that the *real* physical or psychic substratum is made to become the bearer of an *irreal* meaning, the temporal particular exhibits an a-temporal generality. In the present case, the meaning is the irreal noematic correlate of the act. In both cases, meanings are gifts of consciousness. The intentionality of consciousness as much consists in being of an object as in being the source of significations. In fact, for Husserl these are two aspects of the same situation: consciousness refers to its object only through the significations it creates.

This entire doctrine, along with the doctrine of constitution$_1$ which follows from it, is traced by Ryle to a mistaken theory of meaning(61). Husserl's error lies, according to Ryle, in several things the chief of which is to speak of acts as if they have meanings, or of things as being the meanings of acts. Now to be sure Husserl does say so, but the locution is not dangerous if we know what he means(62). Things are the intentional correlates of acts. The acts have meanings in so far as every act has its noematic correlate. The precise sense and justification of such locution have already been elaborated. Neither does Husserl himself confuse, nor need we in all fairness accuse him of having confused between this use of 'meaning' and the sense in which words and sentences have meanings. According to Ryle, Husserl — like other Brentano disciples — "acquired the habit of assimilating the (supposedly simple) relations between acts of consciousness and their intentional objects to the (supposedly simple) relations between symbols and what they stand for"(63). In truth, the former relation is for Husserl neither simple nor a sort of the latter. Further, the theory that meanings are gifts of consciousness follows not from the doctrine that they are intentional accusatives of acts, but from the fact that they exhibit an irreality which is not there in the real thing considered as real. Whether the further thesis that things are "tissues of meaning" correctly represents the Husserlian concept of constitution$_1$, and whether this thesis is entailed by the theory that meanings are gifts of consciousness are questions to which we may now turn. Meanwhile, it should be said that Ryle's further charge that to speak of a thing known as the correlate of an act of knowing implies that we could get to the heart of the thing by analysing our act of knowing it is also unfounded. Ryle hardly needs to remind us that we get to know more about the things not by analysing our acts of knowing them but by knowing the things themselves. Phenomenology is not to be a substitute for the empirical sciences. Phenomenological clarification of the 'constitution' of things is not empirical analysis of its constituent elements or qualities. The former is concerned with explicating the *sense* of thinghood of things, or the sense of any of the other specific essences (materiality, spirituality, etc.). In doing this, phenomenology turns away from the results of the sciences and considers how the thing *quâ* thing (or, *quâ* material body or organic being etc.) is given to consciousness; in other words, it comes to study the acts for which the thing in the generic or the specific character concerned is the intentional correlate. But surely by the explication of these acts you do not come to *know* more about the thing under consideration. You rather discover its sense for consciousness, its constitution.

According to the doctrine of constitution₁, the thing is not surely a "tissue of meanings." It has a sensory and hyletic component that is not a gift of consciousness. Further, there is the thetic character which is not a meaning in the strict sense, although it derives from the nature of the act. The unique particularity of the thing as also the passivity of its experience are thereby taken care of. But what, on this thesis of constitution₁, is constituted? Is it the *noema,* is it the intentional object, or is it the real thing out there? It would seem that it is the *noema* that is constituted by the corresponding noeses. However we have to take into account Husserl's warning, referred to earlier, that the noetic-noematic correlation is not the same as the relation between the acts and the objects they constitute. There are involved here two steps: for one thing, an identical *noema* is constituted by a plurality of noetic acts, and for another a whole series of noemata "close up," through a passive synthesis of *"Deckung,"* to constitute an identical intentional object. What then is constituted₁ is in the long run the intentional object. There remains nevertheless a gap between the intentional object and the thing *per se* (e.g., the real tree out there). The thesis of constitution₁ fails to include the latter within its scope.

(b)   The Conception of Constitution₂

When Fink writes (in 1933)(64) that the psychological intentionality is receptive, the transcendental act-intentionality is indeterminate *(unbestimmt),* i.e., neither fully receptive nor fully creative, and the transcendental constitutive intentionality is productive and creative, he is no doubt drawing attention to a most important distinction between Husserl's early and later works. What we have called constitution₂ is Fink's creative and productive intentionality. However one should be clear right at the outset what 'productivity' does not mean in this context. Though Husserl comes to speak of 'genetic' constitution he never quite abandoned his deep distrust of the notion of creativity of consciousness. One cannot but agree with Berger that the notions of 'production' and 'activity' are mundane concepts, and do not have any validity after the exercise of transcendental reduction which is a necessary presupposition of getting at the notion of constitution$_2$(66). Fink's emphasis on creativity therefore is likely to mislead.

The transition to the concept of constitution$_2$ is made possible through several lines of thought. First, the lectures on time consciousness seek to exhibit the intentional constitution of the hyletic stratum. Second, the supposedly unanalysable act unities are resolved into more primitive intentionalities constituting time-consciousness. Thus while constitution$_1$ with its matter-form scheme was concerned with act intentionalities, constitution$_2$ is concerned with intentionalities other than act intentionalities. With this a host of new concepts come to figure prominently in Husserl's writings. Some of these are: 'genetic constitution,' 'passive synthesis,' 'pre-predicative intentionality,' 'horizon intentionality,' 'operative intentionality,' 'unconscious' and 'anonymous' intentionalities. Let us consider these carefully.

(i) *'Passive synthesis'*: The notion of passive synthesis is not peculiar to constitution$_2$ alone. We have it in the *Ideas I* in the form of that passive synthesis of identification by which various noemata coalesce so as to make reference to one identical object possible. However, the overall importance of passive synthesis comes to light only later on: first in the lectures of 1918-1926(67), then in the *Formale und transzendentale Logik* and in the *Cartesian Meditations*. The *Cartesian Meditations* distinguish between active production of abstract entities like collections, numbers or inference-structures and passive constitution of pre-given things like the physical objects which confront us in life as ready-made(68). The abstract entities are produced — in a sense which approximates more accurately to the ordinary usage of 'production' — by conscious acts (of collecting, counting, or inferring) of an ego or of a community of egos(69). Such entities are in fact given to consciousness as products. They have besides the character of irreality. However, active production of such irreal entities presupposes that some other entities (of a lower type) be given: these latter are in the long run the real things, the physical objects which confront us in life as ready-made. An investigation into the 'sense' of their reality, of their thing-hood or of their physicality brings

to light their constitution, but they are not actively produced
by any act. Their constitution is passive, for otherwise they could
not have been given as if ready-made, they would not have been
passively intuited. To be sure, they are not given in consciousness as products. Whatever else Husserl might have meant by
'passive synthesis,' his ground is covered partly by Kant's notion
of 'transcendental synthesis of imagination' and partly by the
more modern notion of 'logical construction.' Kant's shift from
the originally suggested thesis that all synthesis is the work
of understanding which is characterised by spontaneity to the
thesis that it is really imagination which synthesises the representations and that imagination is a blind and unconscious
faculty of the soul(70) whose achievements are simply made
self-conscious by being brought under the unity of apperception
is an interesting parallel to Husserl's shift from his early emphasis on constitution by acts which confer meaning on pre-
given matter to the later thesis, which we are expounding at
the moment, that the synthesis which constitutes the physical
things and persons constituting the real world is passive. There
are no doubt significant differences between the Kantian thesis
and the Husserlian thesis, but the points of convergence are no
less striking. The fact that Kant regards the transcendental
imagination as 'productive,' while Husserl — at least in the
Cartesian Meditations — speaks only of active genesis as production is not really decisive. Passive synthesis is also genesis.
Equally significant is the role assigned to association by the two
philosophers in this context. Husserl regards association as a
primary form of passive synthesis(71) and refuses to look upon
it as a purely mechanical process: association for him is an intentional connection. Kant does not question the Humean account of association, but only rejects its primacy: association, for
him, presupposes — rather than constitutes — objective experience. More specifically, it presupposes that 'affinity' which is
a product of the synthesis of transcendental imagination. In any
case, a sort of passive synthesis underlies, and is presupposed
by, the higher level constructions.

It has already been said that the Husserlian thesis also
takes into account the insight on which the modern notion of

logical construction is based(72). One might wonder what the passive syntheses are if they are not either logical constructions or conditions of the possibility of phenomena. In the latter case, a condition of possibility again is nothing but a logical construction. Now, such an argument misses the essential point about the idea of passive synthesis. For one thing, whereas Russell regards entities of all higher order types — physical things, other minds, abstract entities — as logical constructions, Husserl is not willing to huddle them together under one heading. For Husserl, there is a fundamental difference between the constitution of entities of higher types and constitution of basic individuals like physical things. The notion of passive synthesis applies only to the latter. For another, the Russellian thesis lacks the fundamental concept of intentionality without which Husserl's notion of passive synthesis would loose all its distinctiveness. On Russell's thesis, to say that an entity A is a logical construction out of other entities a_1, a_2, a_3 . . . . . . a_n is to say — speaking in the formal mode — that statements about A may be translated into statements about a_1, a_2, a_3 . . . . . . a_n, these latter statements not containing the name 'A.' Perfect translatability in principle — ontologically speaking, perfect analysability without residue — is what is entailed. However this is not so on Husserl's thesis. A physical thing is a passive synthesis out of its various perspective appearances, not because the unity of the former is analysable into the series of those appearances as obeying certain laws of arrangement, but because each such appearance intends the same thing, refers to the same thing, and further because these intentions close up and coincide. The unity is realised through the endless series of appearances, but even prior to its fulfillment each appearance intends the unity. Thus the notion of passive synthesis is not to be considered independently of the notion of intentionality. The passive synthesis involved is thus not a mere construct as Cerf seems to take it to be(72). It is capable of being phenomenologically realised through reflection, i.e., brought to *evidence*, not merely inferred as a condition of possibility.

(ii) '*Horizon Intentionality*': The *Ideas* I contains the idea of horizon as what is, in an improper sense, given with all things

(uneigentliche Mitgegebenheit) but with more or less indeterminateness to be determined with a pre-given style *(Bestimmbar-
keit eines fest vorgeschriebenen Stils)*(73). We also find there the
idea of the threefold temporal horizon of every experience(74)
which is worked out in greater detail in the lectures on time
consciousness. The specific sense of horizon intentionality however comes gradually to the forefront in the late twenties. The
Cartesian Meditations refers to the horizon as the objective sense,
implicitly meant and foreshadowed in the actual *cogito*: the
predelineation is never perfect, but in spit of its indeterminateness it does have a determinate structure(75). The object
as *a pole of identity* is meant "expectantly" through the "horizon
intentionalities."

(iii) *'Genetic Constitution'*: The name 'genetic consitution'
is used by Husserl in a more specific sense in which it does not
coincide with 'passive synthesis.' The *Ideas* I contains the notion
of passive synthesis but not that of genetic constitution. The
typically new element in the latter notion is the idea of historical achievement(76). The idea of 'hidden achievements' is
of course common to 'passive synthesis' and 'genetic constitution': what is distinctive about the latter is the notion of historicity. Thus writes Husserl in the *Formale und Transzendentale Logik*:

> "Es ist eben die Wesenseigenheit solcher Produkte,
> dass sie Sinne sind, die als Sinnesimplikat ihrer Genesis
> ein Art Historizität in sich tragen . . . . . . dass man
> also jedes Sinngebilde nach seiner ihm wesensmässigen
> Sinnesgeschichte befragen kann".(77)

Each layer of sense presupposes those which arise before it.
For example, if I once judge that S is p, S will henceforth appear to me as carrying the sense p. Thus, every object carries in
it sedimentations of meaning deposited by previous meaning-
conferring acts. Under such circumstances, the task of phenomenology would be to "reactivate the original encounter"(78)
and to dig up the layers of sense. In the *Cartesian Meditations*,
we are given an example of how intentional references lead back
to a 'history': how in early infancy we had to learn to see
physical things(79). The example is surely from psychology,

but Husserl does not warn us against — on the contrary he seems to be drawing attention to — the analogy between this sort of psychological genesis and phenomenological genesis. Now this is exactly where any talk of 'genetic constitution' is likely to go wrong. However, the notion of historicity of constitution makes use of two theses each of which by itself seems plausible enough. First, there is the already familiar thesis that a thing is constituted by the meaning-conferring function of intentionality. Secondly, this meaning-conferring is not all done by me at this moment of my perception, I already find the thing ready-made, it has *already* been constituted and so is an achievement of past intentional syntheses. I infact do not begin all anew, I inherit achievements to which I might add, but I always find something achieved. To discover the sources of the achievements which I inherit would be the task of a philosophy of genetic constitution.

Now, though all this sounds plausible enough, it does not seem quite clear to what extent such a task can find its place within a phenomenological philosophy. It may perhaps, in tracing the genetic constitution of things, go back into the historical evolution of the meaning of 'thing' — in the manner of Heidegger — and show that what we now find pre-given *as a thing* is really the result of several stages of intentional modifications achieved through the history of human thought, that there are indeed several layers of meaning sedimentation in the *concept* of 'thing.' This would be genetic constitution in one sense of 'genesis.' But whereas such a genetic-historical analysis may apply to our fundamental concepts, it would not apply to the pre-given things themselves — to the case of the things of nature especially which I find before and around me. True, some of them, possibly each of them, has a significance for me — emotional, practical or utilitarian — which is inherited by me from the past. But striped of such overtones, the natural thing is still something whose constitution does not have a history in the phenomenological sense though it, and not its constitution, may have a history in the naturalistic sense.

Thus it appears as if 'genetic constitution' may be of various sorts. It may be historical or not. Further, it may be passive or not. Physical objects are passively and genetically constituted but not historical achievements. With regard to them Seebohm's characterisation of 'genetic analysis' as the exhibition of the connectedness of the various types of conscious states which, within the unity of the stream of consciousness, come to constitute the unity and identity of the object surely holds good(80). Cultural objects have a genetic and historical constitution. It is with regard to them that the notion of historicity and historical sedimentation of meaning most aptly applies, but their constitution is not surely passive. The ego is also constituted by a sort of auto-genesis, by what Husserl calls 'habitus'(81). From this we may conclude that not all genetic constitution is passive, though all passive constitution is genetic. Further, it would be fair to add that not all genetic constitution is historical achievement.

(iv) The ideas of unconscious and anonymous intentionalities emerge in various contexts. The intentionalities which passively constitute the pre-given world are 'anonymously' there; the experiencer knows nothing of them(82). Phenomenology has to rescue them from this anonymity. It penetrates the anonymous intentional life and uncovers its synthetic processes(83).

It would be an error however to equate the anonymous intentionalities with either the unconscious ones or with the intentionalities other than acts. Thus, e.g., the horizon intentionalities are not acts but are neither anonymous nor unconscious. Acts may have contributed to the sedimented sense of a pre-given object, and in such a case it is these acts which have become anonymous. Unconscious intentionalities, on their part, may be either acts or not. There are in fact unconscious desires, love and hatred which are acts. The whole notion of unconscious intentionality makes its appearance in course of Husserl's attempt to take into account the findings of modern depth psychology(84).

(v) All these foregoing concepts — the concepts of passive synthesis, genetic constitution, pre-predicative intentionality, anonymous intentionality and horizon intentionality — all these are brought together, in Husserl's last papers, under the title of 'operative intentionality.' Already in notes to the manuscript

of the *Erste Philosophie,* Part II(85), we are told of the implicit
"*Verflochtenheit aller Intentionalität in einem Leben.*" A note
of 1925 to the now published *Phänomenologische Psychologie*(86)
speaks of the intentional life as *Weltleben.* The adjective '*fun-
gierende*' is used along with '*lebendig*' perhaps for the first time
in the *Formale und transzendentale Logik*:

> "Die lebendige Intentionalität trägt mich, zeichnet vor,
> bestimmt mich praktisch in meinem ganzen Verhalten,
> auch in meinem natürlich denkenden, ob Sein oder
> Schein ergebenden, mag sie auch als lebendig fun-
> gierende unthematisch, unenthüllt and somit meinem
> Wissen entzogen sein".(87)

Operative intentionality is here said to be that mode of the
intentional life which remains unthematic, undisclosed and thus
removed beyond my knowledge although it carries me forward
in my theoretical as well as practical relationship. The title
'operative' seems to suggest the meaning that this intentionality
simply is not, it functions. "*Sie ist nicht schlechthin, sondern sie
fungiert*"(88). The compact unity and simplicity of the 'consciousness of . . . . . .' is the result of a simplification, a "*Verein-
fachungsleistung*" of many different modes of consciousness. The
entire *process* remains anonymous while only the simplified
achievement comes to the forefront. Intentional analysis should
lay these processes bare. They are not acts and also not cognitive.
Yet, they confer sense on the pre-given world, and provide the
basis for further creation of significance.

Both Fink and Merleau-Ponty make use of this notion of
operative intentionality. According to Fink(89), operative intentionality is "*die lebendig sinnbildende, sinnleistende, sinnver-
waltende Funktion des Bewusstseins, welche zu den einfachen
seelischen Einheiten der Akte sich selbst verdeckend zusam-
menschliesst.*" For Merleau-Ponty, it is "that which provides the
natural and ante-predicative unity of the world and of our
life"(90). We learn from Brand(91) that in his later papers
Husserl came to identify operative intentionality with the "*Welterfahrende Leben,*" the world-experiencing-life. One understands

why Merleau-Ponty came to identify the operative intentionality with the pre-objective world(92).

In fine, we could say that the notion of operative intentionality gathers together the various strands of thought which emerge in Husserl's writings at various stages. We have at first the thesis that intentionality constitutes objects, and also the further thesis that not all constitution is active and conscious. These two lead to the position that there is a passive synthesis which, itself hidden and anonymous, constitutes transcendence. Try to uncover this anonymous operation, and you are led from one layer to another till you reach the last ground of all synthesis: this is the world-experiencing-life, the source of all meanings and constitution(93).

Thus, the expression 'operative intentionality' is used to designate two very different things: first the intentionalities other than acts, which are passive, anonymous and synthetic; but also the supposed last source of all meaning and all constitution: the world-experiencing-life.

C. THE DIALECTICS OF INTENTION AND FULFILMENT

Reference has already been made to the notions of intention and fulfilment as bringing to light the essential moment of temporality in intentional life. However, these notions which came into full prominence first in the sixth logical Investigation but which continue to characterise Husserl's thought in all its various stadia deserve closer attention. In fact, for an accurate understanding of the motivation of Husserl's philosophy this dialectic of intention and fulfilment — as Paul Ricoeur so aptly calls it — should be given serious consideration.

If positivism, in philosophy, is that mode of thinking which goes back to the given as its last source of signification and its last court of appeal for questions of validity, there always was an important strain of positivism in Husserl's thought. We have already met this in his notions of 'representing content' and 'hyletic datum.' Every intentional act presupposes some intuitive data to work upon. Some intuitive content or other underlies every objectifying act, though this intuitive content, as we have seen, may function in many different ways. Now these notions have no doubt been subjected to criticisms, chiefly on the ground that they smack of an uncritical surrender to empiricism. We had occasions earlier to defend, as far as it then seemed possible, the notion of the *hyle*. But now let us turn to another form in which the appeal to the given reappears: this is the notion of fulfilment of an intention.

If intentionality is directedness towards an object, it is also a directedness towards a fulfilment. The concept of intentionality is no doubt to be understood as freed from the psychological notion of purposive aiming at. Nevertheless, as directedness towards its own fulfilment, it betrays close affiliation to that psychological notion. I should think the relation intention-fulfilment is not a kind of purposive aiming at satisfaction; but rather purposive aiming at satisfaction is a specific mode of intention directed towards fulfilment, or, better still, the ontic structure of purpose-satisfaction presupposes the universal phenomenological structure of intention-fulfilment.

Consider the following cases of this sort of relationship: An act of desire aims at the fulfilment of the desire. An act of supposal (e.g., that there may be life on the moon) aims at its confirmation by empirical evidence. An act of doubting (e.g., whether the yonder object is a man or a tree) aims at its resolution. An act of judging (e.g., that there are living beings on the Mars) aims at its verification in experience. A mathematical judgment (e.g., that there is a prime number between 1000 and 2000) aims at its fulfilment through construction. Hearing the beginning of a melody arouses expectations which demand fulfilment. Perception of the side of a physical object turned towards me arouses intentions which demand fulfilment through perceptions of the other sides turned away from me.

These examples vary a great deal amongst themselves regarding: (a) the sort of experience which would fulfil, or confirm, or resolve or verify or complete the initial act; and (b) the specific relationship which obtains between the initial act and that towards which it is said to aim. In other words, though in all cases we have spoken of 'aiming at,' this locution does not have precisely the same significance in each case. That this is not so is borne out by the fact that in some of the cases, the talk of 'aiming at' fits into ordinary use, in others it does not; in some cases, it is more nearly literal, in others, more nearly metaphorical. Notwithstanding these differences, there runs a common pattern through all of them: this is what Husserl calls the pattern of intention-fulfilment.

Further, whereas some acts, initially empty, aim at fulfilment as when the initial act is one of what Husserl calls 'symbolic thinking' where the talk of fulfilment is in a sense more apt and approximates not so much to the pattern of fulfilment of a desire as to the pattern of filling in of an empty outline or form with intuitive content; there are also acts which by themselves fulfil other prior intentions but which also press for, demand or aim at fresh experiences which would complete them, carry them forward towards satisfaction: in these latter cases it is not so much a matter of filling in an empty form with intuitive content as of following a pre-delineated tendency towards intuitive completion.

We have thus two broadly distinguishable patterns of intention-fulfilment structure. The first pattern brings to light the tendency of empty thinking towards getting filled with content, and shows a basically Kantian motivation. The second pattern exhibits the essential incompleteness and self-transcendence of all fulfilling experience so that there is always a dissatisfaction, a transcendence, a pre-delineated horizon beyond; there is always a surplus, a more in our intentions over their fulfilment. Together they show that complete coincidence is an ideal, never to be reached but always aimed at. A completely empty intention and a completely fulfilled intuitive act which harbours no partial empty intention within itself — both are ideal limits. Actual intentional life moves between these two limits.

In theory of meaning, we are led to distinguish between intended meaning and fulfilled meaning. "It is the intended meaning of which the language of *entities* holds good. Besides, it is of the intended meaning that we can predicate that identity, objectivity and universality, in short, that ideality which Platonists ascribe to the socalled abstract entities. On the other hand, the idea of meaning-fulfilment seeks to accommodate the phenomenological element in the positivist's emphasis on empirical verification"(94). Actually the two are not separate and sundered from one another. There is rather a living and dialectical passage from the one to the other. Husserl not only found room for both Platonism and empiricism; he saw the dialectical relation between the two. Life of thought is involved in this dialectics. The pure Platonist and the uncompromising empiricist, both err by onesidedness.

As we pass from meaning-intending act to the act of knowing, we meet with a sort of *provisional* limiting situation of the first pattern — an identity between intention and fulfilment, between the intended meaning and the fulfilled meaning, a coalescing of the two into one act as it were. *"Die Reden von Erkenntnis des Gegenstandes und Erfüllung der Bedeutungsintention drücken also, bloss von verschiedenen Standpunkten, dieselbe Sachlage aus"*(95). I have qualified this limiting case of identity as 'provisional,' for complete identity, total fulfilment of intention is an ideal. Actually what we have is not static unity but dynamic and phased identification. In fact, with the progress of Husserl's thought, emphasis shifted from total and static coincidence to the dynamic process of identification. In the *Erste Philosophie* I, Husserl writes: *"Nie aber ist, im gesamten Reiche der Realität, die Erfüllung eine vollkommene."* Furthermore, *"Kein Wissen ist das letzte"*(96). The notion of adequate givenness, of total bodily self-givenness ceases to have any instantiation. Even the self-givenness of consciousness is said, in the *Cartesian Meditations*(97), to be apodictic but not adequate. Intentional life aims asymptotically at this goal.

While the worth of an intuitive experience is to be measured by the intention which it seeks to fulfil (there being no blind experience as such, no bare Humean impression), or the *presence* has to be measured by the *sense* (to use Paul Ricoeur's striking terms), the validity — if not the meaning — of the intention needs appraisal by 'seeing', the sense has to be evaluated by the presence(98).

Two insights dawn upon us through reflection upon this dialectics of intention and fulfilment. First, the intentional act involves an aiming at, a project, an active thrust demanding actualisation, which brings to light the *minimum* core of the temporality of every intentional act. But secondly, we also realise that intention always goes beyond fulfilment, that not only there always remains an unfulfilled surd but there are intentions like absurd intentions which are *a priori* incapable of fulfilment — so that consciousness with its meaning-intending function, its power of creating significations, is not fettered within the limits of mundane experience, is not exhausted by being-in-the-world.

CHAPTER 3

THE EXISTENTIALIST CONCEPTION
OF INTENTIONALITY

THE EXISTENTIALIST CONCEPTION of intentionality, as found in the writings of Heidegger, Sartre, Merleau-Ponty and Ricoeur, has been foreshadowed in those features of Husserl's thought to which attention has been drawn in connection with our discussion of his conception of constitution$_2$. To start with, these are: the conception of the *Welterfahrende Leben,* the world-experiencing-life as the last source of all synthesis which, as Brand insists(1), anticipates Heidegger's conception of *In-der-Welt-sein;* the conception of horizon-intentionality or of consciousness's perpetual self-transcendence, *Übersichhinausmeinen,* which, as Ricoeur suggests(2), is very near the existentialist notion of consciousness as transcendence; the conception of the primacy of intentionalities other than acts over act-intentionalities, which foreshadows the Heideggerean primacy of concern over cognition; and the conception of operative intentionality which leads to a rejection by Merleau-Ponty of the notion of consciousness as pure transparence.

The idea of constitution is not totally rejected but is divested of its idealistic overtones; the idea of noetic-noematic correlation is abandoned in so far as the *noema* pretended to stand in between the act and the being; intentionality comes to be a relation amongst beings (or of beings with Being). The transcendental ego as the *source* of intentionality is dispensed with. It is replaced either by *Dasein* or by body, or even by a pure consciousness, the for-itself, which is not yet an ego. Reduction which for Husserl is an indispensable preliminary for a correct appreciation of the concept of intentionality is now fully abandoned: intentionality becomes an ontic, or an ontic-ontological relation. Existentialism becomes a phenomenological ontology. Most of the existentialists with the possible exception of Ricoeur have found fault with the Husserlian concept of the *hyle* and the consequent hylo-morphic scheme, though they all surely differ in their attitudes towards the doctrine of constitution in any of its two forms. Finally, the problem of the relationship between the concepts of transparence and intentionality has been made to bear on all these discussions.

Let us now take a closer look at the views of the leading exponents of existentialist phenomenology.

A. HEIDEGGER:

Heidegger retains the notion of intentionality, but at first modifies the Brentano-Husserl thesis, and then subordinates his own modified version of it to some other apparently non-intentional principle. Let us follow him in these two phases.

(1) Intentionality is first transformed into concern *(Sorge)* and then into openness *(Erschlossenheit, Offenheit)*(3). These transformations follow upon a rejection of the primacy of theoretic consciousness, of *doxa,* which figures so prominently in Husserl(4). In fact, what happens is more than this. The formulation of the intentionality thesis by Brentano and the early Husserl made use of the distinction between consciousness and Being: a distinction which, for Heidegger, is Cartesian in origin. Heidegger's philosophy is based on an unequivocal rejection of this Cartesian dualism. The basic category for him is neither consciousness nor Being, nor is it consciousness's intrinsic directedness towards Being; it is rather the *In-der-Welt-sein* of the *Dasein*: the Being-in-the-world of the there-being. However, the fact that *In-der-Welt-sein* is Heidegger's substi-

tute for Intentionality is better brought out by de Waelhen's translation of it into 'Being-to-world' *(etre-au-monde)* than by the usual 'Being-in-the-world'(5). This Being-in-the-world is to be characterised as a primal concern, and not as a merely theoretical awareness of. . . . . . The *Dasein* is in the world, not as a neutral being inhabiting it, but ecstatically, by being outside of itself by a kind of self-transcendence. The *Dasein* is not a substance existing in itself. It is ecstatically projected, spatially as well as temporally, into a world-field which it carries around itself like "an overarching pattern"(6).

Further analysis of this being-to-the-world reveals the way the Husserlian analysis has been taken up and transformed in it into something almost unrecognisable(7). Let us recall Husserl's distinction of the hyletic and the noetic components of an intentional act from the noematic correlate of the same. To these three correspond the three structural features of the being-to-the-world: *Befindlichkeit, Verstehen* and *Rede. Befindlichkeit* or ontological disposition reveals the being-contained-in, the pre-given accomplished facticity of *Dasein*, the original situation of being thrown into the world *(Geworfenheit)*. This aspect of being-to-the-world corresponds to the hyletic component of Husserlian intentionality: both are meant to take care of the aspect of pre-given passivity and facticity which characterise all human experience. *Verstehen* or comprehension reveals the prospective dimension of being-to-the-world, the aspect in which *Dasein* projects itself towards others in order to seize and manipulate them and, in doing so, give them meaning and significance. This *Ausser-sich-sein* or self-transcendence, the *Immer-sich-schon-Vorwegsein* corresponds to the noetic, the specifically intentional and meaning-conferring component of an intentional act. The world as "Total Meaningfulness" is made possible by comprehension. *Rede* and *Logos* bring out the aspect of encounter with the present, whose articulation takes place through constituted meaning and language: it corresponds to the Husserlian conception of the *noema*.

However, though the Husserlian analysis survives, it has been changed beyond recognition. For one thing, the concepts have been expressed in the language of feeling, they have been divested of their abstract, theoretical and epistemological garb and dressed in a manner such that they come closer to the everyday concrete human existence. For another, the static analysis of Husserl has been replaced by an emphasis on the temporal character of intentionality as well as of its structural elements. To be sure, Husserl himself had supplemented, as we have seen, his static analysis with a dynamic one which though already present in the Logical Investigations gradually come to prominence in the later works.

The three structural elements of being-to-the-world together constitute the *temporality* of *Dasein*. *Befindlichkeit* or ontological disposition as a mode of disclosure of the facticity of *Dasein*, of its being thrown into the world, has a reference to what has been, to the past that is settled and accomplished. *Verstehen* or comprehension with its prospective project, with its disclosure of the possibilities before the *Dasein*, refers to the future that is yet to be. *Logos* or speech which articulates the encounter with the present refers to the present. Thus being-to-the-world as the basic intentional structure of *Dasein* also reveals the temporality of intentionality.

But the intentional character of *Dasein* is further brought out in the characterisation of *Dasein* as radical openness to Being(8). The *Dasein* is luminous, it is *lumen naturale* in so far as it lets the beings show themselves. The radical openness of *Dasein* is what makes the Being of beings manifest(9). *This* concept of openness (Heidegger would soon give us another concept of openness) entails that consciousness is not a pure inner but a *Her-vor-gang*, an *Aus-sich-gang*, a perpetual self-transcendence towards . . . . . . , all of which is a consequence of that total rejection of a representative consciousness which seems to follow from the intentionality thesis(10). And it has been claimed(11) that the understanding of consciousness as openness helps phenomenology to sidetrack the epistemological problem in so far as the classical alternatives realism and idealism have been overcome *"von Grund auf."*

(2) However, whereas in his earlier works including the *Sein und Zeit* intentionality of consciousness is *explicated* as the being-to-the-world of *Dasein* (though Heidegger also says that

the intentionality of consciousness is *grounded* in the temporality of *Dasein* (12)), in the later works beginning with *Was ist Metaphysik?* intentionality is construed as an ontic relation and so — in accordance with the well-known Heideggerean move — traced back to an ontological principle as the condition of its possibility. Now intentionality is said to have been made possible by "transcendence"(13) and not *vice versa*. To equate *Dasein's* relatedness to beings with this transcendence would be now a mistake. What then is the transcendental condition of the possibility of intentionality? Heidegger now gives us two such conditions: the world-project *(der Weltentwurf)*, and the fact that the *Dasein* has been taken in to find itself in the midst of beings *("die Eingenommenheit* . . . . . . , *die das Dasein inmitten von Seienden* . . . . . . *sich befinden lässt")*(14). These statements are difficult to construe. What they may mean is that *Dasein* is possessed by Being (whereas in the *Sein und Zeit, Dasein* was simply open to Being), that man undergoes this openness, that man's openness is not self-explanatory but derives from a project of Being, that Being thinks in man. The openness is now spoken of as the horizon which makes man's confrontation with beings possible(15).

It is only in the earlier Heidegger that the notion of intentionality (as formulated by him) may be regarded as a primitive one, and it may be supposed that what he has done is to have explicated this notion in his own way. But in the later works he denies to intentionality a primitive status, and derives it from a rather metaphysical notion of the historicity and destiny of Being and its world-project (whatever the latter may mean). Neither the explication nor the derivation would succeed or would have seemed to many as successful unless the notion from which he makes the derivation were itself covertly intentional. The being-to-the-world is clearly an intentional concept; so also is the concept of temporality as Husserl has already shown. The metaphysical notions of the historicity and project of Being are no less intentional.

B. SARTRE

Sartre takes the concept of intentionality more seriously than

Heidegger, and instead of founding it on some other concept makes it one of the primitive notions of his system. He is closer to Husserl in this respect. He is also closer to Husserl in locating intentionality in consciousness rather than in *Dasein*: in fact, he finds Heidegger's concept of *Dasein* unsatisfactory in so far as it excludes consciousness(16). Sartre's for-itself is consciousness. It is defined by intentionality as also by its translucency. Let us examine these two notions as they are to be found in Sartre.

1. Regarding the translucency of consciousness, Sartre holds a view which is very much like the Prābhākara Mimāmsā theory of the self-luminosity of consciousness. In his early essay on "The Transcendence of the Ego," he tells us that consciousness is "all lightness, all translucence"(17). But its primary awareness of itself is not positional, not a reflection. Prior to reflection, prior to what the Nayiyāyikas call anuvyavasāya, prior to the Cartesian *cogito*, every conscious state is also a non-positional, pre-reflective awareness of itself(18). Every intention, he writes later on, is immediately self-conscious. A pleasure, e.g., exists only as consciousness of pleasure(19).

Now one consequence of this theory that consciousness is all translucence is that there could be nothing opaque within consciousness. Husserl's hyletic stratum is thereby thrown out of consciousness into the world(20). The *hyle* could not be in consciousness, for then "it would disappear in translucency." Further, idealism is rejected: the table out there cannot be in consciousness, for the table is not capable of being given completely, it can be given only in a never to be completed series of profiles. Representationalism is also rejected, for consciousness cannot by its nature contain any content, any picture, of the table. Philosophy, Sartre proposes, should "expel things from consciousness" and "reestablish its true connection with the world"(21), which is wholly and entirely outside consciousness(22). It follows that consciousness is utterly empty, but fully transparent. In fact, its emptiness and its transparence are, for Sartre, but two aspects of the same situation.

2. As regards intentionality, the interpretation of it as a constituting function is rejected(23). Consciousness cannot con-

stitute the being of its object, for to be conscious of something is to be confronted with a concrete and full presence which is not consciousness. Sartre does allow however, and this is an important part of his philosophy, that the for-itself makes possible both the totality of in-itself and its differentiated parts, both the *world* and the *this*(24). But he possibly means no more than that the for-itself makes the totality emerge or appear as a totality by distinguishing itself from it but does not "add anything" to being(25). Another reason why consciousness cannot constitute its object is that the supposed constitution of any single object, e.g., of this table on which I am now writing, would involve an infinity (an infinite series of actual and possible data and actual and possible series of acts) and such an infinity could not possibly be given, whereas there could be nothing in consciousness that is not immediately given to itself(26). Husserl's doctrine of the *noema* as an irreal correlate of the noetic act — of the *noema* whose *esse* is *percipi* — is rejected as being unfaithful to the principle that consciousness is transcendence(27).

The essential nature of intentionality is transcendence(28). Transcendence is to be understood here in a two-fold sense: first, as reference to a being outside of itself, but also as consciousness's urge to transcend the ontic being towards the ontological, namely the meaning of being. Now, here Sartre is both close to Heidegger and yet removed from him. In his emphasis on the self-luminosity of consciousness, on its openness to the beyond and on the notion of transcendence, Sartre is closer to Heidegger than to Husserl. But he is also removed from the former in two respects. For one thing, he identifies intentionality with transcendence but does not found the former in the latter. For another, though 'transcendence' is used by Sartre in both ontic and ontological senses yet the later Heideggerean notion of transcendence as the world-project of Being is altogether absent. Intentionality does not require a further grounding. As the essential structural moment of consciousness it is autonomous.

These two contentions — namely, that consciousness is intentional and that it is also translucent — together lead Sartre to the further contention, seemingly the most revolutionary of his theories, that *consciousness is nothing*. By saying that consciousness is nothing, he means to assert all of the following propositions:

i.   'Consciousness is empty of all contents.'

ii.   'Consciousness is wholly transparent, with nothing opaque in it."

iii.   'Consciousness is not a substance, but pure appearance; it is what it appears to be'(29).

iv.   'The entire world is outside of it.'

v.   'Intentionality is transcendence.'

vi.   'Consciousness by affirming the object negates itself, i.e., posits the object as what is other than itself and distinguishes itself as other than the object'(30).

vii.   'Consciousness can detach itself (a) from the object and (b) from the ego.'

viii.   'Consciousness is "a lack of completed possibilibilities"(31). It is what is yet to be. It is perpetually ahead of itself *(Sichvorwegsein)*.'

xi.   'Consciousness also posits the unreal, the absent and the fictitious.

Now whatever else Sartre might mean by his statement that consciousness is nothing, he surely means these, and that statement may be construed as equivalent to these statements taken jointly.

We have seen that the intentionality thesis together with the notion of the translucency of consciousness leads to the thesis that consciousness is nothing. But does Sartre regard the two notions of intentionality and translucency as independent of each other or does he regard them as mutually dependent? It seems that the latter is the case. In *The Transcendence of the Ego*, he writes, ". . . . . . consciousness is aware of itself insofar as it is consciousness of a transcendent object"(32). Later on, he puts this more explicitly. He asks himself, 'Why is it necessary for consciousness to be of something?' and gives the following answer: 'consciousness can be self-conscious only by means of that of which it is conscious'(33). The internal negation — the way consciousness negates itself as what is other than the object or *vice versa* — is constitutive of the essence of consciousness. Thus consciousness is fully intentional because it is fully transparent, it is fully transparent because it is fully intentional. Intentionality and reflexivity of consciousness depend upon each other.

The intentionality thesis also leads Sartre to deny the primacy of the ego. The pre-reflective consciousness being wholly directed towards the other does not contain the 'I' as a constituent of itself: its form or *ākāra* is 'This is a tree' and not 'I perceive a tree.' Now the logic of Sartre's argument here needs a closer look. The Indian school of Nyāya also holds the view that pre-reflective consciousness has the form 'This is a tree' and that it is only the subsequent act of reflection which gives us 'I perceive a tree.' But the Nyāya also holds that the ego, as the permanent self who possesses both the pre-reflective and the reflective awareness, *was* there in the pre-reflective awareness as well. Why then does Sartre deny the ego in pre-reflective consciousness? Is the fact that the latter mode of consciousness does not 'mention' the 'I' adequate to prove this? By itself it is not adequate. One should add to it the further premise that consciousness being all translucent if the ego were there it would have been transparent. The Nyāya school does not regard consciousness as translucent, it rejects the translucence of pre-reflective consciousness and that is why it can combine with its doctrine that the pre-reflective consciousness does not contain an 'I' the further doctrine that the 'I' nevertheless was there. Sartre with his basic thesis that consciousness is all transparent could not hold both these theses together. The 'I' is not *in* consciousness, but when in reflection I discover it, it is found to be as much an object in the world as any other object. Of course, it is difficult to make out what precisely is Sartre's account of the process of emergence of the 'I' as an object of consciousness in reflection. Does reflection create it? Or, does reflection discover it? But one thing seems sure, the ego may be or may not be there in the world prior to reflection, it is in no case within consciousness. Consciousness is in its essence non-egological.

These contentions of Sartre bear striking resemblance with some of the central theses of the school of Advaita Vedānta: that consciousness is *nirguna,* that consciousness and the world wholly exclude each other, that consciousness while immediately revealing itself also reveals the world as its object, and that the self-revealing consciousness is not an ego, the ego being as much an object as any other. However, it is interesting to note the fact that while the Advaita Vedānta derives the *nirgunatva* of consciousness from its essential non-intentionality, Sartre deduces the nothingness of consciousness precisely from its intentionality. This makes us suspect that either the intentionality which Samkara, the great proponent of Advaita Vedānta, denies to consciousness and the intentionality which Sartre ascribes to it are not quite the same, or the *nirgunatva* of consciousness which is the key doctrine of Samkara is not exactly the same as the nothingness of for-itself which Sartre propounds. But this is a point which we cannot pursue further in the present context.

Against Sartre's fundamental thesis, it has been contended that consciousness does not merely negate the object as what is not itself, it also affirms the object as what the latter is — so that it is both affirmation and negation of being(34). But it would be rather odd that Sartre should have missed this simple point. It seems to be the case that he takes the affirmative moment as an aspect of the act of negating. Or, perhaps he regards the act of negating as being the more primitive of the two.

But for more fundamental criticisms of Sartre's philosophy we have to turn to Merleau-Ponty and Paul Ricoeur.

C. MERLEAU-PONTY

Merleau-Ponty's concept of intentionality is developed out of the later Husserlian notion of operative intentionality. The emphasis shifts from the objectifying acts (in the specific Husserlian sense) to the intentionalities other than acts with their passive, anonymous, synthetic functions. At the same time, there is an explicit rejection of the Sartrean antithesis between the for-itself and the in-itself which represents the former as fully intentional and fully translucent and the latter as fully non-intentional and fully opaque. Merleau-Ponty rejects these extremes as abstractions which are not instantiated in experience. He only finds the middle region of ambiguity, the region where there are degrees of intentionality, degrees of transparency and the correlative degrees of opacity. This ambiguous region out of which the Sartrean for-itself and in-itself are abstractions is defined by human existence. The return from the pure for-itself to human existence is a return from Sartre back to Heidegger. But unlike Heidegger, Merleau-Ponty locates human existence in the body, and it is body which cuts across the distinction between the in-itself and the for-itself. Bodily behavior reveals a prospective activity, an intentionality which, contrary to Sartre's thesis, is not yet self-aware(35). The distinction between subject and object is blurred in my body — Merleau-Ponty would say, even the distinction between *noesis* and *noema* is also blurred. But the distinction is also blurred in the thing "which is the pole of my body's operations, the terminus its explorations end up in and which is thus woven into the same intentional fabric as my body"(36).

Consciousness is intentional, and posits objects. But there is no absolute positing, for "the absolute positing of a single object is the death of consciousness, since it congeals the whole of existence, as a crystal placed in solution suddenly crystallizes it"(37). What Merleau-Ponty seems to mean by this is that if there could be an act of consciousness which reveals an object completely, which does not suffer from the limitations of perspectives and profiles, which is not liable to error, inadequacy and doubt, that consciousness would be the same as the object: the two would be indeed identical, the consciousness would be nothing in itself, it would be merged in its object. There would be no interiority at all.

Likewise, consciousness is transparent, but never wholly so(38). If it were wholly transparent, myths, dreams and illusions would have been impossible, there would have been no distinction between the apparent and the real in the subject as well as in the object(39). One errs as much with regard to the object as with regard to one's own inner life. There are true as well as false feelings. The hysterical subject feels what he does not feel and does not feel what he feels(40). Further, if consciousness were as it appears to itself, then both the truth of my perceptions and the falsity of my illusions would have been fully transparent to me — which would have rendered

their distinction pointless(41). For Merleau-Ponty, an absolutely transparent consciousness would not be very much different from the unconscious, for "in both cases, we have the same
retrospective illusion, since there is introduced into me as an
explicit object, everything that I am later to learn concerning myself"(42). An all-transparent consciousness knows everything
about itself though much of what it knows is only learnt later
on, and the same is true of the unconscious which contains ideas
and acts about which one learns only later on. Such a consciousness would not be in time and also would not be in a situation. Temporarily and situation-orientedness place a limitation
on consciousness's coincidence with itself(43).

If consciousness is never wholly coincident with itself, never
fully transparent to itself, it is not also wholly opaque. "Consciousness is neither the positing of oneself, nor ignorance of
oneself, it is not concealed from itself . . . . . . although it does
not need to know this explicitly"(44). If it completely overlooked itself it would be a thing(45).

Thus, what we are left with are degrees of intentionality
and degrees of transparency, as manifested in different levels
of human behavior, in sexuality, and in thought. But the basic
intentionality is bodily movement(46). The notion of bodily
intentionality is an original contribution of Merleau-Ponty. It
is not the case that no one before him saw the intentional directedness of bodily behavior. But those who did see this phenomenon, were too much under the influence of the myth of
the "ghost in the machine" to be able to appreciate the originary
character of this phenomenon. Bodily intentionality was explained as being *due to* the intentionality of the mind or consciousness inhabiting the body. It goes to the credit of Merleau-
Ponty to have emphasized, and established with a wealth of
empirical evidence, that this derivation is not tenable. Bodily
behavior is not amenable to causal explanation. It has to be
understood from within, from the point of view of the person
who is experiencing it(47). But even looked at from within,
movement is not thought about movement. To suppose that
movement directed towards an object is necessarily accompanied by a representation of that object is to commit the

same sort of fallacy as to suppose that to understand an expression is necessarily to have a mental picture of the object for which the expression stands. Both are examples of that intellectualistic fallacy which bases all intentionality on the intentionality of a representing consciousness. But facts disprove such a possibility. "In the action of a hand raised towards an object, there is reference to the object, but not to the object as represented," but "as that highly specific thing towards which we project ourselves, near which we are in anticipation, and which we haunt"(48). Motility is not a handmaid of consciousness. Patients who have good power of representation of movement fail to execute the movement. The body has its own world, and objects may be present to the knowledge not to the body, or they may be present to the body and not to the knowledge.

If motility is the basic intentionality, consciousness which surely is intentional is itself a motility. Consciousness is not primarily an 'I think' but an 'I can'(49). It is not primarily representative, nor is it a collection of mental facts. Intentional consciousness is primarily an active thrust, a project. This primacy of 'motor project', Merleau-Ponty claims, helps us to overcome the dualism between mind and body(50).

Merleau-Ponty retains the Husserlian notions of *Sinngebung* and constitution, but radically transforms them. In Husserl, the notion of *Sinngebung* is connected with that of the meaningless stuff, the *hyle*. Merleau-Ponty is no less emphatic than Sartre in his rejection of this Husserlian notion. There is no mere sensation. The sensation is already charged with a significance. Each colour, for example, has a definite "motor value", a "muscular tonicity," a "motor physiognomy", a "motor halo"(51). "Every sensation is already pregnant with a meaning, inserted into a configuration, and there is no sense-datum which remains unchanged from illusion to truth"(52). If there is no unmeaning stuff, *Sinngebung* is not to be understood as conferring meaning from the pedestal of a transcendent consciousness. We have a new conception of meaning. All meaning is not an act of thought or of a pure ego. Bodily movement also confers meaning, as is to be seen in the case of habit(53) and sexuality(54). The original source of significance is the body which, as it were, secretes significance(55). But body does not impart meaning into an originally meaningless world. On the contrary, there is a sort of pact between the body and the world, and the primary significance derives from body's dealings with the world, from body's world-exploring activity, for example.

If all *Sinngebung,* and surely not the primary form of it, is not an act of consciousness, all constitution is not of the *Auffassungs-Inhalt* type(56). Several features of Merleau-Ponty's concept of constitution should be noted: first, if the body with its peculiar unity of functioning constitutes the unity of the thing, it is also the case that the unity of the thing determines the unity of the body: the constituted and the constituting in a way reciprocally determine each other, so that the question of priority is ruled out ab initio and what is important is to gain insight into the intentional thread which binds the one to the other(57). In the next place, constitution of the world is a continuing process. "The world is already constituted, but also never completely constituted"(58). If the world were already constituted in toto, if it were completely determined with no indeterminacy left, then we in our dealings with the world would have been completely passive and determined and there would be no possibility of freedom. On the other hand, if the world were not at all constituted prior to our act of constituting, if every act of constituting gave it fresh determination, then we would have been completely free (as in Sartrean ontology). Merleau-Ponty, as is to be expected, rejects both these extremes. Complete indeterminacy awaiting determination and complete determinateness awaiting mere manifestation — both are results of one-sided abstraction. What is given in experience is the mid-region between the indeterminate and the fully determinate: it is here that Merleau-Ponty seeks for the "origin" of the world, the process by which the relatively indeterminate gains determinateness through the body's explorations, anticipations, memories, and expectations.

But the notion of 'operative intentionality' with its 'anonymous' mode of working inevitably leads to the notion of forgetting *(Vergessenheit).* The constituting process is forgotten, and we have the illusion of a fully determinate objective world.

The task of phenomenology is to make explicit, to raise into self-awareness this "crypto-mechanism" of consciousness(59), to catch it in the very process of conferring sense and thereby to "foil its trick" i.e. to discover the 'origins' of the world, or to capture the process of emergence of definiteness and meaningfulness.

In this process, there is as it were a body-world pact(60), so that the body's world-finding activity grounds the general features of the world.

Consciousness then is not a opening to the world, but is a movement towards it. Reflexivity is subordinated to intentionality. Being directed outwards, consciousness is not turned towards itself. Intentionality prevents full transparence, just as transparence prevents full intentionality. There are only degrees of both. Neither does consciousness capture its object fully, nor does it coincide with itself completely.

The really valuable and original insights in Merleau-Ponty's concept of intentionality are (a) his notion of bodily intentionaality as an originary phenomenon irreducible to the intentionality of consciousness or of thought; and (b) his notion of degrees of intentionality and transparency.

At the same time, we have to concede that his grand framework suffers from unclarities and difficulties some of which are as follows: First, though he assigns to bodily intentionality a primary status and in fact seeks to overcome the dulism between the in-itself and the for-itself by his conception of body, he nevertheless does continue to speak of the intentionality of consciousness without making it clear what the status of consciousness is in his philosophy(61). Is conscious intentionality a mere epiphenomenon of bodily intentionality? In that case, he would be guilty of a fallacy which is the counter part of the fallacy of reducing bodily intentionality to the intentionality of consciousness. If consciousness is not a mere epiphenomenon of the body, if it exhibits essentially something new, then how is its intentionality related to that of the body? In fact, seeking to understand consciousness in the manner of bodily motility, he construes consciousness as a sort of active thrust, a movement, a project. Now these locutions are both illuminating and misleading. While they fit such phenomena as volition, they do not quite suit such phenomena as knowledge. The temptation to construe all intention as volition is understandable but should be avoided if one is to remain true to the nature of the phenomena as they give themselves to us. But again, while the constituting and meaning-conferring functions of the body should be recognised, one has to account for the universality of the constituted world. And one is left wondering if the constitution by the body can satisfy from this point of view. Perhaps one needs to take recourse to the notion of the bodily *a priori*, meaning thereby certain universal and necessary constitutive structures of any human body. That in itself is an attractive hypothesis, but such an explanation of the generality of body's constituting function would take away some striking features of Merleau-Ponty's existentialistic mode of thinking for we shall be back again in universal constituting functions, if not of consciousness surely of the body! Furthermore, one suspects whether the attempt to overcome the Cartesian and Sartrean dualisms by taking recourse to the ambiguous middle region of body really succeeds(62). One even needs to get clear about what it is worth. The valuable discovery of bodily subjectivity or of the subjectivity of the body does not entail that there is no dualism between the in-itself and the for-itself, between nature which is opaque and consciousness which is transparent. It only shows that there are missing links which traditional dualism failed to take note of. It also shows that the body-mind dualism is not the same as the dualism between the objective and the subjective, and suggests that it is the latter dualism which is fundamental: the dualism namely of the intentional and the non-intentional.

D. PAUL RICOEUR:

Ricoeur is closer to Husserl than the three philosophers whom we have discussed above. He remains precariously poised between Husserlian and existential phenomenologies. His inclusion in a chapter devoted to existential phenomenology is justified by the deep awareness which his works evince of those problems concerning human existence with which the existentialists show special concern: the problems of freedom, guilt,

144 The Concept Of Intentionality

dread and death. Being also an outstanding interpreter of Husserl's works, his own independent thoughts regarding the nature of intentionality are closely linked up with his understanding of Husserl. Through him, we may look forward to have the double advantage of confronting some problems basic to both the wings of the phenomenological movement.

What strikes us first about Ricoeur's phenomenological researches is not merely his overall preoccupation with the problems of will and action, but what we may call his *volitional interpretation of intentionality*. For him volition is intention *par excellence*, for every intention is attention and every attention "reveals an 'I can' at the heart of the 'I think' "(63). Every act, whether specifically volitional or not, is an intentional act in so far as it expresses a power in us which we exercise, so much so that "the analysis of volition places us at the very heart of the intentional function of consciousness." This primacy of the will in intentional life is not recognised by Husserl who, according to a well-known doctrine of the *Ideas*(64), accorded primacy to the doxic act, or, as in the Logical Investigations, to the objectifying acts in general.

Preoccupation with the volitional acts helps Ricoeur to build up a good case against the well known Sartrean criticism of the concept of the ego. Sartre argued(65) that the ego is not a component of the pre-reflective consciousness, that the pre-reflective perception of a tram car has the form 'This is a tram car' and not 'I see a tram car.' Now while it may be true that the reference to the ego does not figure explicitly in pre-reflective cognitive consciousness, the case is surely different with regard to pre-reflective volitional consciousness. In making up one's mind to act in a certain way, I posit myself as the agent of the decision, but this reference to the subject pole is still pre-reflective, it is not an inspection or reflective observation of myself. This is what Ricoeur calls "pre-reflective self-imputation": I figure in the project as the one to whom the action can be imputed(66). Ricoeur is aware that this relatedness of an intention to the self is not revealed so explicitly in other kinds of acts. It is in voluntary intention that it is to be found most clearly. But one could well assume that the reference to the self, the basic self-relation, a certain presence to myself, is implied in all intentionality(67). This conception of self-presence should not be mistaken with Sartre's notion of pre-reflective transparence. The latter does not contain a reference to the 'I,' the former does — without however being either a reflective judgment or even a retrospection or any form of self-observation. This pre-reflective self-presence, far from being reflective, contains the germs of the possibility of reflection.

It may be apprehended that such a self-imputation should actually be incompatible with consciousness's intentional reference to its object, that if consciousness is wholly intentional then it could not possibly contain such a relatedness to the subject pole. Merleau-Ponty seems to have been impressed by such an incompatibility. Again, Ricoeur's close study of voluntary acts shows that this need not be the case. There are in fact acts, such as acts of resolution, where "awareness of myself is involved as an active ferment of the very thrust of consciousness towards its object"(68). Self-consciousness therefore is not as such disruptive of intentional reference. It disrupts intentionality when it becomes self-observation. Such self-observation which disrupts the intentional reference to the object is, for Ricoeur, the "uprooted" consciousness, as contrasted with the original "generosity" of consciousness(69). True reflection is not grafted upon the unreflective act *ab extra*, it is rendering explicit a moment which is already there in a rather diffused manner(70).

It should be obvious that this notion of pre-reflective self-imputation contains, though not identical with, the notion of transparence. Consciousness is transparent, for Ricoeur — but, like Merleau-Ponty, he also rejects the Sartrean doctrine of complete transparence of consciousness(71). In fact, Ricoeur is one of the few phenomenologists who have taken the Husserlian notion of the *hyle* seriously, and have sought to accommodate the psycho-analytic notion of the unconscious within the framework of a phenomenological theory of consciousness. Consciousness always contains within itself affective matter which are never fully transparent to it. "Affectivity is obscurity itself"(72). Presence of affective matter leaves room for indefinite possibilities for self-questioning and self-interpretation on the part of consciousness. Ricoeur singles out three such phenomena: need, emotion and habit. Need is intentional, but the full significance of it can never be clear to consciousness. So also is an emotion into whose hidden meaning consciousness can never fully penetrate. Habit is built up by conscious intentions, but once built up it becomes the "acting, unreflecting body," and to try to understand it is like "an invitation to endless memory which becomes lost in shadows." All these phenomena, but chiefly the phenomena of the unconscious, reveal the inadequacy of the principle of total transparence of consciousness.

Basing on the principle of total transparency of consciousness, Sartre rejected the psychoanalytic notion of the unconscious. If consciousness is all translucency, there cannot be anything hidden in it — neither hidden meaning nor opaque matter. "Existential psychoanalysis rejects the hypothesis of the unconscious; it makes the psychic act coextensive with consciousness"(73). But consciousness and knowledge are different, and though there is a pre-reflective consciousness of all psychic acts, one does not always know them; psychoanalysis should enable a person "to *know* what he already *understands*"(74). Now for reasons already stated above Ricoeur rejects the principle of total transparence of consciousness, but he does not make the opposite mistake of what he calls the Realism of the Unconscious(75), which consists in the belief that the unconscious contains fully formed acts — desires, love, hatred, thoughts — which lack only in the quality of consciousness. Since for Ricoeur every act contains an implicit, diffused, vague self-presence, there cannot be an act of which we are totally unaware. The unconscious cannot think or desire or love or hate. And yet psychoanalysis does give meaning to the unconscious whatever the latter may contain. Dream experience is interpreted not merely by the psychoanalyst, it first becomes a completed image, a completed act only upon awakening as it is recounted(76). Recounting the dream is not merely putting into words an already completed series of experiences, it is to complete that experience for the first time. Here Ricoeur's view closely resembles that of Norman Malcolm(77).

Ricoeur's point seems to be that while the unconscious cannot be said to contain fully formed acts, it yet surely contains something which when brought to consciousness first becomes an act. It contains the hyletic stuff, the affective and impressional matter, which are made significant by the analyst. The affective matter constituting the unconscious is not yet intentional, it is not yet of . . . . . . The psychoanalytic cure suggests that the unmeaning matter which weighed on the mind of the patient ceases to be a burden as soon as it gains meaning, and thereby becomes intentional(78). The patient is disturbed by the presence of unformed matter. When this matter is "promoted" to thought, he is cured. Husserl's notion of the *hyle* is thus rehabilitated by Ricoeur on the basis of his interpretation of Freudean psychoanalysis.

While not unlike Merleau-Ponty, Ricoeur looks upon the world as the intentional correlate of the body and regards the body as essentially open to the world and consequently as intentional(79), he refuses to identify intentionality with being-in-the-world(80). That my existence is not wholly reducible to my being-in-the-world, that my involvement in the world is not total, and that, on the contrary, amidst all my finiteness I also escape it is sought to be brought home through an analysis of that dialectics of intention and fulfilment which Ricoeur never ceases to emphasise. The pertinent point regarding this dialectic which bears on the present issue is that the meaning-intention may, and in fact always does, go beyond all possible fulfilment. If outer perception is always from a point of view and thus reveals that I as the percipient is not a transcendental consciousness but a corporeal being in the world, I also, in perceiving an outer object, anticipate all possible points of view of all possible percipients, and thus come to *mean* the thing itself, and not a perspective of it, as the object being perceived, even if this meaning-intention can never be totally fulfilled. Further, the power which I have of creating absurd significations (e.g. 'roundsquare') shows that my intentionality is not exhausted by fulfilled presence(81), and that I transcend the limitations imposed by the world.

If consciousness, by virtue of its intentionality, transcends being-in-the-world, it is not wholly creative either. Here we may recall Ricoeur's deeply insightful observations regarding Husserl's notion of consciousness. The idea of a total creativity of consciousness, its 'genius,' its exhuberance is, according to Ricoeur, singularly un-Husserlian(82). For Husserl, the creativity of consciousness is tied to a "transcendental guide," the object or the sense: "the life of the *cogito* is not an anarchistic outburst but rather is always guided by permanences of signification"(83). It starts with the total intention, the finished sense (the object claimed to be perceived, or the conceptual meaning claimed to be thought of), and wonders how such an abiding signification could emerge out of the flow of consciousness with its partial intentions and partial fulfilling experiences, actual and possible. Without such a "transcendental guide," "the flux of consciousness would submerge us"(84). Phenomenology, Ricoeur tells us, is a philosophy of "sense," not of "freedom"(85). Constitution of the given or the intended is not creation(86).

The indispensability of the layer of sense only shows that intentionality is not an absolute contact with the world; it is intending a sense which again claims fulfilment. The idea of a total bodily self-givenness of objects (individual or eidetic) which so much dominated the thought of Husserl at one time has to be restated in the light of this dialectics of intention and fulfilment.

E. EXISTENTIAL PHENOMENOLOGY AND HUSSERL:

We have now before us the main criticisms of Husserl's concept of intentionality by the existentialistic phenomenologists. It remains to be seen to what extent these criticisms may be taken care of from the point of view of Husserl's later writings.

Some like Sartre have been concerned with the question of the transcendental ego as the source of intentionality. Others like Heidegger have sought to rehabilitate intentionality as an ontic or even as an ontic-ontological relation, and consequently to do away with the key Husserlian concept of *noema*. Most have found fault with the concept of *hyle* and the consequent hylomorphic scheme, though the critics surely differ in their attitudes towards the doctrine of constitution in any of its two forms. Another central issue has been the question about the *locus* of intentionality, and finally we have the problem regarding the relationship between the concepts of transparence and intentionality which has been made to bear on all these discussions. Let us consider each of these points separately.

1. Sartre's criticism of Husserl's concept of the transcendental ego as the *source* of intentionality may be met in either of two ways. One may argue(87) that Sartre is right in insisting that the ego is not empirically given and that the *mine* is capable of being accounted for within the framework of a non-egological theory of consciousness, but at the same time one may contend that this empirically given intentional structure *presupposes* the transcendental ego. Now this solution surely is not Husserlian. The ego that is merely the presupposition is 'transcendental' in the Kantian sense but not in the Husserlian sense. Husserl however did get beyond the particular version of the doctrine of the ego which Sartre criticised. For, he came to recognise that even the transcendental ego is constituted though in a manner radically different from the way objects are constituted. In the *Ideen II*, he says that the pure ego is not in need of constitution(88), but in a *Beilage* to it he adds that "*schon vorher muss die Lehre vom reinen Ich — zunächst als Pol — revidiert (?) werden*"(89); and expresses the view that though the ego is a pole of identity, it is an "*unselbständiges Zentrum für Affektionen und Aktionen.*" Of course, the ego is not to be found in the stream of experience — and so far Sartre's point is not disputed(90). We are even told, immediately after, that "*Die absolute Identität erkenne ich in der Reflexion.*" However it is in the *Cartesian Meditations* that we come to the explicit formulation of the doctrine of the self-constitution of the pure ego through habitualities(91). In fact, it is important to remember the distinction between transcendental ego and transcendental subjectivity(92). The latter alone is pre-mundane, pre-objective, meaning-giving consciousness; the former is a constituted unity, though its mode of constitution is radically different from the mode of constitution of objects. However, this development of Husserl's thought renders the whole thrust of Sartre's criticism pointless. Furthermore, while it may be true, as Husserl him-

self concedes, that the pure ego is not to be met with within the stream of consciousness, it may still be true, as Ricoeur has shown, that a reference to the ego accompanies all acts, covertly or overtly, and makes subsequent reflection possible. The idea of such a 'pre-reflective self-ascription' or self-imputation is not inconsistent with the doctrine of the self-constitution of the ego.

2. The objections to the effect that intentionality in Husserl's philosophy is no more an ontological relation are also based on a misunderstanding of Husserl. By positing an irreal *noema*, Husserl did not want to deny that intentionality relates to beings, or even to Being (whatever that may mean). As we have shown above, he was clearly aware of the fact that the noetic-noematic correlation was not the same as — nor could it be construed as a phenomenological reconstruction — the intentional reference to object. The *noema* is not the intended object. But such is human consciousness, one could perhaps say that its intention posits the *noema* and through it as it were reaches out to the object beyond. But even this way of putting the matter is misleading. For, the *noema* and the object belong to two radically different dimensions — linguistically, to two totally different universes of discourse, phenomenologically to two radically different modes of givenness. The possibility of turning away from the object-oriented attitude to the *noema*-oriented attitude is an inherent possibility of consciousness. But the introduction of the *noema* should not be regarded as shutting the door for ontological encounter. It may be supposed that Husserl is introducing a sort of the content theory. Possibly, he is doing that. But a content theory should take into account two facts. For one thing, the content is never given together with the object, the two are rather given in two different attitudes. This radical difference in their modes of givenness bears testimony to the radical difference in their modes of being. For another, the content is not another object standing in between the mind and the object, obstructing the reference by its opacity. It is rather a transparent medium which makes intentional reference possible. In defending the doctrine of the *noema*, we have said that perhaps human consciousness is such that its intentionality posits such an irreal *noema*. Hasn't Merleau-Ponty said

that we are condemned to meanings? And yet we are in rapport with the world. It is true that the intentionality thesis requires us to abandon the conception of a representative consciousness. But the *noema* is not a representation, not a Lockean idea, not a copy of the transcendent object. Sartre's for-itself, the totally empty consciousness, fully open to being but emptied of all contents, the consciousness that is out and out nothing — this precisely is not the human consciousness. A theory of consciousness that would be adequate and fair to human consciousness should of course (i) take into account its intentionality and therefore the fact that it is not a representative consciousness; but (ii) it should also recognise that man is nevertheless condemned to meanings, that it is not passive openness but also active *Sinngebung*. The concept of *noema* is an attempt to take both these facts into account.

3. Some of the criticisms made against the interpretation of intentionality as constituting function are not any more sustainable. Sartre's argument that the supposed constitution would involve an infinity which could not possibly be given whereas there could be nothing in consciousness that is not immediately transparent to it would be partly conceded by Husserl(93). There is always a presumption, an element of hypothesis, an 'I can go on . . . . . .' involved in it. The constitution of real things is characterised precisely by this presumptive character. Sartre complains that if this infinity were there it would have been transparent. Here again he is assuming that total transparence of consciousness is an accomplished fact. Were it so, reflection would have been redundant. It is reflection which discovers the 'I can go on . . . . . .,' the infinity involved in the synthesis of an endless multiplicity of perspectives. The infinite series need not be completed. A phenomenology of constitution does not *fully* lay bare the constitution in details. On the contrary, it courts the tragedy of its own failure to complete itself. But this subjective failure has its counterpart in the objective essence of the constituted thing as well. Once we understand this, Merleau-Ponty's charge that a world constituted in consciousness would stand fully revealed looses it biting force. The charge cannot be sustained on the basis of Merleau-Ponty's own

concept of consciousness as ever possessing only a degree of transparence.

Whereas the *Ideas I* restricts the constituting function to the pure consciousness and its intentionalities, the two other volumes of the *Ideas* mark an advance in this respect. With growing awareness of the importance of the body and with growing liberation of his conception of the body from the naturalistic framework, Husserl also came to realise that the constitution of both nature and the psyche is essentially bound up with the constitution of the body. The *Phänomenologische Psychologie* carries this move a step further ahead: here Husserl, possibly for the first time, speaks of "bodily intentionality", and says that the intentionalities in which things come to be given cannot be investigated without investigating the intentionalities of one's own body(94).

4. We have just noted that Husserl came to speak of bodily intentionalities. However, we do not notice in him either of the two possible monistic moves which are likely at this stage. He does not say that bodily intentionality is but a pale reflection of the intentionality of consciousness, that the body only appears to be intentional owing to the intentional consciousness which inhabits it. He also does not say that the basic intentionality is that of the body — as Merleau-Ponty says — and that the intentionality of consciousness is only an epiphenomenon of it. That he does not make any of these two likely monistic moves shows that descriptive phenomenology does not yield ground, even in his later writings, to speculative system-building. We are thus led to the recognition of radically different sorts of intentionality: the precise relationship between these is a matter of descriptive investigation rather than of *a priori* metaphysical speculation. In any case, the body mind dualism seems to get transformed into a dualism of intentional functions.

It remains for us now to consider the problem of the relation between the notions of transparency and intentionality. But with this, we may pass on to the last part of this book, where we shall be confronted with a larger vista of problems emerging out of the concept of intentionality.

PART THREE

CHAPTER 1

INTENTIONALITY AND REFLEXIVITY

I

THERE SEEM TO BE two major conceptions of consciousness in the philosophical traditions of both India and the West. These are: (i) the concept of consciousness as that which exhibits a peculiar property called 'intentionality' or *savisayakatva;* and (ii) the concept of consciousness as that which is characterised by a peculiar property called 'reflexivity' or *svayamprakāśatva.* When I say that these two concepts have dominated philosophical thinking about the nature of consciousness I do not mean that the formulations of these concepts have been always precise and satisfactory. Nor do I mean that those who have accepted one of these characterisations have also accepted the other. In fact, though philosophers as different from each other as the Naiyāyikas, Rāmānuja, Descartes, Brentano and the phenomenologists have recognised intentionality as a defining character of consciousness, they will yet be found to have quite different conceptions of what it means to be intentional. Similarly, though philosophers as different from each other as the

Prābhākaras, the Buddhists, Samkara, Rāmānuja, Brentano and the phenomenologists have looked upon reflexivity as a defining character of consciousness, their conceptions of what it is to be reflexive are sometimes strikingly different. Further, there are philosophers like the Naiyāyikas who have thought it impossible that consciousness which they regard as intentional should also be reflexive./Others like Samkara have thought it *absurd* that consciousness which is reflexive should also be intentional.) For both these groups of philosophers there seems to be an essential incompatibility between these two concepts. But there are also philosophers, Rāmānuja and Sartre amongst them, who recognise consciousness as being *both* intentional and reflexive: for them there is no incompatibility between them, on the contrary there may even be some kind of inner connection.

In this chapter, I propose to investigate precisely into this relationship, but I would like to start with the following statement which is historico-philosophical in content: *The nature of intentionality was not adequately understood in Indian Philosophy, just as the nature of reflexivity was not adequately understood in Western philosophy.* Let me now proceed to explicate it.

(a) Of all Indian philosophers, it is the Naiyāyikas, the Mimāmsakas and also Rāmānuja who came nearest to a clear recognition of intentionality as a distinguishing feature of consciousness. The chief opponents of the intentionality thesis (as pertaining to consciousness) are the Advaita Vedāntists and the Vijñānavādin Buddhists — the first because of their explicit theory of non-intentional consciousness, the second because of their theory of representative consciousness (*sākāravij-ñānavāda*). Let us briefly recount these two theses.

The Advaita Vedāntists not only believe, on grounds which are metaphysical and which will be questioned later in this chapter, that consciousness in its essence is non-intentional (but have also sought to prove that it is not possible to give an intelligible account of the subject-object relation which is *therefore* regarded as false)(in that very peculiar sense in which 'falsity' is used in this system). We get a good account of their arguments for the latter purpose in Madhusudana Saraswati's

Advaitasiddhi(1). Madhusudana first argues that no relation is conceivable which could hold good between the subject and the object *(dṛgdṛśyasambandhānupapatteh)*. Knowledge cannot manifest its object while being unrelated to it; for that would prove too much (i.e., any knowledge would then reveal any object, which is absurd). Nor can knowledge be related to its object, for irrespective of whether knowledge constitutes the essence of the self (as in the Advaita Vedānta) or is a property of it (as in the Nyāya), the relation between them can neither be conjunction *(samyoga)* nor inherence *(samavāya)*, and there is no other relation that is not false(2). Madhusudana proceeds to argue that not even a satisfactory definition of *'visayatva* (or of the property of being an object) is possible and in fact considers and finally rejects a whole series of attempted definitions of it. To mention here only a few of them:

It cannot be said that the object of knowledge is that in which knowledge produces an effect (in so far as the object becomes known and acquires the property of 'knownness'); for, first, it is not possible to ascertain what precisely the supposed effect of knowledge is, and secondly no effect could conceivably be produced in the past and future things which may however be objects of ꞇnowledge. The Buddhists define the object as that which is the source of the form of knowledge *(jñānā-kārārpakatvam visayatvam)*; but since on the Buddhist theory a knowledge and its form are not different things any cause of a knowledge (e.g., the appropriate sense organ in the case of a sense perception) would become, on this definition, a source of the form of that knowledge and so should be counted as its object — which indeed is absurd. Or, the object of a knowledge may be defined as that which 'appears' in that knowledge *(yasyām samvidi yo'rtho'vabhāsate sa tasya visayah)*; but here the source of the trouble, according to Madhusudana, is the preposition 'in.' What could it mean by saying that something appears 'in a knowledge'? It cannot mean that the object is located in the knowledge, for the object is not in its knowledge, it should be other than it. Does the 'in' mean *visayasaptami*, i.e., locative case in the sense of being an object? Is it, in other words, used in that specific sense in which an object alone can

belong to its knowledge? Madhusudana thus comes very near
anticipating the notion of 'intentional inexistence' of the object
in the act when he sees that the 'in' may be construed as
'*visayasaptami*,' but he rejects it as an explication of the concept of 'being an object' for it involves that very notion which
requires to be explained. If the preposition 'in' makes the definition suspect, no less troublesome — and this Madhusudana fails
to point out, at least in the present context — is 'appears' which
hides many important phenomenological distinctions.

A close scrutiny of the definitions of 'object' considered by
Madhusudana as well as of his reasons for rejecting them brings
to light the real source of his difficulty. The trouble is that he
is searching for a *real* relation that could possibly obtain between
knowledge and its object, and he fails to find one. This leads
him to conclude that the subject-object relation is unintelligible.
In a sense he is right. There can be no real relation between
consciousness and its object. But by saying this we are opposing
'real' to 'intentional' and not to 'false.' That consciousness is not
a relation or that intentionality is not a relation shows not that
consciousness is non-intentional or *nirvisayaka* but that its essential *savisayakatva* cannot be construed as a real relation of some
sort. That consciousness of one thing is consciousness precisely of
that thing and not of another thing is a tautologous truth, and
I do not see why if consciousness is of an object without being
related to it then the consciousness of one thing should be consciousness of any other thing as well.

If the Advaita Vedānta thesis regarding the non-intentionality of consciousness is based on the contention that the alleged
subject-object relation is unintelligible and indefinable, the
Vijñānavādin Buddhist's opposition to the intentionality thesis
is based on: (a) his denial of external objects and (b) his
peculiar version of the theory that consciousness is *sākāra* or has
form or content. The Vijñānavādin Buddhist believes that consciousness not only has a form or content (*ākāra*) but is also
self-illuminating. These two contentions taken together lead
him to a denial of anything external to the mind. For, when,
e.g., I perceive a pen there is only one form before me, and my
consciousness being both formed and self-illuminating, that form

which is manifested in my knowledge of the pen is consciousness's own. The alleged external object therefore can only be a merely inferred entity, and an entity that is merely inferred is a fiction. If there is no external object, consciousness cannot be *savisayaka* or intentional. It is non-intentional, though it is *sākāra,* i.e., with a form of its own — which is wrongly supposed to be either the form of the object or derived from the latter.

Now, it is curious and instructive that the answer to the question whether consciousness is *savisayaka* or not, i.e., whether it is intentional or not, has been made to depend upon the answer to the question whether there are external objects or not. The former question is phenomenological, the latter metaphysical, and the independence of the former of the latter has not been properly appreciated. The reason seems to be that both those who recognise intentionality and those who reject it agree in understanding intentionality as an ontic relation, and this precisely is where they go wrong.

The Naiyāyikas who recognise the intentionality of consciousness not only define *buddhi* as *arthaprakāśo* (manifesting an object)(3) but further determine this property as being *svābhāvika visayapravanatva*(4). The reference to object is intrinsic to it. Of course, by this they sought to deny intentionality to other states like desire, pleasure pain etc. and held that the reference to object in these latter cases is derivative and not original. Only in the case of consciousness (which they identified with knowledge) is the reference original. We may emphasise two points in this connection. First, intentionality is here treated as being primarily theoretical and cognitive. Further, consciousness itself is regarded as being primarily cognitive in function. Again, with the Naiyāyikas as with most Indian philosophers who recognised intentionality, the intended reference to an object is a *relation* between two terms: consciousness and its object. The interest is predominantly ontological. Every intended object is *eo ipso* a real object. We of course find the realisation that this relation may be very much unlike other relations. Some Naiyāyikas like Udayana treated it as a sort of *svarupasambandha,* a relation which constitutes the essence of one of the relata(5).

The Naiyāyikas not only defend the *savisayakatva* of consciousness but take great pains to refute the Buddhist theory that consciousness is *sākāra* or has form of its own. In fact, for them there is nothing in consciousness. It is not a container, it has no contents, no form. All its specifications, all that by which consciousness of blue differs from consciousness of yellow lies outside of consciousness in the objects concerned(6) — a view which closely approximates Sartre's rejection of representative consciousness and Moore's emphasis on the diaphanous nature of consciousness.

We find the same emphasis on the *savisayakatva* of consciousness in Rāmānuja: "*Na ca nirvisayā samvit kācidasti, anupalabdheh*" — there is no non-intentional consciousness, for no such consciousness is experienced(7).

Nevertheless, the fact has to be recognised that Indian philosophy did not quite free itself from a relational concept of intentionality. The realists who alone recognised intentionality as an essential feature of consciousness could not free themselves from their own realistic ontologies and so were not able to look squarely in the face of phenomenona. This comment is corroborated not only by the fact to which attention has already been drawn, the fact namely that the issue regarding the intentionality or non-intentionality of consciousness was made dependent upon the realism-idealism issue, but gains additional corroboration from the fact that most Indian philosophers look for an ontological status of the object of illusory experience within their own systems. The search for real entities is never abandoned.

We have already seen that a satisfactory concept of intentionality — whatever else it may imply — has to take care of the fact that consciousness's intentional reference to an object does *not* logically entail the existence of the intended object. For, if it did so entail, then the entire point about intentionality would be lost: it would be but another ontic relation, no matter external or internal. In fact, adopting a relational theory of intentionality — a theory which construes it as a relation between two reals: consciousness and object — would be tantamount to rendering that notion superfluous, and would also give rise to the well known difficulties with which philosophers like Russell have vainly struggled. Fortunately, the relational theory fails on its own account. It fails to account, amongst other things, for intentional acts directed towards fictitious and non-existent objects, and also for what has recently been called by Quine 'referential opacity'.

(b) Western philosophy has again and again felt itself constrained to recognise that peculiar character of consciousness which we have called its reflexivity, but its understanding and formulation of this concept has remained inadequate, partly owing to the predominantly objectivistic outlook. It has of course been clearly realised by many that there is a radical difference between the way objects are given to consciousness and the way consciousness is given to itself. But this difference has been, more often than not, misconstrued either as the difference between outer perception and inner perception (as by Brentano) or as being due to a most peculiar doubling back of consciousness upon itself in a manner that is ruled out in the case of anything other than consciousness. No wonder then that Ryle in his criticism of the self-intimating theory of consciousness should accuse this theory of leading to the hypothesis of an infinite series of onion skins of consciousness. What, in fact, he is finding fault with is not the theory of consciousness as *svayam-prakāśa* but the theory of consciousness as being *eo ipso* an object of inner perception(8). As regards the supposed phenomenon of doubling back(9) we can only say that it retains in essence the idea of inner perception but only makes a state of consciousness its own object, thus exposing itself to the charge of *karmakartrvirodha*, i.e., the incompatibility of the same thing's being both the subject and the object of the same act. The error in all these cases is to be traced to an unconscious attempt to assimilate the reflexivity of consciousness to its intentionality, to look upon, in other words, consciousness's peculiar mode of self-awareness as a function of its intentionality. There is a subtle confusion between 'reflexivity' as an essential character of all consciousness, even of what Sartre calls 'pre-reflective' consciousness, and 'reflection' which is only a higher order intentional act. All consciousness is not reflection, nor is all consciousness reflected upon. But all consciousness is reflexive or transparent.

Just as one needs to free oneself from the prejudice of a realistic ontology in order to be aware of the true nature of intentionality as an intrinsic function of consciousness, so one has to free oneself from the objectivistic attitude and instal oneself in the purely subjective attitude in order to be aware of the true nature of reflexivity or transparency as a feature of consciousness that is irreducible to its intentionality.

That the reflexivity of consciousness is not an inner perception and not also a curious doubling back of consciousness upon itself is what we learn from Advaita Vedānta, Prābhākara Mimāmsā and the Buddhists as also from Sartre and Ricoeur.

II

We may now ask the question: *what* precisely is intentional? What precisely is that to which intentionality belongs? It is good to ask this question, for a great deal of confusion is due to lack of clarity on this fundamental issue.

We have seen that in modern times Brentano introduced this notion of intentionality in course of his search for a criterion to distinguish what he calls 'psychic phenomena' from what he called 'physical phenomena.' However, as subsequent investigations have shown, though the search for a criterion led to a rediscovery of this notion, yet its usefulness as a criterion is only limited. Thus, Husserl raised the pertinent question whether in fact all that is mental is intentional. Others have emphasised that not all that is non-mental is non-intentional. Thus, Merleau-Ponty has highlighted the intentionality of bodily behavior. Taylor and Hampshire have drawn attention to the intentional nature of the concept of action(10). Indian philosophers would introduce a further complexity into the situation by distinguishing between 'consciousness' and 'mind': a distinction that is, broadly speaking, not on the forefront in western thinking on this matter. Making use of this distinction (whatever it may amount to), many Indian philosophers would say that mind or its states are non-intentional and that consciousness alone is intentional.

We have thus at least *three* things of which one could possibly predicate intentionality. These are: *consciousness, mental states* and *bodily behavior*. It may be supposed that intentionality belongs originally to only one of these and that the others are intentional only in a derivative sense. For example, it may be said that consciousness alone is intrinsically intentional and that mental states and bodily behaviour are so, or merely seem to be so, only in so far as they are associated with consciousness. Or, it may be held that mental states alone are intrinsically intentional and that consciousness is said to be so only in so far as it is always *associated* with some mental state or other. But I think there is another and phenomenologically more sound way of looking at the situation. Instead of distinguishing between one original and many derivative ascriptions of intentionality, one may prefer to regard each of these ascriptions as being equally original. On this view, then, each of these — consciousness, mental states, and bodily behavior — is intentional, and in an equally underivative sense. Merleau-Ponty has forcefully argued that the intentionality of body is *not* a reflection of the intentionality of consciousness, that bodily behavior quâ bodily behavior is characterised by a motility which, according to him, is the (we may amend it and say, 'an') original intentionality.

As regards the so-called mental states, we may make the following remarks. As said before, the distinction between consciousness and mind is made almost by all systems of Indian philosophy. But we do not find much light from that source on the problem in our hand. For the Naiyāyikas who draw the distinction with great cogency, the word 'mental state' does not designate anything. Mind, for them, is only an instrument (and a non-conscious one) in the production of such states as knowledge, feelings, and volitions in the *self;* they are states of the self and not of the mind. There are no mental *states*. Of the states of the self, only the cognitive ones, coming under the class *'buddhi,'* are conscious. The rest — affective and volitional states — are non-conscious. Intentionality characterises directly the cognitive states, derivatively the non-cognitive ones. It does not in any sense belong to the mind. The pertinent distinction here, in that case, is between the conscious and non-conscious states of the *self*. It should be added, in order to avoid misunder-

standing, that when the Naiyāyika regards the affective and
the volitional states as non-conscious, he means to deny to them
both reflexivity or transparency and primary intentionality. Denial of the former is not in this system significant, for even
conscious or cognitive states do not, according to the Nyāya,
possess transparency: they are of objects but are not aware of
themselves at the same time. This denial therefore does not
serve to distinguish the non-conscious from the conscious states.
As regards the denial of primary intentionality it should be
noted that primary intentionality, in this system, is nothing
other than cognitive intentionality *(jñānaviṣayatva)*, so that to
say that the affective and the volitional states lack it is not to
say that they are not directed towards their respective objects
but only to say that they are not cognitively directed. Thus the
distinction between conscious and non-conscious states is found
to amount, by definition, to that between cognitive and non-cognitive states of the self. All that the system adds is that a non-
cognitive state's directedness towards an object is necessarily
mediated by a cognitive directedness, which amounts to saying
that if my pleasurable state is of, or directed towards, or about an
object 0, then it is so only in so far as I have also a knowledge
of 0: which is a very doubtful thesis indeed.

Thus we have not found any help from the Naiyāyika in
whose system there are no mental states at all. Let us therefore
approach the Sāmkhya-Vedānta group of philosophies where
we do have a conception of mental states *(antahkaranavrtti)* but
no genuine conception of its intentionality. For, mind is conceived
in these philosophies as subtle matter and the mental state
as a real form it takes up, a real transformation in accordance
with the form of the object(11). The conception then is one
of a mental picture (in the case of cognitive states) or, in general, of a mental modification. Here intentionality is being construed as a real formation which is surely a real relatedness of
some sort involving, amongst other things, a causal process as
well. Such a conception has no room for that peculiar directedness towards . . . . . . , which is the very substance of the notion
of intentionality.

It may be added that in the Sāmkhya-Vedānta philosophies,

'being directed towards . . . .' or 'being *of* . . . . . .' is a property which belongs neither to consciousness by itself (for consciousness, in these systems, is essentially non-intentional(12) but reflexive), nor to the mental states (for reasons stated above), but only to that association between the two, to what has been called in the Advaita Vedānta works on epistemology *'vrttyavacchinnacaitanya'*: a curious, further inexplicable, by-product — illusory and having no primitive *locus standi*.

To sum up: the Naiyāyikas distinguish between mind and consciousness but do not recognise mental states; the Sāmkhya-Vedānta philosophies admit mental states but have no genuine conception of their intentionality. The Naiyāyika distinction between conscious and non-conscious states of the self is really one between cognitive and non-cognitive states: both are non-reflexive, both are intentional, though the intentionality of the non-cognitive states is mediated by that of the cognitive ones. The Sāmkhya-Vedānta distinction between cognitive and non-cognitive mental states cannot be the same as that between conscious and non-conscious states: strictly speaking, in these systems, there are no states of consciousness, all mental states are non-conscious, they derive their apparent intentionality and apparent translucency from their, rather any further inexplicable, association. The appearance of translucency in the non-conscious mental states is thus explicable, but the appearance of intentionality in them remains a most inexplicable mystery.

What we are after is a conception of *mental states* according to which: (i) all mental states are genuinely intentional; (ii) some but not all mental states are reflexive; and (iii) the distinction between mental states and consciousness may be taken care of. Now, mental states are either conscious or unconscious, but in either case they are intentional. An unconscious desire or an unconscious hatred may be said to be of something, it is not an objectless desire or an objectless hatred. Only, it is not conscious in the passive sense, it is not aware of itself. Thus if our concept of mental states has to make room for the modern psychological concept of the unconscious, we have to say that all mental states are intentional but not all are reflexive. Further, we have to take care of the distinction between seeing, desiring, loving or hating, and *reflectively* knowing that one is seeing, desiring, loving or hating. And yet seeing, desiring, loving and hating are not unconscious mental states, they are — to use Sartre's term — transparent. As and when one is seeing, desiring, loving, or hating, one is also aware that one is doing so without being *reflectively* conscious *of* it. It is this pre-reflective transparency which is designated here as 'reflexivity,' it is both different from and yet the condition of the possibility of reflective consciousness.

'Consciousness,' as distinguished from 'mental states,' then means either of two things(13): in a broad sense, it stands for all conscious mental states; in a narrow sense, it stands only for the acts of reflectively attending to the unreflective mental states. In the latter sense, again, all consciousness becomes cognitive. The former allows for cognitive as well as non-cognitive modes of consciousness. We prefer the former use which is comprehensive enough to include the latter. In that case, the distinction between mental states and consciousness would not help us any further. We may replace it by that between:

(i) mental states which are merely intentional but not reflexive;

(ii) mental states which are both intentional and reflexive. The acts of reflection form a subclass of (ii).

In identifying consciousness and mental states, we run the risk of inviting a misunderstanding against which it is necessary to warn at this stage. Many modern philosophers have denied that words like 'knowing,' 'understanding' stand for mental states. What do they thereby deny knowing and understanding to be? They deny first that they are states or modifications of a substance called mind; they also deny that they are observable processes stretching over a period of time. If to be a mental state is to be either or both of these, then surely knowing is not a mental state, nor is understanding so. But they are mental states or conscious states in the sense that they are both intentional and reflexive: whatever is so is a conscious state or an *Erlebnis.*

We may then conclude that conscious states or acts or *Erlebnisse* are intentional, and further that bodily behaviour is also so. Moreover, we find no reason why the intentionality of the one should be derived from that of the other. *Prima facie* there seems to be no harm in admitting two *radically different* types of intentionality. Whether this *prima facie* irreducibility is in the end sustainable has yet to be decided. At least nothing that we have said commits us to an ontological dualism between body and mind, nor do we feel tempted to rush forward to the sort of monism where all conflicts are resolved and where most speculative metaphysicians find their inevitable resting place.

III

Let us now turn to the question, how are the two concepts, that of intentionality and that of reflexivity, interrelated? Or, instead of asking this broad question let us ask the following more specific questions:

(a) Is there a sort of opposition, a mutal incompatibility, between the two, intentionality and reflexivity?

(b) If we answer the question (a) in the negative, then we ask: is any one of the two primary and the other derivable from it?

(c) If (b) is answered in the negative, we have to ask: is any one of the two dependent on the other?

(a) The thought that the reflexivity of consciousness is incompatible with its intentionality finds its most forceful exponent in Samkara. We only need to take a close look at the very opening sentence of his commentary on the *Brahmasutras* to realise this(14). In fact, the central problem of his philosophy may be stated thus; if consciousness is, in its essential nature, self-revealing, if it is thus self-sufficient, why need it refer to an object, how does it at all become *savisayaka?* Starting with the assumption that there is an inherent incompatibility between the two functions, Samkara is led to the conclusion that the *savisayakatva* or intentionality of consciousness could only be apparent, it cannot be real.

But on what grounds does he hold that consciousness is merely self-revealing and not intentional? What leads him to pose this paradox where possibly there is none? Investigating

on these lines, we fail to find a satisfactory answer from Samkara.
We do not find any answer why self-revealing consciousness
cannot be, in reality, also intentional. There is nothing to show
that consciousness is merely self-revealing and, in its intrinsic
nature, nothing else. Whatever self-revealing consciousness we
know of is also intentional. The onus of showing that in its in-
most nature consciousness is self-revealing and nothing more
is therefore on Samkara. This may possibly be shown in either
of these ways: One may try to show that there is a *logical* contradiction in supposing a self-revealing consciousness to be intentional. But such an argument is not of much worth; what
does and what does not involve logical contradiction depends
upon our initial definitions of the concepts involved, and in the
present case a defender of Samkara can only so define his concepts of self-luminosity and intentionality of consciousness that
a logical contradiction would be plain enough. Or, one may
pretend to show that not logic but phenomena point to a level
of consciousness which is non-intentional but reflexive. If this
be so, then the lesson we may learn is that the intentionality
of our ordinary consciousness is a fortuitious character which is
got rid of, once the extrinsic conditions on which it depends
are eliminated. Now the sort of phenomenological evidence
which is supposed to corroborate this conclusion is the traditional gradation of conscious states into waking, dream and
dreamless sleep: the intentional function is gradually thinned
down, *almost* eliminated in dreamless sleep, without the self-
revealing nature of consciousness thereby being impaired. If this
reading of the gradation is correct, then it points to a state of
consciousness where the intentional function is totally eliminated, which is non-intentional but reflexive. Now there are
many flaws in this argument. There is a subtle transition from
what the facts show to what they suggest or point to. There is
also a most controversial step which consists in making use of
the premise that in dreamless sleep the self-revealing consciousness persists, and yet that it persists is curiously enough sought
to be proved by an inference which is only too well known to students of Indian philosophy.

Or, as a last resort one may appeal to faith in the scriptures which speak of consciousness as being pure, unobjective, and merely self-revealing. Now we agree that those who speak of a purely non-intentional consciousness are really grounded on such a faith, which at its best may be understood as a spiritual demand arising out of the belief that the intentional function of consciousness is the source of all pain and suffering *(duhkha)!*

Interestingly enough, the same incompatibility between consciousness's being of an object and its being at the same time self-intimating is felt by the Naiyāyika. But the Naiyāyika makes a different decision. Unlike Samkara, he simply denies the self-luminosity of consciousness. Intentional consciousness, he holds, cannot be selfluminous, just as for Advaita Vedānta, the self-luminous consciousness cannot be really intentional.

There is still another way of dealing with the alleged incompatibility, and we find this in the philosophy of Merleau-Ponty. Perfect intentionality, if we mean by it consciousness's ability to grasp its object fully and in its entirety, and perfect transparence in the sense of absolute coincidence of consciousness with itself — these two are mutually incompatible, and Merleau-Ponty denies both(15). Just as consciousness is never wholly transparent (to suppose that it is so is a mistake of intellectualism), so also the intentional grasping of the object is never perfect. We as much err about ourselves as about the world. Most of our intentionality, indeed the more important part of it, is not act-intentionality, it is operative and mixed up with the motility of the body. But even the bodily motility is not just in-itself, wholly opaque, lacking self-awareness. We always are in the middle region, the region of ambiguity in between the two extremes. Neither the *cogito* nor the *cogitatum* is grasped absolutely. Intentionality as well as reflexivity are always matters of degree.

Insofar as Merleau-Ponty emphasises the need for recognizing the unconscious and the pre-conscious, even bodily, intentionalities, we find his thoughts valuable. Also valuable and to a certain extent original are his notions of degrees of transparence and degrees of intentionality. Only, the two are nowhere fully absent in so far as human reality is concerned. It is not also true that the two are always to be found in inverse proportion. In other words, it is not always true that the more the intentional concentration the less is the reflexivity of a conscious act. As Paul Ricoeur has pointed out, sometimes the reverse may well be the case: there are acts which are such that they attain greater self-awareness with increasing intentional concentration. For example, in acts of decision and resolution self-affirmation may accompany the very thrust of an active project.

Thus we may say that pre-reflective reflexivity accompanies all conscious acts — though in different degrees. Only when reflexivity turns into an explicit reflection, when self-consciousness tends to become observation does it threaten to suspend the original intentionality: such a purely observing reflection is what Ricoeur calls the "uprooted consciousness".

If this be so, we are compelled by the phenomena themselves not to agree with those who posit an incompatibility between the two functions of consciousness. To our first question then we reply in the negative. This leads us to our second question: 'Is any one of the two primary and the other derivative from it?'

(b) Intentionality as we have seen is exhibited in a much wider range of phenomena of which only a subclass exhibits reflexivity. Unconscious intentionalities, bodily intentionalities are not all reflexive; only conscious states are so. It would seem then that the concept of intentionality cannot be derived from that of reflexivity. On the contrary, the reverse may be the case. As has been said before, what we have called 'reflexivity' of consciousnss has been misconstrued either as inner perception (Nyāya, Brentano), or as the possibility of intentionally directing an act of reflection towards the conscious state in question (Husserl), or as a peculiar doubling back of consciousness upon itself. But the reflexivity of consciousness is neither of these, it is prior to all these. It is not a function of intentionality, it is not just another mode of it. The original mode of givenness of consciousness to itself is not its being an object of another intentional act(16). Phenomenology may be, as Thevenez says, a "philosophy of infinite reflection"(17) or even, as de Waehlens says, "a philosophy of incomplete reflection"(18); but to recognise the perpetual inadequacy of reflection is not incompatible with that primary, unreflective coincidence with itself which characterises all consciousness. The pre-reflective transparence of consciousness may still elude the grasp of subsequent reflection, and in so far reflection may fail to restore that original coincidence.

Thus if intentionality cannot be derived from reflexivity, reflexivity also cannot be derived from intentionality. But may we not detect a sort of dependence of the one on the other?

(c) If intentionality were dependent on, or presupposed the reflexivity of consciousness, it would follow that an act could not intend an object unless it were aware of itself as so intending. But the existence of unconscious, preconscious and bodily intentionalities proves that this is not the case. By extending the range of the concept of intentionality beyond conscious intentionality, we at the same time free it from dependence on the concept of reflexivity.

But is not the reflexivity of consciousness dependent on its intentionality? Granted that reflexivity is not reducible to intentionality, granted that it is not just another mode of it, may it yet be said that consciousness could not be aware of itself unless it were also intentional? In other words, can it be said that only an intentional consciousness could be reflexive? Samkara no doubt regards the supposed nonintentional consciousness as being *svaprakāśa*, and yet the being of such a consciousness is borne out neither by direct experience nor by logic — for logic cannot legislate as to what is or is not — but by a covert appeal to *faith!* And the absurdity of having to prove the being of something which is yet claimed to be self-intimating is sought to be explained by an appeal to a concealing agency, to a sort of explanation which Popper calls 'the conspiracy theory of ignorance'(19)!

More true to the phenomena, Rāmānuja clearly sees the dependence so much so that he defines reflexivity of consciousness in terms partly of its intentionality(20). What does Sartre do? Surely, as Thevenez recognises(21), Sartre sees a new dimension of consciousness other than intentionality: in fact one gets the impression that he leaves the two side by side, two independent functions of consciousness, whereas really he does see an inner bond between them. I think it is possible to argue that only an intentional consciousness could be reflexive. The argument which makes use of some of Sartre's notions may be stated as follows:

A consciousness which is non-intentional will consist in *contents* which do not refer to anything. It would be like a substance possessing attributes, or undergoing modifications, or like a container containing 'ideas' which would themselves be non-intentional. Or, it may be a real, non-intentional relation between real non-intentional terms. Such a consciousness, conceived on the analogy of non-intentional substances, qualities, processes or relations, would be no better than them with regard to its mode of givenness. It would share their opacity. One may at most contend that though like any other non-intentional substance consciousness may yet be regarded as exhibiting a most peculiar property of efflorescence or shiningness in a manner analogus to light or other shining substances. However, such an efflorescent property cannot make consciousness reflexive, the analogy with light fails to bring out the positivity of the self-luminosity of consciousness. The point of the argument is that, any non-intentional substance, property or relation would be opaque. Only a wholly intentional consciousness could be completely transparent. For, as Sartre would put it, its whole being would consist in intentional reference, it would have nothing *in* it, no representative content (in fact, a non-intentional consciousness cannot represent except *for* an intentional consciousness), no states, properties, processes! Such a consciousness would be nothing, it would be, as the Advaitins would say, *nirguna* but not *nirvisaya*. It is *nirguna* precisely because it is wholly directed towards an other. Bereft of all opaque contents, it would be wholly transparent. Being wholly directed towards the other would not obstruct its transparency, for transparency does not mean being *directed towards* itself. True — as the Naiyāyikas contend — if consciousness is wholly directed towards an other it cannot at the same time be directed towards itself. But this self-givenness without being directed towards itself, this non-positing, pre-reflective self-givenness of consciousness is exactly what we have called its transparence or reflexivity;

and intentionality of consciousness constitutes a necessary, if not sufficient, condition of its possibility.

IV

The argument sketched in the preceeding paragraph helps us to give some sense to locutions like 'degrees of intentionality' and 'degrees of reflexivity.' We may now say that to the extent to which a state is intentional, i.e., to the extent to which it excludes opacity and approximates towards the completely empty consciousness, to that extent it is transparent. A completely empty consciousness, a consciousness that is in itself nothing, that is fully exhausted in its intentional function, is also the most transparent. This principle helps us to grade the intentional states in a certain scale at the one end of which are the so-called unconscious state, followed by the purely bodily intentionality, the horizon or preconscious intentionalities, conscious intentionalities with their various gradations leading up, at the other end, to *knowledge*, the most free from any content, the most transparent of all intentionalities at the same time.

With a view to elucidate the idea of such a hierarchy, let us recall at this stage Husserl's notion of *hyle* or formless material which "offer themselves as material for intentional informings"(22) and which together with the "animating prehensions" "belong to the 'real' *(reellen)* constitution of the experience"(23). Now it has been seen that this notion of *hyle* as a real component of experience has been subjected to devastating criticism. Sartre, for example, suspects the *hyle* to be "a hybrid being which consciousness rejects and which cannot be a part of the world"(24). It cannot belong to consciousness, for then "it would disappear in translucency." Consciousness cannot conceal anything opaque within it. We need not however so hastily reject the *hyle*, for the translucency of consciousness has its degrees, and one may suppose that the translucency varies in inverse proportion to the presence of the hyletic element. In states that contain more of unformed matter, there is less of translucency, in states that contain less of *hyle* there is more of translucency. The so-called unconscious states are, from this point of view, the nearest approximations to pure hyletic stuff,

and in so far they are the least reflexive. The psycho-analyst
speaks of unconscious desires and of unconscious hatred. Not
that these locutions are mistaken, only they need to be taken in
their true import freed from what Ricoeur has called "the
Realism of the Unconscious"(25). I think one should, in connection with the problem of the unconscious, avoid two extreme
views. There is at one extreme the realism which asserts that
there are unconscious desires and hatred, fully formed but lacking merely in the quality of consciousness. There is at the other
extreme the view according to which the unconscious is the
mere "impressional matter not yet brought to life by an intentional aim" (Ricoeur), it is not yet intentional, it is not yet *of*
. . . . . . On this view, the so-called unconscious desire is what
the impressional matter *would be* when it is fully formed and
thereby made conscious. This latter view, and the explanation
of psychoanalytic cure as the process of bestowing intentional
form on the unformed matter thereby freeing the mind of their
weight, is perhaps the most interesting attempt made to
reconcile the psycho-analytic theory of the unconscious with
Husserlian phenomenology. But it gives rise to certain questions
in the light of which the theory needs to be modified. If there
is no unconscious desire or hatred, if it is the psycho-analyst
who helps to transform the impressional matter in the patient's
unconscious into a desire or a hatred and thereby relieves him
of the "weight" of the unformed stuff, if this were the whole
story, then two things would remain unaccounted for. For one
thing, how is it that the patient gives his assent to the "discovery" and *recognises* that the desire or the hatred was in fact
in his mind? In fact, the patient "recalls" from the depth of his
memory and identifies the disturbing element as a desire or
hatred. For another, if the disturbing state weighing on
the patient's mind were not already 'formed,' is the imposition
of a certain form on it purely an arbitrary act? Why should it,
for example, be interpreted as a hatred, and not as a suspicion?
Why as a love and not as a fondness? We are thus led by reflecting on these two considerations to a view of the unconscious
according to which both unconscious realism and its total denial
are false. The unconscious quâ unconscious is already intentional,

is *of* . . . . . . , and yet the intentional formation is vague and indefinite, the mere pattern is laid down but not its definite meaning. The hyletic stuff predominates over the intentional form. Thus we have an unconscious intentionality which the patient later on 'discovers' and recognizes as a hatred or a desire, this process of discovering or recognizing is also in part one of making the indefinite definite, filling up the outlines into a complete picture, supplying the vague intentional reference with a definite intended object. It is unconscious in the sense of being irreflexive, it lacks translucency; and this lack is explained by the preponderance of the hyletic elements in the mind. Yet the patient recognises the desire or the hatred as somthing which has been all along there, and this is taken care of by the fact that the state concerned is still intentional.

It would indeed be an arduous task to carry out this explanatory schemata right through all the various levels of intentionality: the bodily, the preconscious, the intentionalities of emotional and affective life and the intentionality of knowledge. But we may say a few words about the last which stands at the other end of the scale. In knowledge, in the strict sense, the intention stands fulfilled, the object is given and not merely thought of. In such a state, as in perception, the revelation of the object through which the intention stands fulfilled is the whole thing; the content, the sensedatum in perceptual knowledge, is nowhere in consciousness or before it. The element of *hyle* is conspicuous by its absence, it is formed by the intentional act, completely transformed into a meaningful pattern. No wonder that philosophers would fail to detect a mental process called 'knowing,' or a performance called 'perceiving.' When, e.g.: Ryle insists that perceiving signifies an achievement, not a process(26), he is right. When Ayer says that to describe one's knowledge is not to describe a mental process(27), he also seems, in a sense, to be right. Here consciousness has become so fully intentional, in fact so completely absorbed in its intentional object (for the intention has become fulfilled) that the act has been emptied of all contents approximating to the idea of pure consciousness that is nothing. And it is precisely in knowledge, for that very reason, that we have the highest degree of transparency: one cannot fail to be aware as and when one knows that one knows (though one may have only a dim, vague, confused and even deceptive awareness, as and when one feels an emotion, that one is so feeling).

I may now put forward the thesis, in partial modification of what was said before, that intentionality is a *necessary* condition of reflexivity, and the more that is needed to constitute the *necessary and sufficient* condition is the relative absence of unformed hyletic stuff in consciousness. Since what we always have is a degree of transparency, this negative condition is fulfilled only in degrees but it cannot be formulated quantitatively with mathematical precision.

V

I have earlier accorded recognition to two different kinds of intentionality: the intentionality of mental states (conscious or unconscious) and the intentionality of bodily behaviour. I refused to assimilate any one of these two types to the other, I also refused to succuumb to the temptation of courting an easygoing monism. In view of our subsequent discussion, the following tentative conclusions may now be drawn:

(a) Intentionality is *not* a defining character of consciousness. It is not also a defining character of mental states. But it still does define a certain range of phenomena. It does not, for example, characterise phenomena of outer physical nature, namely the sort of phenomena studied by physics or astronomy. It might be useful to say that the range of phenomena which the concept of intentionality defines is circumscribed by the regional title 'subjectivity.' Intentionality characterises in some degree or other whatever is subjective. The reverse also holds good: whatever exhibits intentionality is to that extent subjective.

Consciousness is also subjective, but not all that is subjective is consciousness. Consciousness is also intentional. But what defines consciousness quâ consciousness, not quâ subjective, is its reflexivity, not its intentionality. Subjectivity is a necessary but not sufficient condition of consciousness.

(b) In view of the conclusion stated in (a) above, we need not stop with a mind-body dualism. It is possible that what we have, in these different types of intentionality, only different *grades of subjectivity,* the body being as much subjective as the mind. I need not enter into this notion of the body as subjective: I would like to regard it as one of the major philosophical discoveries of our age, a philosophical insight sustained and corroborated by the researches of such thinkers as K. C. Bhattacharyya, Marcel, Sartre, Merleau-Ponty and Hampshire. I only wish here to make use of this important philosophical insight without further explicating it and resolve the apparent dualism of body and mind into a notion of grades of subjectivity to be understood in the light of the concept of degrees of intentionality and reflexivity.

It has been suggested that the concept of intentionality defines the concept of subjectivity, or that intentionality is a defining property of the subjective. Further, I have distinguished between the subjective and consciousness. This may be intuitively clear, but if the contention is not to be trivial we have to look for some other character of subjectivity. In other words, it seems intuitively clear that the bodily and the mental all come under the regional title 'subjectivity' and further that they are intentional. But if subjectivity means nothing other than intentionality, then the thesis that the subjective alone is intentional is rendered equivalent to the trivial thesis that the intentional alone is intentional. This charge of triviality can be set aside if we can produce some other property characterising the subjective. Now, I find several different ways of doing this. (a) One may say that the subjective is also that which pertains to, or belongs to — in a sense of 'pertaining to' or 'belonging to' that requires careful specification — man, or better to a person. (b) One may however not want to restrict the concept of subjectivity to that of the person, and try to characterise it as "freedom from objectivity." Now both these moves are beset with difficulties. The first move is faced with the difficulty that all that is owned by a person is not subjective, and to say that amongst those things that may be said to be owned by a person only those are subjective which also exhibit intentionality is to revert to the trivial thesis. The main difficulty here is to define the precise sense of 'belonging to,' and this is a task which cannot be undertaken here. The second line of thought, admirably worked out in Bhattacharyya's *Subject as Freedom*(28), has to reconcile the two apparently incompatible characterisations: namely, that subjective is both freedom from objectivity and also intentional: in fact, this is what Bhattacharryya does when he writes: "The knowing function represents a positive mode of this freedom, the freedom of the subject to *relate to object without getting related to it*"(29). It is not possible to comment on this within the scope of the present work, but it may be remarked that the thesis defended here, that intentionality is not a relation — realised even by Brentano when he says it is not a relation but only relation-like — is not incompatible with Bhattacharyya's thesis that the objective reference of consciousness is not a mode of getting related to the object. However, I must for the present resist the temptation of elaborating these two moves. I have only hinted at the vast problem that opens out after all that has been said.

(c) However, there is still another possible move — one which is less ontologically committed. One may contend that the unifying concept of subjectivity (and so also of intentionality) is to be understood as an *analogical* concept and not as a generic concept. The sense in which I wish to distinguish between analogical and generic concepts may be explicated thus: if G be a generic concept, and m,n,o,p its instances, then of course, m,n,o and p are different Gs (e.g., Plato, Socrates, Aristotle and Kant are different men); they are Gs in so far as they possess some character in common precisely by virtue of which G is predicated of them. But if A be an analogical concept, and b,c,d,e its instances, then b,c,d,e are not only different As but are *as As different*. In other words, A is predicated of each of them but not in the same sense, not by virtue of the possession of an identically common character. Thus not only are mathematical entities and physical objects beings, but they are, as beings, different: the very sense of 'to be' alters as we move from one such domain to another. Nevertheless there is a concept of being which is truely predicated of them all. Now, it may be said that the concept of intentionality is such an analogical concept. Bodily intentionality and conscious intentionality are not only different sorts of intentionality but are, as intentionalities, different. Nevertheless we do have a concept of intentionality, of being directed towards, the precise sense of which alters from one domain to another. In such a case, the very notion of 'grades of . . . . . . ' is essential to the concept. It is not a true account of the situation to say that what we have, in the different domains, is the presence of a common characteristic together with some accidental properties. The notion of intentionality *essentially breaks up* into several *radically* different modes of its instantiation, and these modes together constitute that notion and are not external to it.

CHAPTER 2

ACHIEVEMENTS AND PROSPECTS

I

IN THE LAST CHAPTER, while trying to locate and circumscribe the concept of intentionality, we were led beyond the traditional notion of consciousness to a concept of subjectivity, and it must be admitted that a phenomenology of subjectivity is the task which opens out before us — a task which freely falls outside the scope of the present work. However, it may be argued that a phenomenological study of intentionality should not be independent of metaphysical considerations. Fink, for example, has urged (1) that a problem which Husserl did not raise but which should be asked, concerns the nature of being *(Sein)* of intentionality itself. It is time, as we conclude, to consider some such metaphysically oriented points of view.

But before turning to them, let us briefly recall what may be claimed as positive achievements. Some of these achievements are not results, for some of them emerge as basic issues, and it is good to formulate them precisely.

(i) There is a sort of ontological neutrality about the concept of intentionality which has been stressed on various occasions. We have the linguistic phenomenona of existence-independence, truth-value indifference and referential opacity. Further, the conception of consciousness as openness to the other may be regarded as bypassing the classical alternatives of realism and idealism, for it renders the question of something being either contained within consciousness or not entirely pointless. However, it may still be asked if the concept of intentionality is really *neutral* as between realism and idealism. Using a spatial metaphor, one may ask: 'Granted that taking the concept seriously places us at a point beyond the two opposed schools, is it still the case that this point beyond is equidistant from them both?' We get beyond idealism through the valuable insight that consciousness does not have an inner where the object could possibly find a habitation. But how do we get beyond realism? Of course, if consciousness does not have an inner, if it is not an encapsulated entity, the very question to which realism is one alternative answer is rendered pointless. One cannot any more ask: is the object within consciousness or not? While this is true, it may yet be claimed that realism is not merely an answer to the above question. Were it so, by rendering it impossible to formulate that question we also render its likely answers *ab initio* pointless. But there is a core within the theory of realism which is not a theory but a descriptive phenomenon: this is the fact of consciousness's *self-transcending* reference to the *other*. And this core is taken care of by the intentionality thesis. In this sense, and in this sense alone, we need to modify our initial statement that the thesis is ontologically neutral. There is rather a partiality in favour of realism. Nevertheless, the thesis does preserve an ontological indifference, for the other to which consciousness refers need not be real.

The Indian realists like the Naiyāyikas urged that denial of representative consciousness (*jñānasākāravāda*) and the assertion of consciousness's non-transparency (*paraprakāśatva*) jointly imply realism. For, if consciousness is not transparent, and has no contents within itself, the object that stands revealed through it is a real other and does not belong to consciousness itself. To this, it should be added that while the Indian realists correctly grasped the inner logic of subjective idealism and sought to overcome it by rejecting the theories of representative consciousness and by establishing the *savisayakatva* of consciousness, yet they did not quite appreciate the phenomena of existence independence and truth-value indifference and the consequent ontological neutrality entailed by the intentionality thesis. We may then conclude by saying that the intentionality thesis does overcome the ageold controversy, but in doing so it nevertheless shows a certain partiality towards realism in so far as the latter contains a phenomenological descriptive core.

(ii) But is it not also the case that idealism is more than a mere theory? Is not there also a descriptive core within the heart of idealism? If there is such a core, what is it precisely, and how does the intentionality thesis stand in relation to it? This descriptive core of idealism is nothing other than the fact of correlation between *noesis* and *noema;* it is to be found also in the fact that every object is an identity of many different profiles and perspectives and, as a unity of signification, may be looked upon as a 'guide' to a whole complex of conscious and bodily acts and movements which go to bring it to more and more adequate self-givenness. It is this correlation between subjective functions and the objective sense which is, as we have seen, a component of the intentionality thesis as developd by Husserl.

(iii) The resulting attitude towards realism-idealism issue is reflected in the philosophy of consciousness which emerges out of the foregoing discussion. There are two opposed views about the nature of consciousness. One regards consciousness as wholly passive and the other regards it as wholly creative. According to the former, consciousness like a ray of light simply manifests whatever it happens to fall upon. It is the principle of manifestation, its only function is to manifest the object (*artha-prakāśo*), or perhaps it manifests both itself and the other *svaparaprakāśa*). It does nothing else, it does not modify the object it manifests, it does not create or constitute any objectivity. Now without doubt such a view does take note of an important truth about consciousness, which it overemphasises at the cost of overlooking or even denying other equally important aspects and truths. Consciousness surely reveals what it intends precisely as that is intended. But this neither means that the object intended *eo ipso* stands fully revealed, nor that intending is merely revealing, or as the phenomenologists say, bringing to bodily self-givenness. Consciousness in intending also confers sense, synthesises, unifies, and achieves something. The view which looks upon consciousness as essentially creative rightly sees this aspect of the matter, but again — not unlike the other theory — errs by onesidedness and overemphasis. The creativity of consciousness is not an unbriddled exuberance, it is not an unfettered freedom. It is restricted on the one hand by the data, the *hyle* which it fails fully to absorb into its creative intentions and on the other by the fact that the creative, constitutive functions of consciousness can be discovered *only by* the regressive method of starting with the given (and accomplished) unity of object (and sense). Thus the two aspects of passivity and constitutive creativity supplement each other and go to constitute a total and integral philosophy of consciousness. The thesis of intentionality brings both to light in their essential interconnections.

(iv) The dialectics of intention and fulfilment, especially as it appears in theory of meaning in the form of the correlative notions of meaning-intention and meaning-fulfilment, helps us to bring together elements of truth in both apriorism and positivism in a manner such that each limits and also needs the other(2).

(v) The intentional consciousness is both in-the-world and beyond it. It is in-the-world in so far as its freedom is fettered by limitations imposed by the situation in which it finds itself and which it does not altogether create (e.g., the role of body and of perspective-oriented profiles in perception, and also the role of history). It is beyond the world in so far as its intentions range beyond the domain of possible fulfilment, in so far as e.g. it anticipates a complete synthesis of profiles which can never be verified fully in experience(3). To put it in other words, the intentional consciousness is both finite and infinite. Also, one may say that it is both unhappy and contented, suffering and also enjoying: the former in so far as the gap between intention and fulfilment can never be totally eliminated, and the latter as and when empty intentions come to be fulfilled, bare anticipations more and more turn into presence.

(vi) Should the intentional consciousness be primarily cognitive or volitional? Here great caution is needed, and one should desist from understanding the primitive concept of intentionality on the model of any single sort of mental functioning. Intentionality characterises all mental functions, cognitive, affective and volitional, and to suppose that in its innermost core consciousness or intentionality is either cognitive or volitional is to be guilty of improper generalisation, and even of overlooking differences between orders of concepts.

(vii) This leads us finally to a point regarding the nature of the *concept* of intentionality. It is first a higher order reflective concept emerging in the attitude of phenomenological reflection. The *fact* of intentional reference is pre-reflective as well as post-reflective. The *concept* however arises from a certain type of reflection. It is also not a generic concept but an analogical one: it does not designate a common essence of all those phenomena which are intentional but rather as we move from acts to intentionalities which are not acts, or from mental to the bodily domain, the sense of intentionality radically alters so that we not only encounter different sorts of intentions but also intentions which are as intentions different. The same remarks should, as said before, hold good of the concept of the subjective.

II

The relevance of a philosophical thesis or of a philosophical concept shall be judged not only by its role in overcoming or dissolving interminable philosophical controversies of the past or by its neutrality — deriving from its phenomenological-descriptive core — as between rival theories. These criteria are intra-philosophical. Success in satisfying these criteria generates a strength which is further heightened if the philosophical thesis or concept under consideration could be shown to play a central role in illuminating, coordinating or regulating — whether from the methodological or from the contentual point of view — researches in some special science. In the case of the intentionality thesis, we may reasonably expect success even from this point of view. If intentionality is the distinguishing mark of the subjective, which includes both mental states and bodily behavior, and if the notion of the subjective is intimately connected with that of the person — it may be expected that the intentionality thesis will have profound influence on psychology in particular and on all behavioral sciences in general.

That the concept of intentionality has a profound influence on psychology has been recognised ever since Brentano sought to demarcate the domain of psychology with its help. But it has never been agreed upon as to how precisely it bears upon psychology. We cannot go back to Brentano's delimitation of the domain of psychology. We have also to recognise the tremendous advance of the science of behavior. How then will an intentionalistic psychology be like?

Should it be an introspectionistic psychology? At the first sight, it might seem to be so. For, it might be supposed that since mental states are open only to introspection or inner perception psychology as science of mind has to take recourse to introspection. Though the psychologist may also have to do some outer observation, yet his paradigmatic method should be introspection. Now, with regard to introspectionism, we have to bear in mind two things(4): one, there is a great deal of difference between phenomenological psychology (which operates with the concept of intentionality as its central concept) and introspective psychology. Introspection is a sort of reflection, and introspective psychology limits itself to reflective experience. The pre-reflective experience precisely as one lives through it falls outside the scope of introspective psychology. For another, introspectionism studies mental phenomena as detached from bodily behavior whereas the phenomenologist, for whom bodily behavior is both intentional and pre-reflectively 'lived,' is interested as much in mental states as in bodily behavior. It has also been pointed out(5) that whereas introspectionism assumes that experience is reducible to a finite number of conscious elements, the intentionalist does not have any such bias. On the contrary, the notions of intentional implication, intentional unity and horizon would rule out any such analysis into elements. Furthermore, the introspectionist like Titchener has no place for meaning, whereas for the intentionalist the notion of meaning is central and unavoidable. One cannot therefore agree with the remark(6) that the psychology deriving from Brentano is a sort of "encapsulated introspectionism" which is sought to be contrasted with the functionalism of the American psychologists.

Let us therefore ask, how does intentionalism in psychology stand in relation to functionalism? Titchener gives a list of four main tenets of the functionalist school(7): functional psychology recognises, implicitly or explicitly, the distinction between the activity or function and the content or structure of consciousness. For the functionalists, consciousness is primarily a matter of function and only secondarily a matter of content. Its chief function is to make good the inadequacy or hesitancy of the nervous system. Consciousness comes to our aid when our organic equipments fail. Consciousness is also basically teleological in so far as it is the index of "problem-solving adapting acts." Finally, psychology for the functionalists is directed towards the attainment of some goal beyond itself, e.g., the goal of controlling human life and institutions. Now there is no doubt that both functionalism and intentionalism recognise acts of consciousness, but whereas functionalism understands consciousness as the act of adapting the organism to environment (where the organic functions fail to rise up to the occasion), for intentionalism the concept of 'act' is strictly defined in terms of intentionality. It is true that intentionalism emphasises the function of consciousness rather than the content, but there are functions which are more basic than those of solving problems. In fact, as Titchener rightly insists, all awareness is not directed towards solving problems:

> "There is a consciousness militant, but there is also a consciousness triumphant: more than that, there is a consciousness that, in the midcourse of its campaigning, rests quietly upon its arms, and surveys the terrain it has occupied"(8).

The functions of self-transcending reference, of synthesising perspectives, of conferring meaning and identifying are surely more basic to the activity of consciousness than those recognised by the psychologists of the functionalist school. Morris seems to be right in suggesting that a functionalist theory of mind may well preserve the truth of intentionalism(9), but the weight of this statement would depend upon what sense we give to 'function' and 'intentionality.' If we widen the notion of function and liberate it from the organic-evolutionary point of view, and if we regard intentionality not merely as a property of the mental but as its nature, i.e., if we hold that consciousness *is* intentional openness to the other — then of course functionalism in psychology may be assimilated into intentionalism.

The intentionalist's relationships to the *Gestalt* school and to behaviorism are more intricate. Both the Gestaltist and the intentionalist would reject sensationism, or for that matter all sorts of psychological atomism. Both would reject the constancy hypothesis, i.e., the supposed one-to-one correspondence of sensory stimulus elements and conscious sensations. But the Gestaltist still operates within the frame work of psycho-physical causality. If he rejects constancy hypothesis, he replaces it by the notion of global functioning of the brain as a whole. Further, it still rests satisfied with larger, though structured atoms, the *Gestalten,* and has no conception of the subtle intentional thread which leads one datum to another, no conception of that zone of indeterminateness which surrounds all data. One could even say that both the *Gestalt* and behaviorism are after precise objective knowledge, and do not recognize that pre-objective lived experience within which objective forms emerge, and into which they all tend to go back. Intentionalism in psychology will consist not merely in inspection of the intentional objects of acts, but also in bringing to light the pre-objective lived experience within which both acts and objects come to emerge as determinate unities. Intentionalism will study behavior, but it will seek to rescue behavior from the model of explanation set up by physiological psychology, or even by the S-R formula. It will even try to show that the S-R formula derives its whole sense from the hidden assumption of an intentional situation(10). But all this is possible when the psychologist frees himself from metaphysical and scientific prejudices, and learns to look boldly in the face of facts as they present themselves. This would undo one of the major defects of traditional behaviorism: namely, its failure to account for sentences in the first person present tense and consquently to recover man's status as a subject and as a person(11).

If the notion of intentionality has thus undeniable relevance for psychology, it is to be expected that it cannot be valueless for other behavioral sciences as well. But this is a matter on which I do not feel competent to pronounce judgment at present.

III

We have been treating the concept of intentionality as a primitive. We have refused to reduce it to some more primitive notion. This claim may be challenged by metaphysicians who would try to impress upon us the need of a metaphysical 'foundation' of the phenomenological thesis of intentionality. Such metaphysicians may concede to us the value and the validity of the intentionality thesis, but they may suggest that we better enquire into the conditions of the possibility of intentionality. Or, they may want − like Fink(12) − to raise the question about the mode of being, about the *Sein* of intentionality itself. Various such metaphysical moves are possible, and a few of them may presently be considered.

(a) We have already considered the Heideggerean attempt to derive intentionality from being-in-the-world and afterwards from the Being's world-project. We have found that whatever plausibility this derivation has or may have is due to the fact that the concept of being-in-the-world itself is covertly intentional.

(b) Sellars(13) considers a sort of isomorphism between intellect and the world as "a necessary condition of the intellect's intentionality" and proceeds to distinguish between two dimensions of this isomorphism: an isomorphism of the real order (where both the terms are of the real order) and an isomorphism of the logical order. The former is the relation of picturing, and the latter is the relation of signifying. However, the relation of picturing itself presupposes that there must be two reals, either both external or one mental and the other external. An isomorphism defined in terms of such a relationship cannot be said to be a condition of the possibility of intentionality, for as has been emphasised before intentionality does not imply reality of the intended object, and it surely goes against a theory of representative consciousness. The case with the relation of signifying is different: here we have a genuine intentional situation which, far from providing a presupposition of intentionality, is itself an excellent example of, and a most basic form of it.

(c) It has been maintained by Horosz(14) that the notion of intentionality presupposes man's purposive nature defined ontologically as self-direction. Ordinarily, purposiveness of man would mean man's essential ability to seek goals and to make decisions. But the goal-seeking and decision-making functions are, for Horosz, ontic; they presuppose the ontological nature of man as self-directing, which is man's potentiality for discovering goals and for ordering and correcting the possible anarchy of multiple goals. For this way of thinking, the notion of intentionality presupposes the notion of the human agency (e.g., the *ego* as the source of intentionality), and the notion of human agency is an abstraction from man's power for self-direction and self-ordering. Now to comment on this: if the thesis were that intentionality is but a type of goal-seeking, of aiming at (the world 'intention' may deceive, but there were also ample warnings against it), then it is clearly mistaken. Intentionality is as little definable in terms of will as in terms of cognition ('revelation,' 'manifestation' or *'prakāśa'* as the Indian philosophers would say); it is a higher order (and yet primitive) notion applying to all special modes of mental and bodily 'directedness towards . . . . . . ' Perhaps the thesis under consideration here seizes upon this notion of directedness as such, without bringing in the notion of a goal or end, and takes it as man's purposiveness defined ontologically. If this be the case, two remarks at once suggest themselves: in the first place, as so construed the notion of directedness (or even of self-direction) is hardly distinguishable from the notion of intentionality. But to this must be added a second remark: the relation between the concept of intentionality and the concept of man is not evident enough. So far as the metaphysical notion of the ego is concerned, it can be shown — à la Husserl and Sartre — to be constituted by intentionality. So far as the notions of 'man' and 'person' are concerned, they surely are not simpler than that of intentionality. As we have briefly suggested in the foregoing chapter, intentionality defines the notion of subjectivity, and the notions of 'man' and 'person' are inseparable from the latter concept. It may not therefore be advisable to ground intentionality in man's self-directing nature.

(d) Another recent writer who emphasizes the need for an "ontological guarantee" for intentionality is Gustav Bergmann(15). For Bergmann, "a fact is an act *if and only if* it is a bare particular exemplifying a species and a thought. A character (F) is a thought *if and only if* there is a fact (P), either actual or potential, such that FMP"(16). (Here M is the connection 'intending'; in Bergmann's ontology it is a fundamental nexus(17)). This is further clarified thus: "it is impossible (for Bergmann, an ill-formed expression marks what in its world is impossible$_1$"(18)) for anything to be a thought without there being an existent (though perhaps only in the mode of potentiality) which it is about as well as another (though only a subsistent) which connects the two"(19). Thus Bergmann comes to the conclusion: "As long as ontological status is denied to the mode of potentiality, there are acts without intentions"(20). The intention of an act, the *Gegenstand*, must be, according to him, a fact either actual or potential. The intending or M is a subsistent nexus. The act is a real fact which has a core which is the *Inhalt* or Thought and a fringe which is the act-quality. The core or the *Inhalt* intends the intention(21).

Bergmann considers three possible ways of conceiving of the ground of intending. Either, intending has an ontological ground which is neither in the core nor in the intention. Or, this ground is the *Inhalt* and the intention. Or, the ground is the *Inhalt* alone. Bergmann rejects the latter two alternatives for the reason that they both imply the doctrine of internal relations, the doctrine namely that the ground of a relation lies wholly either in one of the relata or in both the relata(22). The first alternative alone avoids this doctrine, and makes the relation of intending (M) independent of the terms related. It is a subsistent nexus, whereas the act is a real particular, its core is a character belonging to it and its intention is a fact, actual or potential.

What now intentionality presupposes is, according to Bergmann, the notion of potential existence. We know already that an act may intend an object which does not exist. Where the intention, i.e., the intended object does not exist, Bergmann will prefer to say that it exists in the mode of potentiality(23). The two concepts — that of mind and that of potential existence — are for him inseparable. It is this latter concept which provides the "ontological guarantee" for the concept of intentionality.

Bergmann's thesis may mean any one of three things: It may mean that the intended object (the same as Bergmann's intention) must be a *Zwischenentität,* something which is neither existent nor non-existent, neither mental nor extra-mental, and that the intentionality thesis presupposes admission of such curious entities. But this could not be what he means. For, first, some intentions — he allows — are actual facts, and only some are potential facts. Secondly, potentiality is for him a mode of existence. The potential fact is an existent fact. The ontological ground of intentionality is precisely this mode of existence. Bergmann may also be taken to mean that the intended object must be a possible object. He introduces two concepts of possibility, called by him 'possibility$_1$' and 'possibility$_2$.' Something is possible$_1$ (in a world) if it is denoted by a well-formed expression of a language reflecting the ontological structure of that world(24). Thus it is possible$_1$ that a thing both has and has not a certain property, for 'S is both p and not-p' is a well-formed expression. But it is not possible$_2$. What is analytically false or self-contradictory is impossible$_2$, what is self-consistent is possible$_2$. 'S is both red and green all over' is both well-formed and logically consistent. What is denoted by it is both possible$_1$ and possible$_2$. However, it lacks possibility in some sense, and Bergmann has still another notion of possibility: possibility$_3$. What is not a priori false is possible$_3$. Obviously, for him the *a priori* is not always analytic(25).

How does his notion of potential existence stand in relation to these notions of possibility?

Now surely one can intend what is self-contradictory, i.e., what is impossible$_2$. One may also intend what is impossible$_3$, and surely also what is impossible$_4$ (see footnote 25). But what one intends must at least possess possibility$_1$: the impossible$_1$ is also the limit of thought. In this sense, the intention must be-also the limit of thought. In this sense, the intention must be possible$_1$. When therefore Bergmann says that the intention must have at least potential existence he may be taken to mean that the intended object must at least possesss possibility$_1$(26). Now this latter contention by itself does not constitute an ontological thesis: it lays down that our intentional acts presuppose a linguistic framework, and since all intentional acts, in fact all awareness, is propositional(27), nothing can be intended unless it is the referent of a well-formed sentence of the language. If this is what Bergmann means, two remarks may be made at once: for one thing, the interpretation of 'potential existence' as 'possibility$_1$' divests that notion of its ontological significance. For another, while it may hold good of all propositional awareness that the intention must be a fact referred to by a well-informed sentence, it is nevertheless not true that all awareness is propositional. To hold that awareness is always propositional is to be unfaithful to actual experience in order to save one's favoured ontology, and would amount to committing a typical intellectual's fallacy. All intentional objects are not facts: they may be objects, persons, events. There may indeed be a bewildering variety of them.

If then the notion of potential existence is to have ontological relevance, it must be given the sense it has in ordinary parlance as for example when one says that something is potentially in something else, the statute is in the block of marble, the oak in the seed, the promise of greatness in a young scholar. One may in that case ask: in whom does the intention 'centauer' or 'round square' or 'golden mountain' potentially exist? In the act, in its content, or in the intending? To say that it potentially exists in reality, in the world, in nature, in the scheme of things, is not giving any account of how it comes to be intended by this act.

The search for ontological guarantee is misdirected. The basis of intentionality will have to be sought, if anywhere, in the structure of consciousness or of subjectivity, and not in the structure of the world. But then one does not really do much by saying that intentionality is ontologically grounded in the structure of consciousness or of subjectivity: if true, it is trivial and unilluminating, for intentionality reveals precisely that structure.

(e) Various monistic metaphysical frameworks may be set up with the claim that only within such a framework the fact of intentionality could be rendered intelligible and its possibility taken care of. The monistic metaphysician may well start with *a sense of wonder,* of utter puzzlement as to how at all could the sort of self-transcending reference that is intentionality be possible. How could, he might wonder, consciousness or the subjective refer to what is beyond? And the wonder is sought to be removed, the puzzle resolved and the paradox eliminated by supposing that the subject and the object are at bottom one. It is this basic identity which explains the *how* of intentional reference. Such monism may be either subjective or objective. The supposed transcendent object may be but a subjective idea, or the supposed intending subject may be but an object not unlike any other object. The supposed intentional reference is in the one case intra-subjective, in the other intra-objective. The subject's reaching out to an object beyond it is then a mere illusion. The monistic attempt to render intentionality intelligible really ends up by denying what it set out to explain. It is no better with an absolute monism which seeks the point of identity beyond both subject and object. The sense of wonder with which we imagined our monist to have started is uncalled for and derives from hidden preconceptions in favour of a concept of non-intentional representative consciousness. The wonder may be removed, the puzzle resolved and the paradox eliminated by getting rid precisely of that preconception derived from the mainstream of classical thinking, and one does not need to set up a speculative framework for that purpose.

Most speculative frameworks — if not all — owe their plausibility to an initial blindness to phenomena.

IV

If some metaphysicians have sought to provide a basis for intentionality, to offer an ontological guarantee or *Begründung* for it, or even to account for its possibility, others have started with intentionality as an inalienable phenomenon and then proceeded to raise *on its basis* metaphysical theories of some sort or other. Do the latter fare any better than the former? Is it possible to build up a metaphysics on the basis of the concept of intentionality?

To be brief, the point of departure provided by the notion of intentionality for metaphysical thought is the concept of 'transcendence'(28). If intentionality is a reference to what is beyond, if it is openness to an other, or if it is nothing in itself but a perpetual self-transcendence — then surely does the thesis of intentionality entail the concept of a transcendence as that which is the *ultimate* referent, or as that towards which man is perpetually open. This transcendence may be construed from the religious point of view as God, or from the speculative point of view as Being. Intentionality then is in its hidden essence encounter with God or Being. Theology and metaphysics in the grand style are not very far away. As an example of this kind of thinking in its theological form, we may think of Henry Dumery who discovers in intentionality "an energy capable of passing beyond all determination as such" to the One or God(29).

This is not the place to undertake an examination of such modes of metaphysicial and theological thinking. It may be argued, as against them, that if the intentionality thesis be ontologically neutral — as has been amply shown earlier — then nothing could follow from it regarding the being or otherwise of the transcendent. To this, however, there are two replies. First, even if the existence of no particular being is entailed by the fact that an intentional act is directed towards it, surely the inalienable phenomenon of intentionality is incompatible with a total ontological scepticism; even if any specific intended object may or may not exist, surely there must be some being or other, for how otherwise could there be the reference to a beyond if there is no beyond at all? Secondly, if all intentional acts were symbolic and empty intentions, there could be ground for scepticism. But there are also partially fulfilled intentions. In other words, there is also *encounter* with being. Even if such encounter is never complete coincidence, and even if every fulfilment hides unfulfilled intentions, even a partial and incomplete encounter shows a way out of scepticism: *svalpamapyasya dharmasya trāyate mahato bhayāt!*

Thus the room for metaphysics of some kind is kept open. But in what specific form it is admissible is a question which the present work will not investigate. Two heuristic principles may better be remembered here. One: phenomenology need not fight shy of speculative metaphysics, but it should keep it to an unavoidable minimum. Two: the metaphysics which is to be attempted first is descriptive. The intentionality thesis may well be the corner stone of a descriptive metaphysics of subjectivity.

NOTES AND REFERENCES
PART ONE

Chapter I

1. For the history of the concept of intentionality, see: Spiegelberg, F. "Der Begriff der Intentionalität in der Scholastik, bei Brenteno und bei Husserl," *Philosophische Hefte,* Vol. V, 1936, 75-91; and Moreau, J. "The Problem of Intentionality and classical thought," International Philosophical Quarterly, Vol. I, 1961, 215-234.
2. Brentano, F. *Psychologie vom empirischen Standpunkt,* Vol. 1, Leipzig, 1924.
3. *Ibid.,* 110.
4. Cp. Mohanty, J. N. *Edmund Husserl's Theory of Meaning,* The Hague: Martinus Nijhoff, 1964, 94-6.
5. Brenteno, F. loc. cit, § 5.
6. *Ibid.,* §6.
8. *Ibid.,* §8.
8. For more about the notion of reflexivity, see this work, Part Three, Chapter I.
9. Findlay, J. N. *Meinong's Theory of Objects and Values,* Oxford, 2nd edn., 1963, 39-41.
10. According to Kraus, Brentano abandoned this usage, possibly as consequent upon his rejection of this three-fold distinction. cp. Brentano, F. *The True and the Evident,* E.Tr. by R. M. Chisholm and others, London, Routledge Kegan Paul, 166.
11. This is explained by the fact that Brentano uses 'thing' or 'real' in a specific sense according to which a thing or a real need not exist or need not be an actual *(wirkliches). See Kraus' Einleitung* to Brentano's *Psychologie* Vol. I, XLI.
12. Brentano, F., *The True and the Evident,* 78.
13. *Ibid.,* 78 (italics mine).
14. *Ibid.,* 169; also *Einleitung* to Brentano's Psychologie Vol. I, XIX.
15. Brentano, F. *The True and The Evident,* 78.

16. See Ch. 3, Part I of this work.
17. Brentano, F. *Psychologie* Vol. II, 1911 Edition, 13-138.
18. Findlay, J. N. *loc. cit*, 39-41.
19. Landgrebe, L. *Phänomenologie und Metaphysik,* Hamburg, Schroder, 1949, 59-83.
20. Spiegelberg, F. *loc. cit.*
21. *Ibid.,* 86
22. Brentano, F. *Psychologie,* Vol. I, Book 2, Ch. II.
23. *Ibid.,* 172f.
24. See *Ibid.,* 176 fn.
25. *"Die Verstellung des Tones und die Vorstellung von der Vorstellung des Tones bilden nicht mehr als ein einziges psychisches Phänomen, dass wir nur, indem wir es in seiner Beziehung auf zwei verschiedene Objekte, deren eines ein physisches, und deren anderes ein psychisches Phänomen ist, betrachteten, begrifflich in zwei Vorstellungen zergliederten."* (*Ibid.,* 179).
26. *Ibid.,* 181.
27. *"Zugleich seiner Totalität nach für sich selbst Gegenstand und Inhalt"* (*Ibid.,* 182).
28. *Ibid.,* 196-198.
29. *Ibid.,* 200.
30. *Ibid.,* 201.
31. *Ibid.,* 203.
32. In the *Anhang* to the 1911 edition, Brentano modifies this position: *"Seitdem aber bin ich davon zurückgekommen und glaube nunmehr, dass es sogar unter den Sensationen viele gibt, welche diese Gemütsbeziehung, also jede in ihnen selbst beschlossene Lust und Unlust, fehlt."* (*Psychologie,* Vol. II, 139.)
33. *Ibid.,* 219.
34. *"Somit sehen wir, dass überhaupt keine gleichzeitige Beobachtung des eigenen Beobachtens oder eines anderen eigenen psychischen Aktes möglich ist."* (Brentano, *Psychologie* I, 181). In an *Anhang* to the volume II of the *Psychologie,* 1911 edition, Brentano recognises that this point was not explicitly made in the earlier edition though it is not incompatible with what was said there — that a psychic act may be objectified i.e. may be made the primary object of a subsequent act (142).
35. *Psychologie* I, 132-136.
36. See especially, *Ibid.,* 237-240.

******

Chapter 2

1. Chisholm, R. M. "Sentences about Believing," *Proceedings of the Aristotelian Society,* LVI, 1955-56, 125-147; "On some psychological concepts and the 'Logic' of Intentionality" in Castañeda, H. N. (ed.) *Intentionality, Minds and Perception,* Wayne State University, 1966, 11-35; also contribution on "Intentionality" to *The Encyclopedia of Philosophy,* edited by P. Edwards, New York, 1967. Also: "Notes on the Logic of Believing," *Philosophy and Phenomenological Research, XXIV,* 1963, 151-201; "Be-

196   *The Concept Of Intentionality*

lieving and Intentionality: A Reply to Mr. Luce and Mr. Sleigh," *Philosophy and Phenomenological Research*, XXV, 1964, 266-269.
2. Chisholm, R. M. "Intentionality" in Edward, P. (ed.) *The Encyclopedia of Philosophy*, New York, Macmillan, 1967, Vol. 4, 200-204.
3. "Sentences about Believing" (see note 1 above).
4. Chisholm, R. M. *Perceiving*, Cornell University Press, 1957.
5. Heidelberger, H. "On characterizing the Psychological," *Philosophy and Phenomenological Research*, 1966, 529-536.
6. See *ibid.*
7. Cornman, J. "Intentionality and Intensionality," *Philosophical Quarterly*, XII, 1962, 44-52.
8. The definition is taken from Pap, A. *Semantics and Necessary Truth*, New Haven: Yale University Press, Paperback edition, 1966,
9. Referred to in Chisholm's Encyclopedia article.
10. Cp. Chisholm's Encyclopedia article and the contribution to Castañeda (ed), *Intentionality, Minds and Perception*.
11. *Intentionality, Minds and Perception*, 18.
12. Pap, A. *loc. cit*, 173-4.
13. *Intentionality, Minds and Perception*, 29.

****

Chapter 3

1. In Indian Philosophy, this position is advocated by the Advaita Vedānta School of Śamkara.
2. Cp. Bhattacharya, K. C. *Subject as Freedom*, Bombay, 1930.
3. The Buddhist philosophers, specifically the Yogācāra Idealists, hold this view, and are known as sākārajñānavādins.
4. Śamkara, *Brahmasûtra Bhāṣya, Adhyāsabhāṣya*.
5. Cp. Madhavācārya's *Vivaranaprameyasamgraha*.
6. Kant, I. *Kritik der reinen Vernunft* (*Kant Werke*, edited by Cassirer, vol. 3), 200-203.
7. For a defence of this *Satz*, see Hartmann, N. *Grundzüge einer Metaphysik der Erkenntnis, Vierte Auflage*, Berlin; Walter De Gruyter, 1949, 93f., 328f.
8. Gustav Bergmann calls this the 'ground plan test' for an ontology. See his *Realism*, University of Wisconsin Press, 1967 140, 374.
9. *Ibid.*, For further discussions of Bergmann's thesis, see Part Three, chapter 2 of this work.
10. See Addis, L. and Lewis, D. *Moore and Ryle: Two Ontologists*, the Hague: Martinus Nijhoff, 1965, Ch. V, esp. 84-99.
11. Cp. Anscombe, G.E.M. "Intention," included in Gustafson, D. F. *Essays in Philosophical Psychology*, Doubleday Anchor, 1964.
12. For a modern statement, see Sellars, W. *Science, Perception and Reality*, London: Routledge and Kegan Paul, 1963, esp. 43ff.
13. Dharmadhvajārindra, *Vedāntaparibhāṣā, Ch.* 1.
14. Bosanquet, B. *Three chapters on the Nature of Mind*, London, 1923, 43-44.
15. Russell, B. *The Analysis of Mind*, London, 1921.
16. Cp. Titchener, E. B. *Systemic Psychology: Prolegomena*, New York, Macmillan, 1929, 252f.

17. Chisholm, R. M. "Intentionality," *The Encyclopedia of Philosophy* Vol. 4, 200-201.
18. Husserl, E. *Logische Untersuchungen,* 4th edition, Halle, Max Niemeyer, 1928 (to be henceforth referred to as *LU*), II.1., 421-425.
19. Brentano, F. *The True and the Evident,* 159.
20. Titchener, E. B. *loc. cit,* 226.
21. Husserl, E. LU, II.1. 421-425.
22. Contrast Quinton ["Mind and Matter," in Smythes (ed), *Brain and Mind, Modern concepts of the Nature of Mind,* New York: The Humanities Press, 1965] who argues (p. 224) that the Brentano thesis rules out behaviorism. It surely does, if intentionality is regarded, as was done by Brentano, as a criterion of the mental. On our view, this is not so, and so the intentionality thesis does not analytically rule out behaviorism.
23. Feigl, H. "The "Mental" and the "Physical" " in *Minnesota studies in the Philosophy of Science,* Vol. II, esp. see 416-419.
24. Carnap, R. *The Logical Structure of the World and Pseudo-problems in Philosophy,* E.Tr. by George, R. A., London: Routledge & Kegan Paul, 1967, 262.
25. *Ibid.,* 262.
26. *Ibid.,* 263.
27. See Chisholm, R.M., "Intentionality" in the *Encyclopedia of Philosophy,* Vol. 4, for criticism on these lines.
28. Chisholm, R. M., *ibid.*
29. Quine, W. V. O. *The Ways of Paradox and Other Essays,* New York: Random House, 1966, esp. 213-214.
30. Sellars, W., Appendix on Intentionality, *Minnesota studies in the Philosophy of Science* II.
31. *Ibid.,* 522.
32. Popper, K. *Conjectures and Refutations,* London: 1963, 298.
33. Quinton, *loc. cit,* 225.

(10)

Chapter 4

1. LU II, 1, 369.
2. *Ibid.,* 344, 378.
3. *Ibid.,* 370-371.
4. *Ibid.,* 372.
5. *Ibid.,* 375.
6. LU. II. 2. *Beilage.*
7. *Ibid.,* 232.
8. *Ibid.,* 241.
9. Findlay, J. N. *Meinong's Theory of Objects,* 41f.

PART TWO

Chapter 1

1. LU. II, 1, 345-363.
2. *Ibid.,* 347.

3. Husserl E. *Ideas, General Introduction to Pure Phenomenology*, E.Tr. by W. R. Boyce Gibson, Collier Books edition, 1962 [to be henceforth referred to as *Ideas* I], 108.

4. This account would also be in conformity with Dilthey's use of *"Erlebnis"* especially in his *Studien zur Grundlegung der Geisteswissenschaften* of 1905 which was written admittedly under the influence of Husserl's *Logische Untersuchungen*. Thus: *"Das Erleben ist immer seiner selbst gewiss."* Further, *"die Gewissheit des Erlebnisses bedarf keiner weiteren Vermittelung, und so kann dasselbe als unmittelbar gewiss bezeichnet werden."* (*Gesammelte Schriften* VII, 26). The act is inherently conscious. We live through it while we are having the act, and so it is an *Erlebnis*. See also Hogdes, H. A. *The Philosophy of Wilhelm Dilthey*, London: Routledge and Kegan Paul, 1952, 35-39).

5. LU. II.1., 356. The Naiyāyikas who believed in the theory that every *Erlebnis* or *vyavasāya* does as a *matter of fact* become the object of an immediately succeeding inner perception (*anu-vyavasāya*) did not however take this to be a matter of necessity. But of course they did not restrict the use of 'consciousness' only to this inner perception.

6. *Ibid.,* 356.

7. Husserl did not quite see this essentially reflective nature of the cartesian *cogito*. In the *Ideas I,* he talks of the *cogito* as if it were the same as the actual and explicit act as distinguished from the potential and implicit awareness in the modus of non-actuality. See especially § 36. And yet he expresses a *cogito* in the form 'I perform an act of consciousness.' Certainly, the 'I perform' or 'I think' or 'I perceive' does not enter into the structure of the unreflective act even though the unreflective act is aware of itself. It would seem therefore that Husserl's early and non-egological concept of consciousness does justice to the unreflective act, the ego does not enter into its structure though one may still argue that the ego is its presupposition.

8. In *Ideas I,* § 45, Husserl says that although an *Erlebnis* may remain unreflected, yet it is in a sense *always ready* to be reflected upon - a sense in which things are *not* so ready. In fact, we do know something even of the unreflected *Erlebnis,* so much so that when we come to reflect we find that it was all along known to us.

9. LU. II. 1., 399 fn.

10. *Ibid.,* 397/8.

11. *Ibid.,* 399.

12. *Ibid.,* 413-414.

13. *Ibid.,* 415.

14. *Ibid.,* 416.

15. *Ibid.,* 416.

16. See *ibid.,* 477 ff.

17. See Mohanty, J. N. *Edmund Husserl's Theory of Meaning*, The Hague: Martinus Nijhoff, 1964, 80-86.

18. For the distinction between meaning intention and meaning fulfilment, and the correlation distinction between intended meaning and fulfilled meaning see L.U.II.1., 378-379; and Mohanty, J. N. *loc. cit.,* 44-53.

19. LU. II. 2, 96-97.

20. *Ideas* I, 226.

21. *Ibid.*, 231.

22. *Ibid.*, 108.

23. *Ibid.*, 231.

24. *Ibid.*, 261.

25. *Ibid.*, 261-262.

26. *Ibid.*, 335.

27. *Ibid.*, 275.

28. Husserl, E. *Volesungen zur Phänomenologie des inneren Zeitbewusstseins,* herausgegeban von M. Heidegger, Halle: Max Niemeyer, 1928 (to be henceforth referred to as *VPZ*), 367.

29. Cp. Sokolowski, R.: "The doctrine of constitution is an attempt to think about the enigma of intentionality." *(The Formation of Husserl's concept of Constitution,* The Hague: Martinus Nijhoff, 1964, 135)

30. *VPZ,* 460: *"Identität von Zeitobjekten ist also ein konstitutives Einheits-produkt gewisser möglicher Identifizierungsdeckungen von Wiedererinner-ungen."*

31. *Ibid.*, 420.

32. *Ibid.*, 461: *"Das Objekt ist eine Einheit des Bewusstseins, die in wiederholten Akten (also in zeitlicher Folge) sich als dieselbe herausstellen kann . . . . . ."* P. F. Strawson in his *Individuals, An Essay in Descriptive Metaphysics,* London: Methuen, 1959, sees this relation between the nature of individual objects and the problem of identification. But Strawson's orientation of the problem of identification is spatial and linguistic, whereas Husserl's is temporal and phenomenological.

33. *VPZ,* §40.

34. Sokolowski, R. *loc. cit.,* VPZ, 444.

35. Sokolowski, R. *loc. cit.,* 92-3; 100.

36. Fink, E. *Studien zur Phänomenologie,* The Hague: Martinus Nijhoff, 1966, 25.

37. *VPZ,* 371. The English translation by J. S. Churchill unfortunately leaves room for ambiguity by not adding the conditional 'when.' See Husserl, E. *The Phenomenology of Internal Time-consciousness,* Bloomington: Indiana University Press, 1966, 25.

38. Cp. Husserl, E., *Zur Phänomenologie des inneren Zeitbewusstseins* (1893-1917) (Husserliana Band X), herausgegeben von Rudolf Boehm, The Hague: Martinus Nijhoff, 1966, especially p. XXXIX, foot note.

39. VPZ, 371 fn.

40. Sokolowski, R. *loc. cit,* 92-3, 100, 114-115.

41. *Ibid.*, 98, 105.

42. Compare Iso Kern on Fink's characterization of Husserl's early distinction between *hyle* and intentional act as being merely provisional: *"Diese an sich völlig richtige Bemerkung Finks scheint uns einen wichtigen Punkt zu vernachlässigen: In Husserls Problematik der genetischen Konsti-tution der transzendentalen oder realen Welt sind für ihn die Empfin-dungsdaten trotz allem das "lezte Material," das den formenden Funk-tionen zugrunde liegt. Erst indem er über diese Problemsphäre hinausgeht, fragt er, wie im immanenten Zeitbewusstsein das reell immanent Empfin-*

dungsdatum konstituiert wird, und weist es als gegeben auf in der Zeitigung der Urpräsentation, Urretention und Urprotention. Es handelt sich hier um eine völlig neue Problemsphäre, in der auch die Begriff der Konstitution und Intentionalität, weil sie sich nicht mehr auf Transzendenz beziehen, eine neue Bedeutung haben: es kann nicht mehr von "formenden Funktionen" oder von "Sinngebung" gesprochen werden; auch der Unterschied von statischer und genetischer Konstitution fällt weg. In seinem Problem der Konstitution der Transzendenz ist Husserl also mit Kant hinsichtlich des in Frage stehenden "Dualismus" einig." (Kern, I. *Husserl und Kant,* The Hague: Martinus Nijhoff, 1964, 274.)

43. *VPZ,* 468.
44. *Ibid.,* 435.
45. *Ibid.,* 467.
46. *Ibid.,* 464.
47. *Ibid.,* 466.
48. *Ideas* I, 131.
49. *Ibid.,* 138.
50. *Ibid.,* 139.
51. *Ibid.,* 153-4, *VPZ,* 39, 40.
52. *Ideas* I, 127.
53. *VPZ,* 400-1.
54. *Ibid.,* 436.
55. Max Scheler distinguished between the lived experience and the living of it, and held that though the lived experience is temporal, the living of it is non-temporal. Fundamentally, our interpretation of Husserl agrees with Scheler, except that we would not like to separate the two levels as radically as Scheler would do. For us the lived experience is what the living of it *appears to itself* in accordance with its intrinsically intentional nature. This is the view we would here ascribe to Husserl. Compare and contrast Dufrenne, M. *The notion of the Apriori,* E.Tr. by E. S. Casey, Evanston: Northwestern University Press, 1966.

****

Chapter 2

1. *Ideas* I, 332.
2. Gurwitsch, A. *Studies in Phenomenology and Psychology,* Northwestern University Press, 1966, 138.
3. *Ibid.,* 139.
4. *Ibid.,* 157.
5. *Ideas* I, 335.
6. *Ibid.,* 271, 335.
7. *Ibid.,* 109.
8. *Ibid.,* 110.
9. *Ibid.,* 356.
10. *Ibid.,* 335.
11. *Ibid.,* 238.
12. *Ibid.,* 261.

13. *Ibid.,* 264.
14. *Ibid.,* 240.
15. See Kern, I. *loc. cit,* 212-213; also Böhm, R. "Basic Reflections on Husserl's Phenomenological Idealism," *International Philosophical Quarterly,* V, 1965, 183-202.
16. Husserl, E. *Die Idee der Phänomenologie,* The Hague: Martinus Nijhoff, 1950, 7.
17. *Ideas* I, 142.
18. Husserl, E. *Ideen zu einer reinen Phänomenologie und phänomenologischen Philosophie, Drittes Buch,* herausgegeben von M. Biemel (to be henceforth referred to as *Ideen III*), The Hague: Martinus Nijhoff, 1952, §16.
19. Cp: *"Dinge aktuell setzen ist nicht Dingvermeintes setzen, ist nicht Dinggesetztes als solches setzen. Ebenso: Wesen aktuell setzen ist nicht Wesenvermeintes als solches setzen usw."* (*Ideen III,* 88-89). This distinction, Husserl adds, is a generalization of the distinction between positing a meaning and positing objects (*Gegenstände*).
20. Gurwitsch recalls a remark by Berger to the effect that the category of *noema* is more fundamental than that of being or of non-being. (Gurwitsch, A. *loc. cit,* 156)
21. *Ideas* I, 241.
22. *Ibid.,* 240.
23. Cp. Mohanty, J. N. *Edmund Husserl's Theory of Meaning.* This book was primarily concerned with the *Bedeutungslehre* which is, in reality, a part of a theory of *Sinn* and thus of a theory of intentionality.
24. *Ideas* I, 320.
25. *Ibid.,* 333.
26. *Ideen* III, 89.
27. Adorno, T. W. *Zur Metakritik der Erkenntnistheorie, Studien über Husserl und die phänomenologischen Antinomien,* Stuttgart: Kohlhammer, 1956, 171.
28. *Ideas* I, 228; also, 262.
29. *Ibid.,* 230.
30. *Ibid.,* 260.
31. *Ibid.,* 237.
32. Dufrenne, M. *The Notion of the Apriori,* E.Tr. by E. S. Casey, Evanston: Northwestern University Press, 1966, 21.
33. *Ideas* I, 266.
34. *Ibid.,* 250.
35. *Ibid.,* 266.
36. Gurwitch, A. *loc. cit,* 138.
37. *Ideas* I, 262; also 250.
38. *Ibid.,* 267.
39. Cp. Mohanty, J. N. *loc. cit.*
40. *Ideas* I, 262.
41. *Ibid.,* 226.
42. Sartre, J. P. *Being and Nothingness,* E. Tr. by H. E. Barnes, London:Methuen, 1957, lix [to be henceforth referred to as *BN.*]
43. *Ibid.,* lix.

44. Gurwitsch, A. *loc. cit*, 253-258.
45. Merleau-Ponty, M. *Phenomenology of Perception*, E.Tr. by C. Smith, New York, 1962, 243; also the same work, 213, 267, 405.
46. Asemissen, H. U. *Strukturanalytische Probleme der Wahrnehmung in der Phänomenologie Husserls. Kantstudien Ergänzungshefte* 73, Köln: Kölner Universitätsverlag, 1957, 22-34.
47. *Ibid.*, 24-25.
48. *Ideas* I, 39, 54.
49. Landgrebe, L. "Prinzipien der Lehre vom Empfinden," *Zeitschrift für philosophische Forschung* 8, 1954, 195-209. Compare also Straus, E. *Vom Sinn der Sinne*, Berlin, 1935.
50. Cp. Chapman, H. M. *Sensations and Phenomenology*, Bloomington: Indiana University Press, 1966.
51. Ricoeur, P. *Freedom and Nature: The Voluntary and the Involuntary*, E.Tr. by K. V. Kohak, Evanston: Northwestern University Press, 1966 [to be henceforth referred to as FN], 373-409.
52. *Ideas* I, 53.
53. *Ibid.*, 53.
54. Husserl, E. *Ideen zu einer reinen Phänomenologie und phänomenologischen Philosophie*, Zweites Buch, herausgegeben von M. Biemel, *Husserliana IV*, [to be henceforth referred to as *Ideen* II], The Hague: Martinus Nijhoff, 1952, Zweiter Abschnitt, Dritter Kapitel.
55. *Ideen* II, 56, 158f.
56. *Ibid.*, 151.
57. *Ibid.*, 151f.
58. *Ibid.*, 153.
59. *Ideen* III, 118.
60. *Ibid.*, 124. From this point of view, Ricoeur's statement (in his *Husserl: An Analysis of his Phenomenology*, E.Tr. by E. G. Ballard and L. E. Embree, Evanston: Northwestern University Press, 1967, 61) that the distinction between existence and objectivity is not known to Husserl may only be conditionally accepted.
61. Ryle, G. "Review" of M. Heidegger's *Sein und Zeit*, Mind N.S.XXXVIII, 1929, 355-370.
62. On this, see earlier this chapter.
63. Ryle, G. "Review" of M. Farber's *Foundation of Phenomenology, Philosophy*, XXI, 1946,263-269.
64. Fink, E. *loc. cit*, 143f. Fink recognizes that the three are not different intentionalities, but one and the same intentional *life* in different stages.
65. Thus in his *Philosophie der Arithmetik*, Husserl writes: "*Im eigentlichen Sinn schöpferische Akte . . . sind psychologische Undinge*" (p. 42). G. Berger, bearing witness to Husserl's later opinion on this matter, refers to "how much the word 'construction' could irritate Husserl." (quoted in A. Gurwitsch, *loc. cit*, 160). For an account of the different stages in Husserl's attitude towards the notion of productive synthesis, see I, Kern, *Husserl und Kant*, The Hague: Martinus Nijhoff, 1964, 249 ff.
66. The same difficulty is faced by the Advaita Vedānta philosopher who cannot literally say that *Brahman* creates the world. Nor can he say that the

world is a transformation of *Brahman*. For, 'creation' and 'transformation' are mundane concepts.

67. Husserl, E. *Analysen zur Passiven Synthesis* (1918-1926), The Hague: Martinus Nijhoff, 1966.
68. Husserl, E. *Cartesian Meditations*, E.Tr. by D. Cairns, The Hague: Martinus Nijhoff, 1960, [to be henceforth referred to as CM], § 38.
69. Husserl speaks, in this connection, of ego-acts being "pooled in a sociality," but recognises that the 'transcendental sense' of this sociality remains to be clarified. Cp. CM, §38.
70. Kant, E. *Kritik der reinen Vernunft, Kant Werke* ed. by Cassirer, vol. 3, 97 (A78 = B103).
71. *CM*, § 39.
72. Cp. Cerf, W. "A Metaphysical Phenomenology," *The Review of Metaphysics*, V, 1951, 125-144.
73. Husserl, E. *Ideen I (Husserliana* III), 100.
74. *Ibid.*, 82.
75. *CM*, §19.
76. Cp. Sokolowski, R. *loc. cit*, 162-163.
77. Husserl, E. *Formale und transzendentale Logik*, Halle: Max Niemeyer, 1929, 184.
78. Sokolowski, R. *loc. cit*, 172.
79. *CM*, § 38.
80. Seebohm, T. *Die Bedingungen der Möglichkeit der Transzendental-philosophie*, Bonn: Bouvier, 1962, 104.
81. Funke, G. *Zur transzendentalen Phänomenologie*, Bonn, 1957, 12-13; also see p. 61.
82. *CM*, § 64.
83. *CM*, § 47.
84. Husserl, E. *Die Krisis der europäischen Wissenschaften und die transzendentale Phänomenologie*, The Hague: Martinus Nijhoff, 1954 (to be henceforth referred to as *Krisis*), 240.
85. Husserl, E. *Erste Philosophie* II, The Hague: Martinus Nijhoff, 1959, 318-319.
86. Husserl, E. *Phänomenologische Psychologie*, The Hague: Martinus Nijhoff, 1962, 428.
87. *Formale und transzendentale Logik*, 208.
88. Brand, G. *Welt, Ich und Zeit, nach unveröffentlichten Manuskripten E. Husserls*, The Hague, 1955, 23.
89. Fink, E. *loc. cit*, 219.
90. Merleau-Ponty, M. *Phenomenology of Perception*, Introduction.
91. Brand, G. *loc. cit*, 25.
92. Cp. Dreyfus, H. L. and Todes, S. J. "The Three Worlds of Merleau-Ponty," *Philosophy and Phenomenological Research*, XXII, 1962, 559-565.
93. Kockelmans, J. J. *Phenomenology and Physical Science, An Introduction to the Philosophy of Physical Science*, Duquesne University Press, 1966, 61-63.
94. Mohanty, J. N. *loc. cit*, 54.
95. L.U.II.2., 33.
96. Husserl, E. *Erste Philosophie* I, The Hague: Martinus Nijhoff, 1956, 273.

97. *CM,* § 9.
98. Ricoeur, P. *Husserl, An Analysis of His Phenomenology,* 192.

****

Chapter 3

1. Brand, G. *loc. cit,* 25ff.
2. Ricoeur, P. *Husserl, An Analysis of His Phenomenology,* 99.
3. de Waelhens, A. "Reflections on the Development of Heidegger: Apropos of a Recent Book," *International Philosophical Quarterly,* V, 1965, 475-502.
4. See also Ryle, G: in *Mind,* 1929, 355-370.
5. de Waelhens, A. *loc. cit,* 480, fn 7.
6. Wild, J.: "Man and His Life-World," Tymieniecka, A. T. (ed.), *For Roman Ingarden, Nine Essays in Phenomenology,* The Hague: Martinus Nijhoff, 1959, 90-109.
7. For the following, see Diemer, A. *Edmund Husserl, Versuch einer systematischen Darstellung seiner Phänomenologie,* Meisenheim, 1956, 33-38.
8. Heidegger, M. *Sein und Zeit,* Tübingen: Max Niemeyer, 1953 [to be henceforth referred to as *SuZ*], 133, 220.
9. *Ibid.,* 133, 350, 351.
10. Cp. De Waehlens, A. "Die phänomenologische Idee der Intentionalität," Van Breda, H. L. and Taminiaux, J. (ed), *Husserl und das Denken der Neuzeit,* The Hague: Martinus Nijhoff, 1959, 129-142.
11. *Ibid.,* 135.
12. *SuZ,* 363 fn; also §69c.
13. Heidegger, M. *Vom Wesen des Grundes,* Frankfurt Am Main: Klostermann, 1931, 15, 44.
14. *Ibid.,* 44.
15. Cp. de Waelhens, A. and Biemel, W. "Heideggers Schrift 'Vom Wesen der Wahrheit,' " *Symposion, Jahrbuch für Philisophie,* III, 471-508, esp. 486.
16. *BN,* 85.
17. Sartre, J. P. *The Transcendence of the Ego, An Existentialist Theory of Consciousness,* E.Tr. by F. Williams and R. Kirkpatrick, New York: Noonday, 1957, 42.
18. *Ibid.,* 45.
19. *BN,* liv.
20. *Ibid.,* lix.
21. *Ibid.,* li
22. *Ibid.,* lvi.
23. *Ibid.,* lx.
24. *Ibid.,* 180.
25. *Ibid.,* 181.
26. *Ibid.,* lxi.
27. *Ibid.,* lxi.
28. *Ibid.,* lxi, 109.
29. *Ibid.,* lvi.
30. *Ibid.,* 217.
31. Cp. Warnock, M. *The Philosophy of Sartre,* London: Hutchinson, 1965, 45.

32. Sartre, J. P. *The Transcendence of the Ego,* 40. Compare Rāmānuja's view, stated in Part Three, Chapter 1, this work.
33. *BN,* 173.
34. Luijpen, W. A. *Existential Phenomenology,* Pittsburgh: Duquesne University Press, 1962, 107.
35. Merleau-Ponty, M. *The Primacy of Perception,* E.Tr. by J. M. Edie, Evanston: Northwestern University Press, 1964 [to be henceforth referred to as *PP*], 4.
36. Merleau-Ponty, M. *Signs,* E.Tr. by R. C. Mc Cleary, Evanston: Northwestern University Press, 1964, 167.
37. Merleau-Ponty, M. *The Phenomenology of Perception* [to be henceforth referred to as *Ph. P.*], 71.
38. *Ibid.,* 124-125.
39. *Ibid.,* 294, 343.
40. *Ibid.,* 378-379.
41. *Ibid.,* 294.
42. *Ibid.,* 380-381.
43. *Ibid.,* 381, 426.
44. *Ibid.,* 296.
45. *Ibid.,* 404.
46. *Ibid.,* 137.
47. *Ibid.,* 120.
48. *Ibid.,* 137-138.
49. *Ibid.,* 136-137.
50. *Ibid.,* 138fn
51. *Ibid.,* 208-209.
52. *Ibid.,* 297.
53. *Ibid.,* 143.
54. *Ibid.,* 156-157.
55. *Ibid.,* 197.
56. *Ibid.,* 152fn.
57. *Signs,* 173-176.
58. *Ph.P.,* 453.
59. *Ibid.,* 58-59.
60. Cp. Langan, T. *Merleau-Ponty's Critique of Reason,* New Haven: Yale University Press, 1966, 23f.
61. Cp. Kwant, R. C. *The Phenomenological Philosophy of Merleau-Ponty,* Pittsburgh: Duquesne University Press, 1963, 156: "Merleau-Ponty hovers between the affirmations of the pre-conscious and the realisation that consciousness itself has to be original, without being able to arrive at clarity."
62. Ballard, E. G. "On cognition of the Pre-cognitive," *Philosophical Quarterly,* 11, 1961, 238-244. See esp. 242.
63. Ricoeur, P. "Philosophy of Will and Action" in E. W. Straus and R. M Griffith (ed), *Phenomenology of Will and Action,* Pittsburgh: Duquesne University Press, 1967, 7-33; esp. 16.
64. *Ideas* I, §§114, 115, 117.
65. Sartre, J. P. *The Transcendence of the Ego,* 41-42.

66. Ricoeur, P. "Philosophy of Will and Action," 18-19.
67. *FN*, 56.
68. *Ibid.*, 61.
69. *Ibid.*, 62.
70. *Ibid.*, 387.
71. *Ibid.*, 376-380.
72. *Ibid.*, 378.
73. *BN*, 570.
74. *BN*, 571.
75. *FN*, 384-394.
76. *Ibid.*, 389.
77. Cp. Malcolm, N. "The concept of Dreaming" in O. F. Gustafson (ed), *Essays in Philosophical Psychology*, New York: Doubleday Anchor, 1964, 265-276. Malcolm writes: "What we must say, although it seems paradoxical, is that the concept of dreaming is derived, not from dreaming, but from descriptions of dreams, i.e., from the familiar phenomenon that we call 'telling a dream' " (266).
78. *FN*, 390.
79. Ricoeur, P. *History and Truth*, E.Tr. by C. A. Kelbley, Evanston: Northwestern University Press, 1965, 307.
80. *Ibid.*, 309f.
81. *Ibid.*, 311.
82. Ricoeur, P. *Husserl, An Analysis of His Phenomenology*, 98.
83. *Ibid.*, 94.
84. *Ibid.*, 100.
85. *Ibid.*, 41.
86. *Ibid.*, 21.
87. This is the argument of M. Natanson in his "The Empirical and Transcendental Ego" in Tymieniecka, A. T. (ed), *For Roman Ingarden, Nine Essays in Phenomenology*, The Hague: Martinus Nijhoff, 1959.
88. *Ideen* II, 28. But the doctrine of the autogenesis of the ego is surely suggested in the same work, 102.
89. *Ibid.*, 310f
90. Husserl, E. *Phänomenologische Psychologie*, 207-208.
91. *CM*, § 32. On 'habitualities', see Ricoeur, P. *Husserl, An Analysis of His Phenomenology*, 54-55.
92. Funke, G. *loc. cit*, 22-23.
93. *CM*, § 28.
94. *Phänomenologische Psychologie*, 197.

****

PART THREE
Chapter 1

1. Madhusûdana Saraswati, *Advaitasiddhi*, edited by Ananta Krishna Sastri, Bombay, 1937, 2nd edition, 453f.
2. *Ibid.*, 453.
3. Vallabhācārya, *Nyāyalīlāvati*, Chowkhamba edn., 408

4. Vācaspati, *Tātparyatīkā*, 108; Vallabhācārya, *loc. cit*, 812-814.
5. For the concept of 'svarupasambandha', See Ingalls, D. H. *Materials for the Study of Navya Nyāya Logic*, Harvard, 1951.
6. Thus Udayana: *"Arthenaiva Viśeṣohi nirākāratayā dhiyām"* (*Nyāya-Kusumānjali*, 4.4.)
7. Rāmānuja, *Sri Bhāṣya*, Nirnayasāgara edition, Bombay, 1916, 87.
8. See Mohanty, J. N. "Gilbert Ryle's Criticisms of the concept of Consciousness," *The Visva Bharati Journal of Philosophy*, III, 1966-67 [now included in the author's *Phenomenology and Ontology*, The Hague: Martinus Nijhoff, 1970].
9. Geiger, M. *Fragment über den Begriff des Unbewussten und die psychische Realität*, Sonderdruck aus *Jahrbuch für Philosophie und phänomenologische Forschung*, IV, 1930. See esp. 46ff.
   Also Thévenaz, P. *What is Phenomenology?* E.Tr. by J. M. Edie, London, 1963, 114 ff.
10. Taylor, C. *The Explanation of Behaviour*, New York: The Humanities Press, 1964, especially 55 ff. Hampshire, S. *Thought and Action*, London, 1960.
11. Dharmarājādhvarīndra, *Vedāntaparibhāṣā*, edited by S. C. Ghosal, Calcutta, 1919, 21.
12. Morris wrongly ascribes an intentional theory to the Sāmkhya in his *Six Theories of Mind*, Chicago: the University of Chicago Press, 1950; see page 149. He is misled by the fact that the Sāmkhya distinguishes between consciousness (or *puruṣa*) and *prakṛti*. Notwithstanding this distinction, consciousness, for the Sāmkhya, is non-intentional.
13. Compare the first two senses of 'consciousness' distinguished by Husserl. See Part Two, chapter 1, this book.
14. Śamkara writes: *Yusmadasmatpratyayagocarayorviṣayaviṣayiṇostamaprakāśavadviruddhabhāvayoritaretarabhāvānupapattau siddhāyām . . . mithyeti bhavitum yuktam."* (*Adhysāsabhāṣya*). Also see Part One, ch.3, this book.
15. Merleau Ponty, M. *Ph.P.*, 404-405.
16. Compare the definition of selfluminosity (*svayamprakāśatva*) given in Advaita Vadānta: *"avedyatve sati aparokṣavyavahārayogyatvam."*
17. Thévenaz, P. *loc. cit.*, 121.
18. DeWaelhens, A. in *Husserl und das Denken der Neuzeit*, 134.
19. Popper, K. *Conjectures and Refutations*, Harper Torchbook edition, 1968, 3ff.
20. Rāmānuja writes: *"Yattvanubhuteh svayamprakāśatvamuktam, tadviṣayaprakāśanavelāyām jñāturātmanastahaiva, na tu sarveṣām sarvadātathaiveti niyamo'sti,"* (*Sri Bhāṣya*, 84).
21. Thévenaz, P. *loc. cit.*, 69.
22. *Ideas* I, § 85.
23. *Ibid.*, § 97.
24. *BN*, lix.
25. *FN*, 385f.
26. Ryle, G. *Dilemmas*, Cambridge; Cambridge, University Press, 1954.
27. Ayer, A. J. *The Problem of Knowledge*, London: Macmillan, 1956, 13.
28. Bhattacharya, K. C. *The Subject as Freedom*, Amalner: Indian Institute of

Philosophy, 1930 [included in Bhattacharya, K. C. *Studies in Philosophy,* second volume, Calcutta: Progressive Publishers, 1958].
29. *Ibid.,* 23.

****

Chapter 2

1. Fink, E. "L'analyse intentionelle et le problème de la pensée spéculative," Van Breda (ed), *Problèmes actuels de la Phénoménologie, Brussells:* Brouwer, 1952, 74ff.
2. Mohanty, J. N. *Edmund Husserl's Theory of Meaning,* 54.
3. Ricoeur, P. *History and Truth,* 308-309.
4. Kaam, A. V. *Existential Foundations of Psychology,* Pittsburgh: Dusquesne University Press, 1966, 247f.
5. Macleod, R. B. "Phenomenology: A challenge to Experimental Psychology" in T. W. Wann (ed), *Behaviorism and Phenomenology, Contrasting Bases for Modern Psychology,* Chicago: University of Chicago Press, 1964. See esp. 54-55.
6. Brunswick, E. "The Conceptual Framework of Psychology" in Neurath, Carnap, Morris (ed), *International Encyclopedia of United Science,* Volume I, nos. 6-10, Chicago: University of Chicago Press, 1955; esp. 663f.
7. Titchener, E. B. *Systematic Psychology: Prolegomena,* New York: Macmillan, 1929, 179-193.
8. *Ibid.,* 184-185.
9. Morris, C. W., *loc. cit,* 152.
10. Cp. Straus, E. *The Primary World of Senses,* Free Press of Glencoe, 1963, 50.
11. Malcolm, N. in Wann (ed), *loc. cit,* 153.
12. See note 1, this chapter.
13. Sellars, W. *Science, Perception and Reality,* London: Routledge and Kegan Paul, 1963, 50f.
14. William Horosz has defended this view in his *The Promise and Peril of Human Purpose,* St. Louis: Thomas Warren Green, 1970, and in personal communication to me.
15. Bergmann, G. *Realism. A Critique of Brentano and Meinong,* University of Wisconsin Press, 1967, 273 f.
16. *Ibid.,* 273.
17. *Ibid.,* 127-128.
18. *Ibid.,* 24.
19. *Ibid.,* 274
20. *Ibid.,* 271.
21. *Ibid.,* 214.
22. *Ibid.,* 152.
23. *Ibid.,* 214.
24. *Ibid.,* 23-24.
25. Compare similar distinctions made by Husserl in *LU* II.1. 326-328. For Bergmann there is a fourth notion of possibility: that is possible₄ which does not contradict a synthetic *a posteriori* generality called a natural law (Bergmann, *loc. cit,* 88).

26. There is at least one place (217, line 33) where 'potential' is said to be the same as 'possible.'

27. Bergmann, G., *loc. cit,* 146.

28. Cp. Farber, M. *Phenomenology and Existence, Toward a Philosophy within Nature,* Harper Torchbooks, 1967, Ch. VII: "The Vehicle of Trans-cendence."

29. Dumery, H. *The Problem of God in Philosophy of Religion,* E.Tr. by C. Courtney, Evanston: Northwestern University Press, 1964, 53.

INDEX

211